The Architecture of the Anglo-Saxons

THE
Architecture
OF THE
Anglo-Saxons

ERIC FERNIE

HM

HOLMES & MEIER PUBLISHERS, INC.
NEW YORK

For Catherine Reid and Sidney Robert Fernie

ACKNOWLEDGMENTS

It is a pleasure to express my thanks to my colleagues for the study leave during which this book was written, to Alison Wardale who typed the manuscript and Michael Brandon-Jones for his assistance with the reproductions, to Don Johnson for his expert draughtsmanship, and especially to Stephen Heywood for many enjoyable discussions and field trips. I would also like to record my indebtedness to the British Academy and the Leverhulme Trust, whose financial assistance enabled me to visit most of the buildings discussed in the following pages, as well as to the numerous incumbents and church wardens who made those visits both profitable and enjoyable.

Eric Fernie *Norwich, 1982*

The figures listed below are reproduced by kind permission of the following:
British Archaeological Association: 38; British Library: 23; Cambridge University Press, H. M. and J. Taylor, *Anglo-Saxon Architecture*, 3 vols., 1965 and 1978: 18, 60, 63, 67, 69, 70, 74, 81, 92, 95, 96, 98; Courtauld Institute: 41, 45; Crown Copyright: 4, 5, 7, 10, 11, 28; Landesamt, Schleswig: 6; National Monuments Record: 1, 61, 71, 82, 90; A. D. Parsons: 34, 76, 78, 79; Royal Archaeological Institute: 13, 22, 24, 92; Society for Medieval Archaeology: 19, 81; Society of Antiquaries of London: 8, 9, 99; Dr H. M. Taylor: 54, 63; University of East Anglia: 72, 100; (S. Heywood) 46, 62, 66, 77, 88, 97; (T. Heslop) 49; (M. Thurlby) 87; (J. Onians) 83; L'Université de Louvain: 55, 68; Zentralinstitut für Kunstgeschichte, Munich: 17, 21, 25, 27, 43, 52, 53, 58, 64.

Grateful acknowledgment is also made to the Oxford University Press for permission to use the quotations from Bertram Colgrave's translation of Bede's *Historia Ecclesiastica* used on pp. 17–18, 42–3 and 47, and to the Royal Archaeological Institute for the quotation from R. Quirk's translation in the *Archaeological Journal* 114, 1957, p. 44, used on p. 98–9

First published in the United States of America 1983 by
Holmes & Meier Publishers, Inc.
30 Irving Place
New York, N.Y. 10003

Library of Congress Cataloging in Publication Data
Fernie, E.C.
     The Architecture of the Anglo-Saxons.
     Bibliography: P.
     Includes Index.
     1. Architecture, Anglo-Saxon. I. Title.
NA963.F4   1983   720'.941   83-12915
ISBN 0-8419-0912-1

Printed in Great Britain

1 *Frontispiece* Cambridge, St Benet, mid eleventh century. Tower arch

CONTENTS

LIST OF ILLUSTRATIONS

INTRODUCTION

When William of Malmesbury, writing around 1120, described Edward the Confessor's mid eleventh-century church at Westminster as built in a new style, the Norman, 'which now almost all men emulate at great expense' (*Gesta Regum*, i, 280), he was merely stating what must have been the accepted view ever since the 1060s, namely that Anglo-Saxon architecture was a thing of the past. From this time onwards, like the English language itself with the ending of the Anglo-Saxon Chronicle in 1155, all mention of the architecture of the Anglo-Saxons vanishes from the documents. This state of affairs remained more or less unbroken until the early nineteenth century when Thomas Rickman began the scholarly study of the subject, engendering a lively ecclesiological debate over the next 70 or 80 years, as a result of which such basic questions as the very existence of stone buildings before the Conquest were definitively answered, and scholars like Micklethwaite were enabled to write about Anglo-Saxon churches in the same terms as would be used today. Indeed Baldwin Brown's *Anglo-Saxon Architecture*, published just after the turn of the century, is still the only treatment of the subject to combine an attention to detail with an attempt to see it as a whole, a fact which may go some way to explaining the number of his conjectures which have subsequently been substantiated, most recently and dramatically at Barton-on-Humber.

In the 1920s Sir Alfred Clapham set the material in an even wider context, incorporating both the Mediterranean and non-architectural sculpture, while at the same time adopting a shorter format and, perhaps as the inevitable result, what Stuart Rigold called 'a wide-angled but selective art-historical viewpoint'. Then in 1965 the Taylors published their massive two-volume catalogue of all the standing structures which they believed contained Anglo-Saxon fabric, followed in 1978 by the third volume, in which Harold Taylor approached the same material typologically, with separate chapters on arches, doorways, windows, etc. In the process a large number of questions have been clarified, both in these volumes and in numerous articles which Dr Taylor has published since 1965, often spurred on by the provocative contributions of Jackson and Fletcher. One can note with particular pleasure his papers on the nineteenth-century documentation and the dating of Bradford-on-Avon and, on a more parochial level, the modern history of the west door at Barton-on-Humber. The debt which any writer on Anglo-Saxon architecture owes to the Taylors is indicated by the fact that, with almost every single building mentioned in the following pages, it can be taken for granted that reference is made to their work, for observations, descriptions, measurements or documentation.

The 1960s and 1970s have seen a veritable explosion of information derived from material excavated or uncovered in various ways and, one is happy to note, expeditiously published. An excellent synopsis of this material is provided by David Wilson's collection of chapters of 1976, among which the contributions of Rahtz, Biddle, Cherry and Cramp are the most relevant here. Contributions of fundamental importance have also been made by Richard Gem, and it is to be hoped that many more of his views, with the evidence which so copiously supports them, will soon be added to his published bibliography. Lastly, Jean Bony's review of Taylor and Taylor is, for the eleventh century, as important as it is brief.

Apart from Baldwin Brown, whose text even in its second edition is nearly 60 years old, this literature, as far as it concerns churches, is of two very different kinds, being either the broadest of outlines, like Clapham, or a detailed analysis of the minutest of archaeological and textual minutiae, Taylor in particular expressly restricting himself to the material remains to the exclusion of monuments known only through texts. There may then be this justification for the present volume, that it attempts to place the quantities of newly available detailed information of both a documentary and a material nature into a broader framework.

The form of the book, what has been included and what excluded, is also largely a response to the earlier literature. Taken at face value the volumes of Baldwin Brown, Clapham and the Taylors might lead the innocent reader to suppose that Anglo-Saxon architecture consisted solely of churches, but of course this impression of our forebears as pious to a degree is erroneous. As other remains such as their jewellery amply testify, they were no less interested in worldly things than the Romans or the Edwardians.

The reason for this disjunction in the literature is the fact that almost all secular buildings of the period were constructed in wood and have consequently been lost, but, thanks to the meticulous uncovering, recording and analysing of features such as post-holes and the beds of sills which has characterized the excavations of the last two decades, there is now a wealth of information that cannot be ignored. Nor should it be, given the importance of architecture in wood indicated by the oft-quoted fact that the Anglo-Saxon verb for 'to build' is *timbrian*, so that in the parable in Matthew 7.24 the wise man *his hus ofer stan getimbrode*. I must however, admit to a lack of expertise in this field, so that the first and second chapters are no more than a précis of some aspects of the evidence, and the history of the wooden church still remains to be written.

The remainder of the book deals with ecclesiastical architecture in stone, firstly, in chapters three, four and five, in the pre-Danish period, where special attention is paid to the function of the buildings in question. Next, chapter six sets out the continental background to the post-Danish period, with reference to the growth of the Romanesque style in the Rhineland and Normandy, out of the architecture of the Carolingian Empire. Chapter seven examines the revival of religious life, and hence of church building, under Alfred and his successors, in conjunction with churchmen such as Dunstan and Ethelwold.

The final four chapters attempt to show that the later church architecture of the Anglo-Saxons, building on the largely Carolingian experiments of the monastic revival, was a part of the early Romanesque style in north-western Europe. In the course of this, particular stress is placed on the crossing formed by the nave and transepts, on the tower, and on architectural decoration, while in the last chapter any sharp distinction between 'Saxon' and 'Norman' in the mid eleventh century is rejected.

The title *The Architecture of the Anglo-Saxons* does not offer the same thing as a history of architecture in England between the sixth century and the eleventh, as the Celts and the Vikings, for example, receive scant attention except in so far as they may be relevant to the English. Equally, and unlike 'Anglo-Saxon Architecture', the title has no necessary stylistic connotation, but indicates simply the buildings erected by or for the Anglo-Saxons.

One final aspect of the approach adopted here needs a word of explanation, although it is significant that it should. Throughout I have attempted to assess the effect which the buildings were intended to have as works of architecture or as functioning objects. In an architectural history on any other historical period such an approach would be taken for granted, if not as the main theme then as one of the most important. That it does not hold this position in Anglo-Saxon studies may be due in part to a belief that the Anglo-Saxons themselves were too 'earthy, laborious and stolid' to bother their heads about such continental fripperies as aesthetics,[1] to which one need surely respond with no more than a reference to Sutton Hoo, the Ethelwold Benedictional and, for that matter, Bradford-on-Avon and Great Paxton.

A more important contributory reason for the existence of this restricted approach to Anglo-Saxon studies is the almost complete lack of standing structures, whether secular or ecclesiastical, from the early period of the seventh and eighth centuries. This is not true of churches in the tenth and eleventh centuries, but perhaps because of the ground rules established by the study of the early period, they tend to be treated in the same way. As a result the buildings have come to be considered primarily as puzzles. This can be illustrated from a recent essay on the historiography of Anglo-Saxon architecture which approvingly contrasts an article delighting in the opportunities provided by work of more than one date in the church at Monkwearmouth, with Baldwin Brown's complaints about such buildings and his preference for churches obviously of one date, like Escomb.[2] Clearly in this period it is impossible to date, let alone appreciate in a proper context, buildings such as Escomb without the detective work which can only be conducted at places like Monkwearmouth. But on the other hand it should not be lost sight of that, enjoyable though the detective work always is, the aim of the exercise is to understand what the Anglo-Saxons made and why, and that this must involve an assessment of the finished structure.

Chapter One

HALLS, HOUSES AND PALACES

The history of the domestic architecture of the Anglo-Saxons begins on the European mainland, where the sources of most of the building types used in England are to be found. The relevant area lies between the Zuider Zee and the Skagerrak, comprising present-day Friesland, the coastal plain of north-west Germany, Schleswig-Holstein and, though less certainly, Denmark (fig. 2). The evidence for this is derived from Bede, linguistic connections, place-names and the building types themselves.

Bede (*HE*, i, 15) refers to 'the newcomers', that is his own people, as the Saxons, the Angles and the Jutes. The first he says came from the land of the Old Saxons, presumably equivalent to the German province of Saxony which can be traced back at least to the ninth century, while Ptolemy in the second

2 Sites of halls, houses, palaces, towns and defences

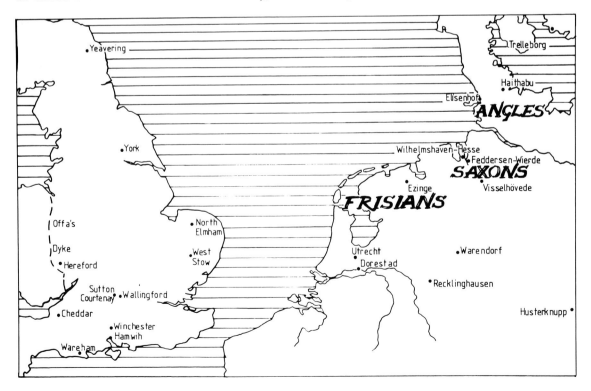

3 Ezinge (Groningen),
fourth century BC –
fourth century AD. Layers
V (top) and I (bottom)
(Van Giffen, *Germania*,
1936)

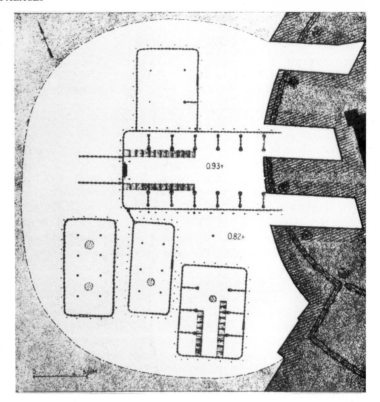

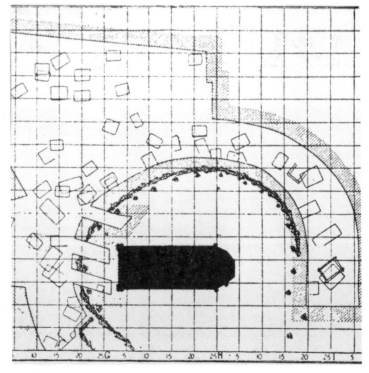

century places the *Saxones* at the neck of the Cimbric, that is the Danish, peninsula. Less precisely, the Romans used the term *Litus Saxonicum* for the coasts of Britain and Gaul open to attack from further north and east. The Angles, Bede says, came from Angulus 'between the provinces of the Jutes and the Saxons', while the town of *Haithabu* in Schleswig-Holstein is referred to in the tenth century as the *oppidum capitale* of *Angeln*. One might expect the Jutes to have something to do with Jutland, but this tribe is the most difficult of the three to pin down, and Bede is significantly silent beyond placing them further away than the Angles. As the material remains of their subsequent history in Kent do not point to a home so far north, and as Jutland has not produced any relevant parallels in plans of buildings, it is as well to place a question mark over this extremity.

Conversely at the southern end we can add Friesland to Bede's list, because of the close relationship between the Frisian and Anglo-Saxon languages and the existence of a type of pottery with characteristics which have attracted the label 'Anglo-Frisian ware'. When in the seventh century the English returned to convert the peoples whom they saw as their cousins, it was in this area that they began, establishing their first missionary see at Utrecht, the nearest Roman town to Friesland.

Buildings in these areas reflect the uncertainty of some of the divisions, so that the architecture of the homelands is best treated as a whole. The settlement at **Ezinge** in the Dutch province of Groningen, with its six successive layers of habitation between the fourth century BC and the fourth AD, provides a representative selection of the most characteristic and noteworthy type, the large three-aisled hall (fig. 3).[1] Layer V, for example, has structures consisting of wooden supports set at regular intervals along lines marking the side walls, with two rows of stouter posts dividing the interior into a central area and two narrower flanking aisles, enabling the roof-timbers to span the width. The outer rows of posts are supplied with angled struts resembling flying buttresses to help take the weight and even, in a wind, the thrust of the roof.

In some plans the struts line up with the pairs of free-standing posts and in others they do not, a variation which can be interpreted in two ways. In the first case the correspondence is accidental so that all buildings are of the same type, with no intimate connection between the inner and outer rows of posts except that they both support the roof. In the second the alignment is intentional and implies a different form of roof from those instances lacking alignment. Here each pair of free-standing posts would support two rafters forming a gable the lower ends of which rest on the outermost posts, with the struts then buttressing what look like points of stress.

The walls of wattle and daub or plaited branches are sharply differentiated from the posts themselves as they have no load-bearing function, serving only to keep out wind and rain while defining the interior space. From the fact that they extend some way beyond the ends of the rows of large supports it can be inferred that the ends of the roof were hipped, requiring less support beyond the gable. The corners are for the most part rounded, and entrances are situated on both the long and short faces.

The halls at Ezinge vary from 13 ft to 23 ft (4 m to 7 m) in width and from 26 ft to 80 ft (8 m to 24.5 m) in length, with most between 35 ft and 40 ft (10.75 m and 12 m), producing proportions from just over a square to 1:3 and more. Differences in length seem to depend on differences in function, though status may also have played its part. In most cases there is at least one hearth, showing that they were used as dwellings. Some examples have a living space at one end and a barn at the other, the latter indicated by the presence of matting designed to catch the droppings of the animals, which stood in the aisles with their heads facing the side walls. In a few cases the free-standing supports at the end which was probably the barn are set further apart than those in the living quarters, presumably to facilitate the turning of the beasts.

It has been suggested that buildings of this type were placed with their barn ends facing the prevailing wind.[1a] This is a sensible notion as it would provide improved shelter, but the structures in the four earliest layers at Ezinge, VI to III, are in many cases set at right angles to one another, while those in layer II are arranged radially, centring on what lies under the later village church. From these two layouts it would appear that the inhabitants preferred visual and social order to physical comfort.

The halls at Ezinge are virtually indistinguishable from those of similar date at Einswarden near the mouth of the Elbe (though the latter have the refinement of an entrance bay slightly larger than those flanking it), at Hodorf in Schleswig-Holstein, at Feddersen-Wierde near Bremerhaven (with one hall over 100 ft, 30.5 m, long), at Zeijen in the Dutch province of Drenthe, at Recklinghausen near Essen (where one hall has a transverse space at one of the short ends) and, much later, in the seventh, eighth or ninth century AD, at Wilhelmshaven-Hesse over the estuary from Bremerhaven, and at Elisenhof in Schleswig-Holstein (which has a set of well-preserved walls and sloping external struts – fig. 6).

These halls are known only from marks left by their uprights and in a very few cases by the bottom two or three feet of walling. Apart from length and breadth, therefore, and a hint of the standards of construction, it might be thought impossible to be certain that they ever achieved any particular quality as works of architecture. Any doubts on this score can however be dispelled, at least in principle, by the description which Venantius Fortunatus, bishop of Poitiers in the sixth century, gives of wooden buildings in the Rhineland:

Wall built of stone, begone! I esteem higher the work of the craftsman in wood. In their mass the great timber palaces strike the sky and in the firmly built structure no church can be seen. However sure a protection is stone, gravel, limestone or clay, yet here a propitious wood has itself built the house: higher it is and vaster, surrounded on all sides by a portico, and the builder has given free play to his fancy in the carving.[2]

There are of course many smaller buildings, constructed on the same principles as the halls, but lacking aisles, of which there are examples at Ezinge and Höhlbek, and even some, at Zeijen and Gielde, reduced to eight, six or four posts. At Warendorf in Westphalia the halls of the seventh and eighth centuries, the period at which the Saxons were advancing into the area, are all aisleless, and there are also some very small structures of a type to which, because of its importance in England, we must now turn. This is the sunken hut, only slightly longer than broad, nearly always small and sometimes reduced to two poles, like a tent. Ironically the earliest examples are known from literary sources, since Tacitus (*Germ.*, 16) describes buildings in Germany excavated below floor level to provide space for storage and a refuge from the weather in the winter, while Pliny (*N.H.* 19.2) says that the Germans used buildings with the floor sunk below ground level as rooms for weaving. Though these are two different types their archaeological remains are very similar, so that they can often only be distinguished by the presence or absence of objects such as loom-weights.

Around the year 400 the spacious huts of layer II (the penultimate one) at

Ezinge were destroyed by fire and replaced by something very different, in the form of small, not to say mean, sunken huts no more than 10 ft by 13 ft (3 m by 4 m) in size and set down without any order (fig. 3). The burning of buildings need not always be a sign of incendiary attack, as it can be done simply to clear the way for rebuilding and, presumably, as a form of pest-control. This is the likely explanation for the signs of fire between layers VI, V, IV, III and II, since these layers are all characterised by the same types of hall. In layer I, conversely, there are only the sunken huts and none of the halls. This change could be explained as the result of the community falling on hard times, but the complete lack of the other building type on either side of the divide makes this unlikely. An alternative hypothesis is that Ezinge was attacked by Anglo-Saxons moving west from the Weser and the Elbe and that layer I represents a new form of building superimposed on the old by a different group.

The prevalence of the sunken hut can be attributed either to poverty or the requirements of a people on the move, since, if they were Anglo-Saxons, it is unlikely that they stayed for long. This area had for centuries been subject to floods, explaining Pliny's description of dwellings north of the Rhine standing on tumuli or tribune-like platforms (*N.H.* 16.1). During the third century AD many settlements were abandoned, so that the newcomers at Ezinge may have arrived only to find it necessary to continue their migration westwards.

The Anglo-Saxon invasion of England shows no signs of having been either heroic or coordinated. The presence of Germanic mercenaries in towns and garrisons before the withdrawal of the Romans conforms to a pattern well-known along other parts of the northern boundary of the Empire. Even after the departure of the Roman army the advances of the newcomers were fitful and opportunist, more the activities of pirates than invaders, in striking parallel to the depredations of the Danes in the ninth century. This, coupled with what was thought to be the overwhelming preponderance of sunken huts in early villages, provides some justification for the long-standing view that the first settlers had a low level of material culture. The assessment is, however, false.

There are two ways in which to approach this reassessment, firstly in terms of the worth of the sunken hut itself, and secondly by questioning the extent of its preponderance. As to the first point, it is difficult to avoid the suspicion that the low esteem in which the sunken hut is held has in part been caused by the effect on the English ear of the original German archaeological term *Grubenhaus*. Though this means almost literally 'pit-house' its overtones of indigent scavenging are adequately realised in the infelicitous form 'grub-hut' recently offered by way of translation.

As to its preponderance, more refined excavation techniques have brought about a revision of earlier views on the relative numbers of this type. In the nature of things ploughing is more likely to destroy the remains of buildings with their floors at ground level than those with excavated interiors, and as the sunken technique seems to have been almost entirely restricted to smaller buildings, an inaccurate picture can easily be obtained.

At Sutton Courtenay in Berkshire excavations conducted by Leeds in the 1920s led him to conclude that the site consisted of nothing but sunken huts and, what is worse, that their walls were not even of wattle-and-daub but of straw and mud. Yet the centre of the site has not been explored, and as recent excavations nearby have revealed large and small buildings of early Anglo-Saxon date together, what Leeds found may have been nothing more than the industrial estate of the settlement.[3]

West Stow in Suffolk, of the fifth and sixth centuries, can be taken as representative of the villages of the period.[4] It has six halls of middling size, used for living accommodation like the continental halls, and 34 small sunken huts, 8 ft by 10 ft (2.4 m by 3 m), with two posts and wattle-and-daub walls like those at Ezinge I and elsewhere, including the two types described by Tacitus and Pliny. Examples which have been reconstructed to full scale prove to be quite commodious, though the discovery of a dead dog under the floor of one building and the complete lack of rubbish pits on the site raise some doubts about the occupants' standards of hygiene.

The halls at West Stow range in size between 16 ft by 32 ft (5 m by 10 m) and 23 ft by 46 ft (7 m by 14 m) and have no internal subdivisions. Those at the sixth- and seventh-century site at Chalton (Hampshire) are more like proper halls, with a separate section at one end occupying about a quarter of the interior, while the main area has two flanking doorways and a third in the end wall. The opposing doorways are set in the centres of the longer walls as these are seen from outside, implying an interest in the visual effect of the building. It is also possible, though not certain, that the walling consisted of planks set horizontally between the posts, rather than of wattle-and-daub.[5]

Despite this alteration to Leeds's picture of a society of hovel-dwellers, it might still be argued that standards here were significantly below those on the Continent. Sunken huts are much more common in England, where they occur in over a hundred villages, while conversely the three-aisled hall is almost unknown, and no structure earlier than the ninth century is particularly long, especially in comparison with giants like that at Feddersen-Wierde. But again this view must be challenged. It has for instance been suggested that halls in England are smaller because the milder climate obviated the need for winter shelter for the animals, a hypothesis which, if correct, removes the stigma from the absence of internal dividing walls. Similarly, the 80 ft (24.5 m) length of the Sutton Hoo ship proves that the size of the halls was a matter of choice rather than limited ability.

The third and clinching argument lies at the only royal site of the early period so far uncovered, that at **Yeavering** in Northumberland, which offers an excellent illustration of the possible effects of excavation on our view of a period.[6]

The oldest element of any consequence on the site is the rampart of an iron-age hill fort (fig. 4). This is linked by pottery finds with one or two structures of post-Roman but pre-Germanic date, and is therefore likely to be the work of northern Britons under Roman influence. In the second half of the sixth century the English struggled for control of Northumbria and achieved it under Ethelfrith (592–616) and under Edwin (616–32), the first Christian king, by which time Yeavering emerges from pre-history as Bede's *Ad Gefrin* (*HE*, ii, 14). The buildings erected by the Anglo-Saxons lie outside the fort and are therefore unlikely to date from the unsettled years of the late sixth century, while according to Bede the site was abandoned 'under later kings', that is therefore before he wrote in the early eighth century and, to judge from the vague tone of the remark, probably some time before. All the relevant buildings are consequently datable to the seventh century and the majority may belong in the reigns of Ethelfrith and Edwin.

There are two groups, a series of large halls to the east lying on a single axis and a more loosely arranged number of small halls to the west, with a wedge-shaped structure standing between, facing the more important buildings. The largest and the most complicated plans are those of the two main halls. That labelled A2 measures 36 ft by 81 ft (11 m by 24.75 m) and has an entrance in the

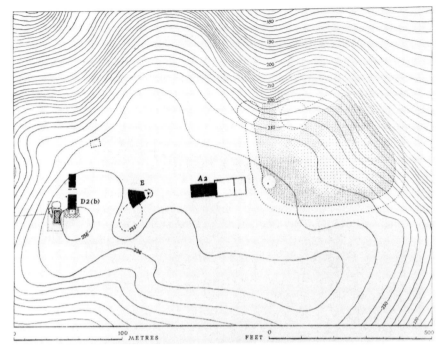

4 Yeavering
(Northumberland),
palace, seventh century
Plan (Hope-Taylor,
1977). *Crown copyright –
reproduced with permission of
the Controller of Her
Majesty's Stationery Office*

centre of each wall with two cross-walls separating off an oblong section at each end, while the main space is divided by free-standing supports into a central area and two aisles (fig. 5). Rows of post-holes set at an inward-sloping angle two or three feet beyond the walls suggest a series of buttresses or props like those surviving at Elisenhof, (fig. 6), the angle of which supplies the likely height of the walls. The end chambers could have formed part of the main space under a gable extending to their outer face, or they could have been hipped in some way, like the roof system reconstructed for buildings at Hodorf and Einswarden. Between the posts the walls were palisaded, that is, they consisted of tongued and grooved planks set straight into the ground without a sill. They were also plastered white, certainly on the inside and probably on the outside.

For an idea of the appearance of the building one has to resort to analogies, some of the oddest sort. The king's cauldron at Sutton Hoo, for instance, would have needed a free height of 14 ft (4.2 m) with its suspension chains, and the presence of something similar at Yeavering would prevent the interior from being very low. This observation at least coincides with the evidence of the angled posts. Next, Bede (*HE*, ii, 14) tells how Paulinus, the Christian priest who was responsible for converting Edwin, spent 36 days teaching and baptizing during a visit to the royal palace at Yeavering. He does not mention any of the buildings, but a few lines earlier (*HE*, ii, 13), when recounting the scene of Edwin's conversion in York, he puts into the mouth of one of the noblemen the well-known story, or parable as one might almost call it, of the sparrow:

Another of the king's chief men agreed with this advice and with these wise words and then added, 'This is how the present life of man on earth, King, appears to me in comparison with that time which is unkown to us. You are sitting feasting with our ealdormen and thegns in winter time; the fire is burning on the hearth in the middle of the hall and all inside is warm, while outside the wintry storms of rain and snow are raging; and a sparrow flies swiftly out through the hall. It enters in at one door and quickly flies out through the other. For the few moments it is inside, the storm and wintry tempest cannot touch it, but after the briefest moment of calm, it flits from your sight, out of the wintry storm and into it again. So this life of man appears but for a moment; what follows or indeed what went before, we know not at all. If this new doctrine brings us more certain information, it seems right that we should accept it.'

5 Yeavering (Northumberland), model of hall A2, seventh century. (Hope-Taylor, 1977). *Crown copyright – reproduced with permission of the Controller of Her Majesty's Stationery Office*

6 Elisenhof (Schleswig), excavated hall, ninth century

From this it is possible to surmise, in a building which was probably of the same type as hall A2, that the hearth lay in the centre of the main space, necessitating a louvre or at the very least an opening in the roof above it, and that, despite the contrast between the warmth within and the wintry weather outside, there were no doors in the doorways, otherwise the sparrow could have flown neither in nor out. Unfortunately the second of these two nuggets of information is contradicted by the description of Hrothgar's hall in Beowulf, since Grendel is there described as bursting the portal which was made of iron. This building also had a porch with inner and outer doors, a steep roof, a gleaming wooden floor and, on an unspecified surface, gold lining.[7]

Almost all the smaller structures are built on the same lines as hall A2, but without aisles. A1b for example has a central room in the shape of a double square, with a doorway in the centre of each long wall and a square annex on each of the short walls, while A3 has the main space divided into three by screens. D3 is of interest in having a floor below ground level like the sunken huts, while being large enough to constitute a proper hall comparable to the larger buildings at West Stow and Chalton. D2 has the distinction of having been rebuilt with the new walls encasing the old, as if there was a need to preserve the interior for unbroken use, the sort of requirement which is only likely to apply to a building such as a temple or shrine.

The most surprising find of all is without doubt the cone-shaped structure, one cuneus or wedge of a Roman theatre, which was probably used for councils rather than entertainments. It was built of wood in the standard manner of Yeavering, though with the addition of metal clamps, a technique which can be read into the description of the hall in Beowulf.

The sources of the halls, the palisading and the theatre can be considered separately. The halls clearly belong to the same broad category as those on the Continent, where both aisled and unaisled types occur, as well as opposing entrances in the long walls (at Feddersen-Wierde), central areas forming a double square (at Einswarden and Ezinge), angled posts (at Ezinge and Elisenhof) and the space separated off at the end (at Recklinghausen). The smaller, aisleless halls can be paralleled at Warendorf.

The origins of palisading are hotly disputed. Although Hope-Taylor claims a British source, no examples survive and its absence from the buildings of the fourth and fifth centuries at Yeavering is particularly eloquent. The only indication of its use in this context is documentary, as Bede (*HE*, iii, 25) describes Finan's church at Lindisfarne as built in the manner of the Scots, from hewn oak. In the Germanic world, however, examples are both better attested and older, including a house of iron-age date built of split logs discovered in Württemberg and another, with a sill, in the early medieval settlement at Husterknupp near Erfurt. As Visselhövede near Bremen belongs in the eighth century, Yeavering may be the earliest known north Germanic example.[8]

Lastly, the wooden amphitheatre represented on Trajan's Column and that excavated at Chester indicate that the sources for the wedge-shaped theatre are certainly Roman.[9]

The pattern of the country-wide distribution of sunken huts and middle-sized halls has not yet revealed any significant regional variation, so that an understanding of secular building does not at present involve a study of political geography. Yeavering, however, is a stunning contrast to this observation, providing evidence for an extraordinary mixture of the Celtic, the Roman and Germanic. Both the theatre and perhaps the plastering of the wood illustrate a Roman influence on the Anglo-Saxons shortly before they were christianized.

The Britons are the obvious intermediaries, and there is no shortage of evidence for their presence. The kingdom of Bernicia, that is the northern half of Northumbria extending from the Tyne to the Forth, apart from having a Celtic name is also an area of heavy British settlement with very few pagan Saxon burials, and very little Anglo-Saxon pottery. Yet despite this, the kings from Ethelfrith onwards were Anglo-Saxons, producing a picture of a British community with Germanic rulers and, to judge from the buildings, an Anglo-British culture.

This highly satisfactory solution is also rather surprising, given Bede's silence on the subject, the apparently unalloyed supremacy of English as the language of the kingdom, and the lack of defences at the site. No obvious explanation suggests itself for the first point (other than perhaps national, tribal or even local pride), nor for the second, considering the fate of the languages of the Langobard and Frankish conquerors, which bequeathed no more than a few hundred words to Italian and French respectively. The evidence on the provision of defence is equally conflicting. On the one hand the Germanic rulers of a Celtic populace at Yeavering apparently needed no protection at all, conspicuously setting their accommodation outside the walls of the fort which

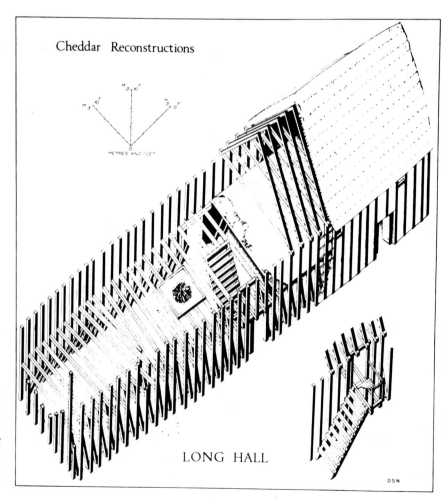

Cheddar Reconstructions

LONG HALL

7 Cheddar (Somerset), hall, ninth–tenth century. Reconstruction, 1:200 (Rahtz, 1979). *Crown copyright – reproduced with permission of the Controller of Her Majesty's Stationery Office*

enclosed an area not a great deal smaller than that which they occupied outside, while on the other hand, Heorot in Beowulf was hardly built for peaceful social intercourse, and the Viking camp at Trelleborg had defences on a massive scale.

Before the Danish invasions of the ninth century the secular architecture of the Anglo-Saxons is explicable almost entirely in terms of what they brought with them from the Continent, but thereafter this is no longer so, as new influences make themselves felt and building in stone becomes common. One aspect remains consistent however, in that evidence of grand structures is so slight that continental parallels are difficult to draw. Even the wills which start to appear are singularly unforthcoming about standing property. One of 1014, for example, mention swords, horses, shields, money and hides of land, but the closest it gets to buildings is 'estates'.[10]

Leaving aside Redwald's seventh-century palace in East Anglia and Offa's eighth-century one in Verulamium as mere references, **Cheddar**, near Alfred's headquarters at Athelney, stands alone as an excavated royal site in the later period just as Yeavering does in the early.[11] Remains begin in the middle of the ninth century and extend well beyond the Conquest, the earliest structure of any consequence being a long hall with irregularly bow-shaped sides, about 18 ft wide by 79 ft long (c. 5.5 m by 24 m) (fig. 7). The main uprights are accompanied by sloping struts as at Yeavering, but here placed inside and sloping inwards, which suggests that they supported an upper floor. That such floors existed is illustrated by the account in the Anglo-Saxon Chronicle, for the year 978, of the collapse of a first floor at Calne, depositing King Edward and all his councillors on the ground beneath, all, that is, except for the lucky Dunstan who found himself standing on a surviving joist. Nothing is known of the function of the hall at Cheddar, but with an upper floor and stucco rendering it too could have served as a council chamber.

It is possible that it dates from the reign of Alfred, but all that can be said for certain is that it was built before about 945, the date of a coin found in the context of the chapel erected in the same place after the hall's demolition. Both this chapel and the new hall, perhaps attributable to Athelstan, are more impressive than the earlier hall and would have provided fitting accommodation for the Witan, which met at Cheddar in 941, 956 and 968, while leaving unanswered the question of where the people attending such meetings would have lived.

One of the most interesting features of this phase at Cheddar is of a much more lowly character, namely the enigmatic sunken arrangement in the form of a circular track with two rectangles leading off it at opposite sides. Rahtz, the excavator, has ingeniously surmised that this was a fowl-run with the fowl-house and the fowl-keeper's dwelling, by analogy with the circular structures for the fowls and geese in the south-east corner of the early ninth-century plan of an ideal monastery conserved at St Gall in Switzerland (fig. 42).

The bow-sided form of the main hall can be traced back as early as the neolithic period at Zwenkau-Harth near Liepzig, in the iron age in Sweden and at Telemark in Denmark. These provide the background for the Viking examples at Lindholm Høje, Trelleborg and Fyrkat, though oddly enough, thereafter, just as it becomes popular elsewhere it ceases to be used in Scandinavia.

Apart from the neolithic examples, bow-sided buildings make their first appearance outside the Viking sphere in the ninth century, among the latest phases at Warendorf and at Dorestad, which may have been a Viking trading post. From here they can be traced to *Hamwih*, the original site of Southampton, where the posts are set in trenches. This is less advanced than the separate bedding of posts at Cheddar, which in turn gives way to the use of sills in the eleventh century at Buckden, St Neot's and Sulgrave. In spite of its connection with the Vikings, the form has nothing to do with boats and is difficult to explain functionally.[12]

There are no standing domestic buildings in stone, and only one or two have been excavated, the earliest of which is that at Kingsbury, Old Windsor, of around 800. The glazing which this appears to have had is not so surprising given the existence, already in the late seventh century, of the fine monastic refectory at Jarrow, with stone walls and glazed windows. It is unclear whether such structures were common at this period – especially those with a secular purpose – but they had certainly become so by the time of Alfred. Asser states that the king 'did not cease ... to erect buildings to his own new design more stately and magnificent than had been the custom of his ancestors', and asks what he should say 'of the royal halls and chambers constructed admirably in stone and timber at his command? Of the royal residences in stone, moved at the royal command from their ancient sites and beautifully erected in more suitable places?.[13] As this is the only evidence we have it is not certain whether such structures would have borne comparison with those of the Frankish and Asturian kings at Aachen and Oviedo.

In conclusion, the paucity of information on the subject of secular buildings in stone is underlined by the jump that is necessary to the next substantial piece of evidence, namely the Bayeux Tapestry, a suspect source made after the Conquest under Norman direction, even if by English hands, in which the houses near Hastings and Harold's hall at Bosham are as likely to represent anachronistic Norman as Anglo-Saxon types.

Chapter Two

TOWNS AND FORTIFICATIONS

Having examined a representative selection of the types of buildings constructed for secular purposes by the Anglo-Saxons from pre-history to the eleventh century, we can now turn to the effect which these produced on a larger scale, when grouped together to form a town. During the period in question this requires three characteristics to be worthy of the name, that is some administrative importance of which a mint is a common indication, a dependence, at least in part, on trade for its existence, and use as an ecclesiastical centre.[1] None of these requirements, of course, need imply any desire for visual effect on the part of the founders or builders, so for present purposes we shall draw a distinction between those towns which have clearly been planned according to some pre-conceived system such as a grid of streets or a rectangular boundary, and those which appear to have grown as demand required. Of course it does not necessarily follow that towns lacking right angles are unplanned, but because of the paucity of documentary evidence it is only safe to assume the presence of a design in those cases with some sort of geometrical basis, hence it is to this type that we shall restrict ourselves.

The study of towns in England has since the 1930s seen the steady advance (or retreat) of the institution into the centuries before the Conquest, starting with the refutation of the view that there was no such thing as an Anglo-Saxon town, proceeding to an acceptance of the urban nature of many of the fortified settlements or *burhs* of Alfred or his children and successors, and now toying with the idea that the origins may lie in planned layouts of the eighth and ninth centuries in Wessex and Mercia. Needless to say, the further back in time one follows this sequence the less concrete the evidence for it becomes, to the point where it is almost non-existent in the 300 years separating the departure of the Roman legions from the century of Bede. Despite this, Roman Britain is where any investigation of Anglo-Saxon towns must begin, because, whether any of them maintained their urban existence or not, a large number survived as physical entities through the first millennium.

Roman Britain boasted over 60 towns. Of these sufficient remains at about 12 sites to enable one to describe them with reasonable accuracy. The arrangement of streets is always rectilinear, with one of the main axes and at least half of the other marked by a wider road (fig. 8). Minor roads are narrower, but follow the same grid as the major ones, and the centre is marked by important civic structures such as a forum and baths. The perimeter is defined by a stout masonry wall, and, even though in almost every case this is an addition, the way in which it coincides with the features inside it and the lack of

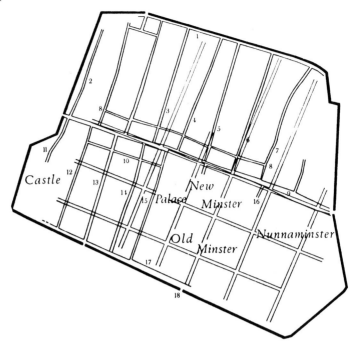

8 Winchester (Hampshire). Plan of the Roman (regular) and Saxon (less regular) street layouts (Biddle, 1971)

features outside indicates that, with some exceptions like Silchester, it was built on a pre-existing line. The rectilinear, and sometimes rectangular, outlining wall can therefore be added to the grid of streets as a characteristic feature.[2]

The decline of these centres began before the fifth century and accelerated thereafter to the extent that continuity between Roman and Anglo-Saxon civic life remains a possibility at only a handful of places such as London, Canterbury, York and, from the fountain still admired there in the seventh century, Carlisle. The number is so small that for all practical purposes it can be left out of account, a conclusion supported by the fact that neither of the earliest Anglo-Saxon settlements which might command the title of 'town', *Hamwih* in Wessex and Hereford in Mercia, lies in or on a Roman centre.

Hamwih is first mentioned in 721 while its decline was well advanced by the late ninth century, at which stage it appears to have been moved a short distance to become the centre of medieval Southampton. The disposition of the buildings of this period suggests a network of roads and a regular layout resembling a grid. It has been suggested that this might result from a following of the shore-line, but this explains neither why such a phenomenon should arise, nor why in the interests of trade or anything else transverse streets should cross at right angles. At Hereford, conversely, there is no evidence of trade and only the faintest of traces of a street plan, but the settlement is defined as a rectangle by a ditch and rampart. As additions to these defences can be dated to the tenth century, the original layout must be earlier and as Mercian charters start to refer to borough work in the middle of the eighth century, it could be considerably so.

The late ninth and tenth centuries bring us to the period of greatest growth in the number of Anglo-Saxon towns, the scale of which can be gauged from the assessment that, against the 60 or so towns in Roman Britain, by the Conquest there were over 100 such settlements. These are situated across the length and breadth of the country, but they can be separated almost without exception into those in the areas of Scandinavian conquest east of Watling Street, where there is no clear evidence of planning (as defined above), and those in the south and west where geometric planning, while by no means the rule, at least occurs.

The centre of our interest lies in the kingdom of Wessex during the time of Alfred and his son and daughter Edward and Aethelflaed, that is broadly speaking in the last quarter of the ninth century and the first of the tenth. The *locus classicus* for the relevant towns is the document referred to as the Burghal Hidage, the text of which can be dated to the second decade of the tenth century.[3] It lists 31 places whose location reveals a strategic intent to put every hamlet in Wessex within 20 or 30 miles of such a defended site. Many of these are simply forts or defended promontories, but eight have a regular plan, namely Winchester (fig. 8), Chichester, Bath and Exeter, which are all Roman (though with no continuous existence as towns), and Wareham (fig. 9), Wallingford (fig. 10.), Cricklade and Oxford, which are new settlements.

In the case of every one of these plans it has on occasion been argued, as with *Hamwih*, that the grid was not an intended element but the accidental result of following the demands of extant features, either the old pattern of streets in the Roman towns, or the terrain in the new ones. The following description of a representative pair of sites is intended to disprove these arguments and to establish the grid as a normal part of Anglo-Saxon town-planning.

Winchester is by far the best known of these examples.[3a] The major elements of the present street plan can be traced back at least to the twelfth century, while some of the subsidiary roads were sealed by the building of the castle in 1067. Radio-carbon dates between 850 and 950 have been provided by these smaller roads, coins found at some levels make a date after the mid-tenth century unlikely, and the resurfacing of some streets a number of times before the Conquest equally implies a date before the eleventh century for the earliest surface.

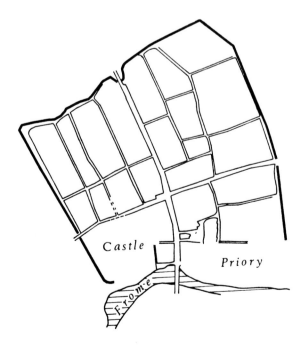

9 Wareham (Dorset). Plan (Biddle, 1971)

10 Wallingford (Berkshire/Oxfordshire). Aerial view. *Crown copyright reserved*

There are two reasons why the grid which these streets form could not have arisen from the old Roman one. First, and oddly enough, except in the case of the High Street (which is conditioned by the positions of the two gates in the east and west walls), the two grids do not coincide. The disjunction between the two plans cannot be explained as the result of streets shifting as buildings collapsed, since that occurrence normally produces kinks and steps and not straight roads on a wholly new alignment. Colchester may afford an illustration of this kind of development, with a Roman plan very like that at Winchester and a later street plan of the tenth or eleventh century often following it, but also diverging at odd places. The second reason is that the flint used in different parts of the earliest layout at Winchester is of a uniform, finely broken quality, implying that the whole system was laid out at one time. From these observations and the dating evidence the conclusion seems inescapable that the

Anglo-Saxons re-designed Winchester using the Roman street plan not as a specific guide, but as a representative of a type.

Wareham in Dorset is an ancient settlement with Celtic and Roman remains, but no Roman street plan or boundary. The town was founded probably shortly before the date of the Burghal Hidage, with an earth rampart with timber facing enclosing a rectangle of some 85 acres, the two main streets crossing at right angles near the centre and numerous smaller streets following the rectilinear pattern.[4] The proposal that this regularity arises from the parallel courses of the rivers Piddle and Frome which define the site to north and south can be answered in two ways. First, there is the general objection that, even conceding the accuracy of this description, as at *Hamwih* there is no obvious reason why such regularity should arise from these restrictions, while conversely any sensible planner will make use of natural features where these fit his purpose. Secondly, the two rivers by no means run parallel. On the contrary the western half of the town lies at what might be called the waist of the land between the rivers, while the eastern half is considerably wider because the Frome turns quite sharply to the south only a few yards east of the western wall. In other words while the site might suggest the use of a grid in the first instance, regularity is only achieved by compromising with the terrain in some places and in others ignoring it. It has also been argued that, because some of the blocks contained no buildings (the outermost ones at Cricklade for example were only built on in the present century), therefore the grids of the new towns were developed piecemeal without any overall plan. Yet Anglo-Saxon towns had a strongly, not to say predominantly, rural aspect, and the provision of pasturage and ploughed fields within the walls would have been quite normal.

There is then a respectable case for considering the grids in these Wessex towns as the result of a decision about planning, and the question that then arises is, what were the reasons behind that decision, or what was the purpose of the grid?

Before attempting to answer this question it might be as well to confront an issue of wider significance, namely the importance of function in design. It is possible to argue, and indeed it has been argued by architects among others, that design is only a matter of finding a means of satisfactorily fulfilling a given function. This may be so with certain types of machinery which are not normally visible, such as the interior of an electric motor or a nuclear reactor, but it has never proved adequate in any case where the successful use of an object includes an assessment of its efficiency by a human being. In this case, and it represents the vast majority of cases, the appearance of potential functional efficiency may be as important as its reality.

Thus a sword, being well-balanced and sharp, may have a particular curve to its blade which is traditional rather than functional, or a symbol on its haft to increase its psychological rather than its practical power. Similarly the twentieth-century soldier's helmet has as much 'art' as 'science' about it, and different types seem to be adopted by different armies as much on the basis of an admiration felt for military prowess as on the results of ballistic tests.

The contribution which the visual aspect makes to the extent to which an object is thought of as functional is nowhere better illustrated than in the productions of the Modern Movement and the Bauhaus in the 1920s which preached the functionalist ideal mentioned above. Far from adhering rigorously to this ideal however, from the start of the movement function, as might have been expected, took on a stylistic character of its own, with the result that objects had to look 'functional' whether such treatment aided, or hindered, their actual efficiency. In this way Le Corbusier's houses resemble the superstructure of a ship so that they will look like machines for living in and food-mixers appear as if designed in a wind-tunnel to reach speeds in excess of Mach 1. The architectural grid may also be used to represent an efficiency which is more apparent than real.

There seem to be few periods where the grid is either used exclusively or not at all, since among Roman towns Ferentino can be set against Aosta, in tenth-century England Canterbury against Winchester and in the twentieth century Peterlee against the centre of Milton Keynes. This variety suggests that whatever the reasons are for choosing the grid, they do not preclude the use of other systems. The centuriation of colonists' plots and the layout of the camp imply that the Romans at least thought the grid was militarily efficient. Yet there is no obvious reason why such thinking should be transferred to towns, and on the contrary there are grounds for believing that the Roman camp only adopted the formula from the town. This in turn conflicts with the value which Vitruvius himself (I, VI) puts on radiating streets in windy regions. A desire for a simple system of property taxes, a wish to reduce the incidence of boundary disputes, or the need to speed up military or commercial traffic can all be inferred and proposed, but in the last analysis it seems likely that the grid was used, at least in part, for the effect of order which it conveyed, and that towns were designed as much for the benefit of the designers as for that of the populace or the bureaucracy.[4a]

As to sources for the Anglo-Saxon grids, it seems obvious that these should be Roman, but while this is probably broadly speaking correct there is an important if unexpected element of rectilinear design in indigenous Anglo-Saxon planning. As already noted, neither *Hamwih* nor Hereford with their rectilinear elements stand on Roman centres, while the middle-Saxon site at North Elmham is arranged in bays, Sutton Courtenay in the fifth century is 'laid out in almost straight rows of houses nearly all orientated in the same direction', and the third- and fourth-century settlements at Wijster in Holland, probably of Anglo-Saxon or related occupation, have houses in parallel rows and blocks formed by streets and palisades, giving the lie to the oft-repeated calumny (or accolade) that the Anglo-Saxons preferred disorder to order.[5] It is probably in the same sort of context as Wijster that one should see *Haithabu* in Schleswig-Holstein as a parallel to what was happening in England, with a village laid out in more or less ordered rows in the eighth and ninth centuries becoming a fully-fledged town in the tenth, with a rampart, a church and a mint.

Turning from the question of sources to that of function, the existence of *Hamwih* in the eighth century has effectively discounted the possibility that Anglo-Saxon towns were military in origin. Nor, if Asser is to be believed, were Alfred's motives purely to do with defence, since he expostulates 'What shall I say . . . of the cities and towns he restored, and the others which he built where none had been before', while at Worcester according to a charter of the 890s Ethelred and his wife Aethelflaed, Alfred's daughter, when ordering 'the borough to be built for the protection of the people', included a mention of the rights of the same people in the town market.[6] Yet even if defence was not the whole reason for their existence, it must have been one of the most important, so that the *burhs* founded by Alfred and his son and daughter can with profit be examined as a military type in their own right.

To begin with, though it may not answer many questions, the terminological quagmire surrounding the term *burh* should be reconnoitred if not assaulted.

The place-name elements 'bury' and 'borough' are far too common, in the Danelaw as well as in the south and west, to permit any narrow definition. This is borne out by contemporary documents which use it for things as different as towns and residences, the only proviso being that they are fortified in some way. Examples of the two extremes are provided by the Anglo-Saxon chronicle, which under 754 refers to Canterbury as *Cantwaraburh*, and under 755 to King Cynewulf's trysting-place as a *burh*, meaning perhaps no more than a bower. In the same century the 45th law of King Ine defines penalties for breaking into the *burh* of a king, bishop, ealderman, king's thegn or gesith, while the term *burhbryce* is used in the laws of Alfred for the offence of unlawfully entering the premises of a nobleman. In fact one suspects that most places must have been fortified, apart from the odd exceptions like those at Yeavering, *Hamwih* and Cheddar.[7]

At this point we begin to trespass on the definition of a castle. Clearly it is wrong to deny that *burh* can describe a fortified residence, but that does not mean that the whole hoary question of the origins of the castle in England need be re-opened. If a distinction can be attempted in a nutshell it is that Anglo-Saxon 'fortified residences' were exactly that: their prime function was as a place to live, and to be secure they had to be fortified. Conversely the Norman castle, at least in England, is in most instances first and foremost a military tool, but one which is also the residence of an individual.

Everywhere in western Europe during the ninth and tenth centuries urbanization increases at least in part as a result of invasion, so that Wallingford owes its existence to the Norsemen, Magdeburg to the Slavs and the enclosing of the Trastevere in Rome to the Muslims. From this one might assume that at least the defensive parts of Alfred's *burhs* would derive their character from the Continent, yet this is not the case, as there is no comparable form on the European mainland earlier than the late ninth century, while conversely the ramparts forming a rectangular boundary around Hereford can almost certainly be dated much earlier.

Until recently it was thought that, whatever the case with the *burh* as a town, the *burh* as a double fortification flanking a river was Frankish in origin. Alfred built one on the Lea in 895 and raised a more permanent structure at Athelney. According to Asser the king founded a monastery there at a place 'which is surrounded on all sides by very great swampy and impassable marshes, so that no-one can approach it by any means except by punts, or by a bridge which has been made between two fortresses. At the western end of this bridge a very strong fort has been placed of beautiful workmanship, by the King's command'.[8]

One may note in passing that such structures were clearly able to excite at least Asser's appreciation, but the main point is that this type of fortification has been derived from similar erections used against the Norsemen by Charles the Bald on the Seine, Marne and Oise in 862 and 885, among other years.[9] The flank of this argument has, however, been turned by the existence of two charters, one from Kent of 811 which includes, among its reserved obligations, 'the setting up of bridges against the pagans', and one from Worcester of similar date which considers bridge- and fortress-work as a single obligation. Taken together these indicate the existence of Anglo-Saxon *burhs* flanking rivers a half-century before those used by Charles, a conclusion which is in fact hardly surprising, considering that the earliest Norse attacks on Frankish territory, those on Dorestad, Witla and Walacria, took place only in 834, 836 and 837, 30 or 40 years after the first appearance of the Vikings in England.[10]

To conclude this chapter we can return to the question of utilitarian and

symbolic function raised in connection with the planning of towns, but in the context of fortifications. Offa's Dyke marks the border between England and Wales. It is traditionally ascribed to Offa, king of Mercia from 757 to 796, on the grounds that Asser, who was Welsh, says he built it and because the king claimed descent from a quasi-historical ruler of the Angles in the continental homelands, also called Offa, who was celebrated in verse for establishing just such a boundary between his own territory and that of an enemy.[11]

The Dyke runs 149 miles across the neck of Wales, *mari usque ad mare*, of which 81 miles are earthworks and the remainder natural features such as dense forest and the River Seven (fig. 11). This length is greater than that of the Hadrianic and Antonine Walls combined, but such a statistic hides the real nature of the feature. Although it is 50 ft (15 m) broad it is a rampart rather than a wall, consisting of a ditch and bank rarely rising much more than a few feet above ground level, constituting a definite but hardly insurmountable barrier. Hadrian's Wall properly speaking, that is excluding the *vallum* which is more strictly comparable with the Dyke, was for most of its length built of stone reaching a height of some 15 ft and presenting a vertical face to the enemy, in addition to the ditch in front of it. Even more important, it was manned in such a way that, with the aid of milecastles and forts, it could be subjected to continuous surveillance.

Offa's Mercian earthwork was obviously designed to give the clearest view to the west and the best protection from attack from the same direction but its great length would have made such manning on the Roman model impracticable. The conclusion seems to be that it was not only a military barrier, but equally and perhaps primarily a giant mark indicatiing unequivocally where the boundary between Mercia and the Welsh Kingdoms lay. As such, apart from representing a staggering feat of organisation amounting almost to administration, Offa's Dyke is the largest single object with a partly symbolic intent ever made in the British Isles.

11 Offa's Dyke, eighth century. Aerial view. *Crown copyright reserved*

Chapter Three

CHURCH BUILDING IN THE KINGDOMS OF KENT, ESSEX AND WESSEX

Whereas among secular buildings Yeavering and the Alfredian *burhs* stand out as exceptions to the lack, as yet, of any clear means by which to set the material into a regional and dynastic framework, in the case of ecclesiastical architecture the position is very different. There is a striking and direct relationship between the churches and their patrons and hence with the localities in which they are situated, and since the ruling families were intimately involved in the spread of Christianity, it will be of use to begin this chapter with a brief outline of the dynastic history of the seventh century. As was evident in Chapter 1, Bede is an unparalleled source for the events of the period, so that what follows is drawn largely from his *Ecclesiastical History* and one or two other works.

In the two or three centuries before the coming of the Danes England was divided into many small kingdoms. While these varied continually in both status and number, the traditional tally of seven does little violence to the truth, namely Kent and the kingdoms of the East, West and South Saxons, the East Angles, the Mercians and the Northumbrians (fig. 12). Broadly speaking Kent was the most powerful south of the Humber from the mid-sixth century into the first half of the seventh, with Ethelbert (king 560–616) holding the title of *Bretwalda* or overlord of the English, Northumbria during the seventh century under Edwin, Oswald and Oswy, the first of whom ruled over the whole of the country except Kent, and finally Mercia during the eighth century, under Ethelbald (716–54) and Offa (757–96).

When Augustine arrived in Kent in 597 he did not come to a kingdom ignorant of either his purpose or his message. The pagan king Ethelbert was married to Bertha, a Christian of the Frankish royal house, whose presence must have helped to smooth the path of the missionaries. On the eastern outskirts of Canterbury she had for her own use the church of St Martin, which she shared with the new arrivals. After the king had been baptised he provided Augustine with a cathedral in the form of a church already standing in the centre of the city, which according to Bede had survived from Roman times. From this auspicious start and with only one relapse the conversion of Kent was complete within a generation (*HE*, i, 25–6, 32–3).

The first attempt to christianize the North Angles was undertaken by the Roman Paulinus who travelled as a priest in the entourage accompanying Ethelburga, daughter of Ethelbert of Kent, on her marriage in 625 to Edwin of Northumbria. He succeeded in converting the king and then his followers and much of the populace at York and Yeavering among other places, but after Edwin's defeat and death at the hands of Penda of Mercia in 632 he and

Ethelburga returned to Kent. Two years later King Oswald, new ruler of Northumbria, invited a mission from the Celtic establishment at Iona off the west coast of Scotland, in response to which Aidan came to Northumbria and within a few years succeeded in christianizing the kingdom. The dominance of Celtic Christianity did not last long. In the late 650s missionaries from the south as well as a number of Northumbrians began to introduce the liturgy of the Roman Church, starting a conflict with the Celts which was resolved in favour of Rome at the Council of Whitby in 664 (*HE*, ii, 9–14, 20; iii, 3, 25).

In the early seventh century the kingdom of the East Saxons lay under the control of Kent, so that when Kent was converted Essex soon followed, Ethelbert building St Paul's in London as the episcopal church of the area. After a long relapse into paganism Christianity was re-introduced in the 650s by King Sigeberht who was converted by Oswy (king of Northumbria 645–70), and by Cedd who came from the north and established himself as a bishop at Bradwell-on-Sea (*HE*, ii, 3; iii, 22).

Another Sigeberht, king of the East Angles, was baptized in Gaul before his accession to the throne in 630. The conversion of his kingdom was carried out by Felix, a Burgundian, whose see Sigeberht set up at *Dommoc*, now identified as Felixtowe, and Fursa, an Irishman, to whom the king gave the Roman fort at Burgh Castle as a base (*HE*, iii, 18–19.[1] The conversion of Wessex was begun by Birinus in the reign of Cynegisl (king 611–42), with Oswald of Northumbria (633–41) acting as godfather at Cynegisl's baptism. The two kings founded a see at Dorchester (*HE*, iii, 17). Christianity came to Mercia after the death of Penda in 654, while Oswy of Northumbria had control of the kingdom. The South Saxons were the last to receive the faith, in the late seventh century (*HE*, iv, 13).

The establishing of the Church in England was largely the result of royal initiative, and in particular that of royal women. Just as Clovis king of the Franks had been converted by his Christian bride from Burgundy, so Bertha introduced Christianity to Ethelbert, and Ethelburga her daughter introduced it to Edwin. Ethelbert saw to the conversion of Kent and Essex, founding cathedral sees at Canterbury, Rochester and London. Edwin and Oswald did the same for Northumbria. Oswald also aided in the christianizing of Wessex, and Oswy in that of Mercia and, after the relapse, Essex.

While the physical remains of churches are extensive in comparison with those of residences and fortifications, Christian sites established before 850 with some material as opposed to purely documentary evidence not only represent a small proportion of the whole, but many are in addition extremely fragmentary, like the short lengths of foundation excavated at Glastonbury. In these circumstances any statistical analysis can be misleading. East Anglia has no surviving monuments despite being one of the most densely populated areas, Mercia has no more than four and Wessex three. Kent and Northumbria are better off, with about half the buildings, of the total known from documentary evidence, remaining in some form. These were the first two parts of the country to be christianized, but even acknowledging this the survival rate has probably thrown them into greater prominence than they deserve.

The early churches of Kent and Essex can conveniently be considered together, given the architectural evidence and the political dependence of one kingdom on the other. Despite being separated by 70 years or more, the earliest dated building, SS Peter and Paul in Canterbury, and the latest, St Mary's at Reculver, are almost identical in those parts which survive. Since more remains at Reculver it is easier to examine it first and to use it as a basis for analysing the more equivocal evidence of the Canterbury church.

According to the Anglo-Saxon Chronicle, in the year 669 King Egbert of Kent gave a grant of land to a priest called Bass for the founding of a *mynster* in the Roman fort at **Reculver**.[2] This survived as the core of the parish church until 1805 when, because of the erosion of the nearby cliff-top, a new church was built further inland and the old one demolished. Today all that remains are the foundations, some descriptions and engravings, two columns and a few feet of wall, yet this is sufficient to provide a remarkably complete reconstruction.

The church is set near the middle of the once-square Roman fort, but since it is correctly oriented it ignores the alignments of the earlier walls. There can have been no intention of using these walls for purposes of defence, as they extended for a third of a mile and would have required a small army to render them effective. There may have been some advantages in having a shelter from the wind, but the over-riding reason is more likely to have been symbolic than utilitarian, that of reposssessing the Roman past.

The eastern cell of the plan (fig. 13) consists of a stilted apse curved on the interior and formed on the exterior from nine sides of a regular 16-sided polygon. The nave is short, only about one and a half times as long as broad, and has entrances in the centres of its northern, southern and western walls, each doorway and each corner being marked by a pair of buttresses. At the east end, just in front of the triple arch separating the nave from the apse, are the remains of a base 7 ft (2.1 m) long by 3 ft (1 m) wide set on a floor of *opus signinum* (or crushed brick mortar), suggesting an altar which would have been framed by the central arch.[2a] Churches at this date were often restricted to a single altar on the main axis, and if that was the case at Reculver then the eastern end of the nave must have acted as the sanctuary. This would in turn make the apsed room beyond, normally referred to as the chancel, into a presbytery for the clergy, furnished as it is with a bench running round the curve of the apse. The carved stone cross-shaft seen under the central arch and described by Leland in the sixteenth century is likely to be an eighth- or ninth-century addition to this arrangement. Originally the celebrant would have faced the congregation westwards across the altar. When the practice changed to the priest facing east

13 Reculver (Kent), St Mary, 669. Plan and axonometric reconstruction, 1:400 (Taylor, 1969)
14 Ravenna (Emilia), Sant'Apollinare in Classe, mid sixth century. Plan of north-east chapel, 1:400

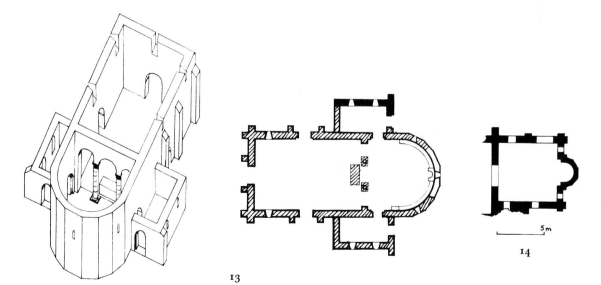

5 m

13

14

in the same direction as the laity, an opening would, literally, have occurred for the erection of a feature like Leland's cross.

The triple arch can be reconstructed from an engraving made during demolition and from two columns conserved in the crypt of Canterbury Cathedral, along with some fragments of the cross-shaft. The columns have cable-moulded bases, triple-collar capitals, and drums forming shafts markedly narrower at the tip than at the bottom. They carried three arches of radially set brick voussoirs, while the responds like the walls were of small but well-cut stone with layers of bricks at every fifth or sixth course. Two subsidiary rooms, of a type referred to by Bede and others as *porticus*, flank the main body in line with the triple arcade. Peers, the excavator, considered these to be part of the original fabric, but the masonry of the surviving north wall is so poor that it is unlikely to have formed part of the same build as the walls of the nave illustrated in the engraving. Small rooms of this type continued to be added until the whole church except for the apse was surrounded by them.

Shortly after the founding of the cathedral at **Canterbury** and probably before the year 600 King Ethelbert provided Augustine with land for a monastery between the city and St Martin's and money to pay for building it 'from the foundations' (*HE*, i, 33). The abbey church was completed and consecrated to **SS Peter and Paul** some 15 years later.[3] Because of its position outside the city walls it rather than the cathedral was intended to be the burial place of 'all the bishops of Canterbury and the kings of Kent' (*HE*, i, 33).

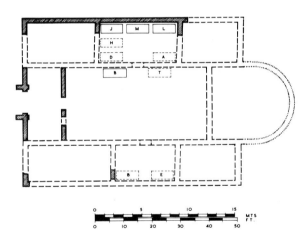

15 Canterbury (Kent), SS Peter and Paul, early seventh century. Plan, 1:400

16 Rome, Janiculum, Temple of a Syrian Goddess, second–fourth century. Plan, 1:400
17 Altenburg (Alto Adige), St Peter, fifth century. Plan, 1:400. (Oswald, 1966)

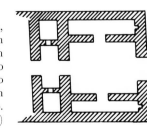

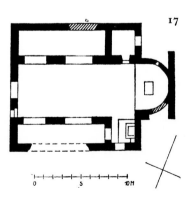

Around 620 King Eadbald built the church of St Mary a few feet to the east (*HE*, ii, 6), of which only the base of a western wall remains, and in the eleventh century Abbot Wulfric built an octagon linking the two churches, destroying the apse of SS Peter and Paul in the process (fig. 18). East of St Mary's stands the brick church of St Pancras, un-dated but probably also of the early seventh century, which as originally planned had the same shape and elements as Reculver in its first state, without any porticus.

The remains of the main church are fragmentary, but combined with the documentary evidence they are sufficient to establish the layout of the western half of the building (fig. 15). The nave had at least three doorways, two to north and south leading into a pair of porticus and that to the west into an entrance porch. Two further porticus filled the gaps left in the north-west and south-west corners, so that from the start the nave was surrounded with chambers, like Reculver in its finished state. The walls were of Roman brick and some 2 ft (0.6 m) thick, and the western door was flanked by buttresses.

In all these respects SS Peter and Paul is the same as Reculver. It is therefore reasonable to reconstruct the east end on the same basis, with an apsed chamber separated from the nave by a cross-wall, as all the authorities have done. They have, however, placed the dividing wall in line with the eastern wall of the north-eastern porticus, whereas the parallel with Reculver requires that it lie much further east. This is because, firstly, the pair of porticus flanking the apse at Reculver also flank the east end of the nave, and there seems to be no reason why similar porticus at Canterbury, signalled by the stub of wall in the north-east corner, should not have done the same.

Secondly, the doorways to north and south out of the nave at Reculver lie a little to the west of the centre of the nave length, and those at St Pancras', the only other Kentish church in which the doorways in the side walls survive, lie in the centres of those walls (fig. 18). At SS Peter and Paul the doorways to the porticus have been lost beneath the sleeper walls of the Norman nave, but a tomb set against the nave wall prevents the door to the main north porticus from lying any further west than the centre of that porticus. If this doorway followed the pattern of St Pancras' or even more of Reculver, then the east end of the nave would lie about 10 ft (3 m) beyond the end of the porticus. This reconstruction has a striking effect on the appearance of the plan, changing it

18 Canterbury (Kent), St Augustine. Site plan, 1:1200. M: Wulfric's rotunda; J.L.N.: the Anglo-Norman church (Taylor and Taylor, 1965)

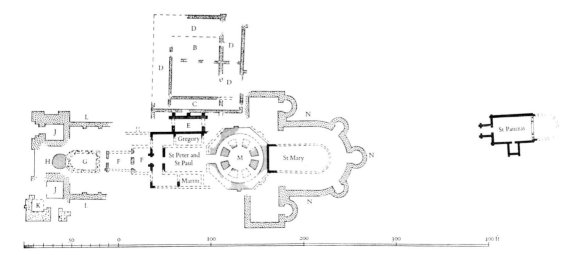

from a stubby and unattractive form to something with the elegance of Reculver. The apex of the apse would lie near the centre of the octagon added in the eleventh century and, it may be relevant to add, the proposed eastern wall of the nave would bear exactly the same relationship to the octagon as does the west wall of St Mary's.

Almost nothing remains of the elevations of these buildings, apart from one or two low fragments of wall at Reculver and St Pancras', but some idea of what they might have looked like can be gained from Minster-in-Sheppey, Bradwell-on-Sea and St Martin's in Canterbury.

Between 664 and 670 Sexburga, queen of Kent, founded and became first abbess of a monastery on the **Isle of Sheppey**. There is no good reason to doubt that the core of the present building belongs to this foundation. The east and west ends are lost but the side walls of the nave exist to a height of no less than 37 ft (11.25 m). Since this is almost one and a half times the width of the nave it probably represents their full height. This is also supported by the four remaining windows of a single splay with arches of brick and stone voussoirs, the apexes of which are 21 ft (6.5 m) above the floor and 16 ft (5 m) below the top of the wall.

St Peter's at **Bradwell-on-Sea** in Essex stands today as a simple rectangular structure looking much like the barn it was used as for many years. Originally it had an apse at the east end separated from the nave by a triple arcade on either piers or columns, and flanked by a pair of porticus. There are remains of prominent buttresses and the masonry consists of rubble, cut stone and brick. All this is as at Reculver, while the greater length of the nave (50 ft by 22 ft, 15.25 m by 6.75 m against 37 ft by 24 ft, 11.25 m by 7.25 m, at Reculver) can be paralleled at Minster-in-Sheppey (50 ft by 26 ft, 15.25 m by 8 m), which also has a comparable height (26 ft by 37 ft, 8 m by 11.25 m, or 1:1.4 against Bradwell's 22 ft by 26 ft, 6.75 m by 8 m, or 1:1.15).

This church has long been identified as that built by Cedd after he arrived from Northumbria in 653 to embark on the re-christianizing of Essex (*HE*, iii, 22), but its Kentish character, and especially the parallels with the proportions of Minster-in-Sheppey, must cast some doubt on this. St Peter's is also set in an odd place, straddling the line of the wall of the fort through the opening of the west gate, whereas at Reculver and Burgh, and probably at Richborough and Walton, the mission church was built fully within the walls. Fragments of rubble still visible in the nineteenth century in the south-east corner of the fort at Bradwell could be the remains of Cedd's church, leaving St Peter's to be an addition made after 669 when Theodore, archbishop of Canterbury, brought Essex over to obedience to the Roman rather than the Celtic Church, and hence firmly back into the Kentish sphere of influence, where it had been before the relapse over 50 years before.[4]

Before the arrival of Augustine in Canterbury, Queen Bertha had the use of **St Martin's**, which Bede claimed was a Roman survival (*HE*, i, 26). The nave of the present building is broad and low in contrast to Minster-in-Sheppey, but is built of the same sort of material and constructed in a similarly rough manner, suggesting that it dates from the seventh or eighth century.[5] Its foundations overlay those of the chancel, which is therefore earlier and is in any case of very different character (fig. 19). Firstly, it is built entirely out of well-laid Roman brick, and secondly its apse-less shape and the position of its buttresses can best be paralleled in the Romano-British temple at Stone-by-Faversham a few miles west of Canterbury, which has also been incorporated into a church to act as the chancel.[6] St Martin's stands near the Roman road leading east out of the city,

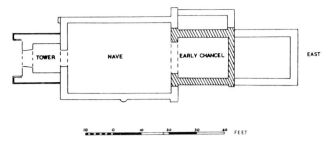

and within or near the bounds of a Roman cemetery. It is therefore quite likely that the chancel is Roman, but even if it was built for Bertha in the late sixth century, it still has the distinction of being the oldest standing Christian structure in the country.

There are a number of other sites in the south-east with early remains, but as they are all meagre and open to widely differing interpretations, they can only be mentioned in passing. Excavations at the west front of **Rochester** Cathedral have revealed the east end of a nave separated from a stilted apse by a sleeper wall which may or may not have carried an arcade. Rochester became the seat of a bishop in 604 and Ethelbert built a cathedral for Justus, the first incumbent (*HE*, ii, 3), but there are no means of telling if these remains go back to the seventh century or even if at any date they formed part of the cathedral. On her return from Northumbria after the death of her husband Edwin in 632 Ethelburga, Ethelbert's daughter, founded a monastery at **Lyminge**. The site awaits re-excavation, as the published plan, like that of Rochester, has been over-interpreted to appear as a close relative of Reculver or St Pancras'. The foundations may however be more interesting than that since they include a large western apse-like area (not on the same axis as the church) which could be part of a Roman villa or even of the new Saxon foundation.[7] From all this it is possible to discern a Kentish 'school' of early churches, characterised by SS Peter and Paul, St Pancras', Reculver and Bradwell, with Lyminge hinting at a greater diversity.

Nothing is known of the first cathedral of Wessex, that founded at Dorchester in the 630s by Cynegisl, Oswald and Birinus, and the earliest church in the kingdom of which anything survives is the Old Minster at **Winchester** built by King Cenwalh after his return in 648 from exile in East Anglia, where he had been baptised.[8] In the same year it was consecrated to SS Peter and Paul (fig. 20). This was a large building about 30 ft (10 m) wide and, if the chippings found in the holes for the scaffolding are to be believed, constructed in cut stone. It consisted of a rectangular nave with an altar at its east end and three porticus leading north, south and east from this area. There are no signs of an altar in the eastern porticus, and as the one in the nave is surrounded by four posts for a canopy it appears to be the main altar, as at Reculver. The Old Minster was used for coronations, and since, from at least the tenth century, the royal palace stood just to the north-west of it, it may have been built as a palace church (fig. 8). In the 660s Winchester became the seat of a bishop and Cenwalh's church was raised to the status of a cathedral, apparently without any structural alterations.

Glastonbury only fell into Saxon hands near the end of Cenwalh's reign (643–74) and the first stone church there was built by Ine, king from 688 to 726.[9] The fragmentary excavated foundations indicate no more than that this building had a nave with some complicated subdivisions, a pair of flanking

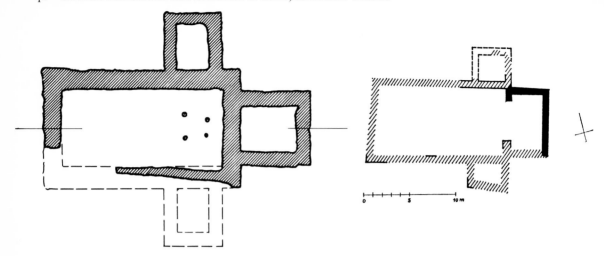

20 Winchester (Hampshire), Old Minster, 648. Plan, 1:400
21 Speyer (Rhineland-Pfalz), St German, seventh century? Plan, 1:400 (Oswald, 1966)

porticus and, to the east and separate from the church, a mausoleum of indeterminate date. The *opus signinum* floor may indicate a link with Kent, probably through the agency of Aldhelm, who was trained at Canterbury and who in the early eighth century became the first bishop of Sherborne.

The monastery of **Muchelney** in Somerset was in existence by 762 when it received a grant of land from King Cynewulf of Wessex and was refounded in the tenth century either by King Athelstan (924–39), or by Dunstan when he was abbot of Glastonbury between 944 and 956. A small early building remains under the Norman chancel consisting of a stilted apse curved on the inside and polygonal on the outside, and a rectangular nave with a section of cross-wall at the west end suggesting an entrance chamber. It is impossible to date with certainty, but the regularity of the hexagon on the exterior of the apse stands in sharp contrast to the irregular forms added to Deerhust and Brixworth in the tenth or eleventh century, while conversely it shares that regularity with late seventh-century Reculver, and on the Continent with late Roman basilicas at Metz and Trier.[10]

These ten or eleven sites represent the material remains of church building in southern England in the pre-Danish period. Meagre though they are, between them they provide a sufficient framework around which to construct a discussion of three general questions, concerning 1) minsters and different types of plan, 2) altars, and 3) porticus with particular reference to burials.

1 Minsters

One of the most striking things about all of these buildings is the lack of any clear variation paralleling differences in function. Reculver, which the Anglo-Saxon Chronicle calls a *mynster* and says was founded for a priest, has the same plan as SS Peter and Paul in Canterbury, a *monasterium* built in the shadow of the cathedral (and hence one might suppose with very different parochial duties from Reculver), while Cenwalh's church at Winchester, whatever purpose it was designed to serve, underwent no major change when it became a cathedral. This is an indication of the diffuse and undefined character of church organisation in the period, nowhere better exemplified than in the ubiquitous occurrence of the term 'minster'. This is clearly a derivation from *monasterium* (and nothing to do with 'minister', from *administrare*), yet it survives in far too many place-names to mean that in any straightforward sense. It appears to imply two requirements, a priest and a religious community, which could be monastic or secular. This vagueness arises from the fact that, in the early period, across the whole country many monks were both missionaries and priests, and also because monasticism was not as codified as it became in the eighth and ninth centuries on the Continent and in the mid tenth century in England. The situation was exacerbated by the position of bishops. Most of these were in monastic orders, and in addition there was the Celtic notion of the peripatetic prelate without a fixed seat, or even a clearly defined diocese, a type who made his way, in the person of the Saxon Cedd, as far south as Essex.[11]

2 Altars

The early churches of Kent and Wessex were built at a time when both the numbers and use of altars were undergoing significant change. Before the sixth century a church was as a rule restricted to one altar, but by the late eighth century, with the growth in the cult of relics and the idea that the mass was a private act of the priest, numerous subsidiary altars became common. The late eighth-century church of the *Alma Sophia* in York had 30 altars and the early ninth-century plan of St Gall illustrates graphically how every available piece of floor area could be taken over for altar sanctuaries (fig. 42).[11a] It is therefore no surprise to find that, in the transitional period of the seventh century, a building like SS Peter and Paul in Canterbury had at least two altars, the main one in a position on the axis which has not been determined, and one to St Gregory in the north porticus.

But while there may have been subsidiary altars in side chambers it is unlikely that in the seventh century the main altar would have been accompanied by another lying further east or west on the central axis of the church. Three churches are described in the eighth-century Northumbrian poem *De Abbatibus*, two real and one visionary, the visionary church having a number of altars but the real ones being restricted to one each. This suggests that the altar at the east end of the nave at both Reculver and Winchester was the main one warranting a prominent position and, at Winchester at least, a canopy.[12]

The eastern room at both buildings would consequently be neither a chancel nor a sanctuary, but a chamber for the use of the clergy, like the others lying to north and south. This is particularly clear at Reculver where the clergy bench around the apse survives. Neither can the triple arch be seen as a chancel arch or primitive iconostasis. It becomes in effect a backdrop, a kind of theatrical setting out of which the protagonists, the celebrant and his acolytes, proceed.

Reculver is by no means alone in having this arrangement. A number of churches in North Africa, which have often been used as a parallel because of their triple arches, also have the altar in the nave and none in the apse. The well-known mosaic rendering of a church at Tabarka in Tunisia has been reconstructed along these lines, with the apse area on a raised platform reached by steps through the central arch.[13] Apart from the question of how it was used, the triple arcade related to a sanctuary is a common feature in Antiquity and throughout the Middle Ages, from parallel triple sanctuaries giving onto a single nave in pagan temples as far apart as Si in Syria and Lydney in Gloucestershire, to the entrances to radiating chapels in early Gothic churches such as those at Auxerre and Reims.

The apex of the apse has been lost at Reculver, making it impossible to say whether there was a throne set at the centre of the curve flanked by the two arms of the bench, though this is very likely. A complete and nearly contemporary example survives at Laubendorf in Austria with, in addition, the base for the altar just outside the apse at the east end of the nave. This sort of arrangement, and especially the position of the bishop's or abbot's seat, makes sense in terms of a derivation from the seat of the Roman tribune set in the apse of a forensic basilica.

3 Porticus

Almost every one of the buildings discussed above, where the evidence is unequivocal, had subsidiary rooms attached to the main body of the church, either from the start or added shortly afterwards. These *porticus* had a variety of functions connected with the mass, with burial and with private prayer, though it is often impossible to specify which in any particular case. The earliest porticus at Reculver communicate with the exterior and with the apsed area and hence can be assumed to have had a rôle such as that of a sacristy, in the conduct of the service. At Bradwell the doorways of the two porticus are set differently, one to the east and one to the west of the triple arcade, which may be a unique survival in this country of a type common enough in the eastern Mediterranean. The *prothesis* and the *diakonikon* (though the labels are by no means consistent) were there used respectively for receiving the gifts of the laity which formed part of the eucharist, and for robing as well as storage of accessories, one requiring access from the nave and the other from the sanctuary, as in the fifth-century Syrian church of Qalb Lozeh. This may however, be a red herring as far as Bradwell is concerned since, if the altar was placed at the east end of the nave as at Reculver, then both porticus would have led onto the sanctuary and the presbytery, and neither would have had any more to do with the laity than their counterparts at Reculver or Winchester.

Numerous texts indicate that porticus were used for burials. According to Bede, for example, Bishop Tobias of Rochester, who died in 726, was buried in a chapel (*in porticu*) which he had built for that purpose, and in 721 John of Beverley was buried 'in the porticus of St Peter in his monastery' (*HE*, v, 23, 6). In the same way Paulinus of Nola, writing of his early fifth-century church in central Italy, describes how the side chambers were used for prayer and burials.[14]

As SS Peter and Paul at Canterbury is particularly illuminating on this subject it is worth while examining it in a little detail. More is known about the arrangement and identification of burials in this church than in any other building of the early Middle Ages in Britain and possibly in Europe. Together, the writings of Bede in the eighth century and Goscelin in the eleventh permit the identification of the north porticus as that of St Gregory which housed the archbishops, and the south porticus as that of St Martin which received the bodies of King Ethelbert and Queen Bertha (*HE*, i, 33; ii, 3, 5). Nothing is known of the relative positions of the burials in the royal chamber, but in the porticus of St Gregory the three tombs surviving along the north wall are those of archbishops Laurence, Mellitus and Justus, while that in the nave just outside the porticus door is Berhtwold's (fig. 15). Here is Bede's contribution on the subject:

On the death of our father Augustine, a man beloved of God, his body was buried outside but close to the church of the apostles St Peter and St Paul mentioned already, for it was not yet either finished or consecrated. But as soon as it was consecrated, the body was carried inside and honourably buried in the chapel on the north side. In it the bodies of all succeeding archbishops have been buried with the exception of two, Theodore and Berhtwold, whose bodies were placed in the church itself because there was no more room in the chapel. Almost in the middle of the chapel is an altar dedicated in honour of the pope St Gregory. (*HE*, ii, 3).

As with the use of altars, so the practice of allowing burials in churches underwent a significant change in the course of the seventh century. The very earliest churches contained no burials, the dead being laid to rest in cemeteries and those considered especially worthy having memoria or martyria built over them. Through a complicated and dimly understood process beginning with the catacombs, the placing of relics in altars, and the dismemberment of holy bodies, the type of church used for eucharistic purposes began to elide with the commemorative martyrium. This development occurred more quickly and more completely in the Latin than in the Greek Church, until by the sixth century the independent martyrium was almost unknown in western Europe, and the eucharistic basilica had become firmly linked with the idea of burial, albeit only of saints.[15]

This situation lasted, broadly speaking, until after the time of Pope Gregory the Great in the early seventh century. Pressure was always intense for burial to be as close as possible to the holy relics held by a church, and in the course of the seventh century exceptions began to be made to the rule preventing burial in church. The Council of Nantes in 658 pronounced that 'no bodies whatsoever are to be buried in church, but in the atrium or in a porticus or outside the church' and such prohibitions imply the existence of the malpractice.[16] Both this edict and the use of side chambers at Nola indicate that these porticus were thought of as technically outside the church, and Bede's description of SS Peter and Paul given above provides eloquent testimony of the erosion of this view in the course of the seventh century. Augustine and his successors were all buried in the north porticus of St Gregory, except for the last two, Theodore who died in 690 and Berthwold who died in 731, whose bodies, due to the lack of room in the chamber, were placed 'in the church itself' (*HE*, ii, 3; v, 8), showing at one and the same time that the nave was still considered to be the church proper and that the prohibition was being weakened by the placings of graves in it.[17]

Turning now to the question of sources, there appear to be three possible ways of explaining the forms of these churches, or at least those of Kent, namely through the shrines and other buildings of the Germanic tribes themselves, Romano-British buildings, or contemporary late Roman building on the Continent, of which the last is by far the most convincing, in particular with reference to Italy rather than Gaul.

Support for the first proposal comes from a letter to Augustine in which Pope Gregory recommends that 'The idol temples of that race [the English] should by no means be destroyed, but only the idols in them. Take holy water and sprinkle it in these shrines, build altars and place relics in them. For if the shrines are well built it is essential that they should be changed from the worship of devils to the service of the true God' (*HE*, i, 30). The pope practised what he preached, as he acquired the Pantheon in Rome from the Emperor Phocas and turned it into a church 'when the multitude of devils had been driven out' (*HE*, ii, 4). This widely-quoted liberal advice opens the possibility that the Christian architecture of Kent grew out of the indigenous building of the kingdom. However, apart from the fact that we know nothing of the religious structures of the Germanic tribes, the churches in question betray not the slightest trace of a development out of wooden forms. Equally important, Gregory was not consistent, since in a letter to Ethelbert of about the same time as the one just quoted he urges the king to 'suppress the worship of idols [and] overthrow their buildings and shrines' (*HE*, i, 32). The Romano-British temple at Stone-by-Faversham, which was incorporated as a chancel into a Saxon church, may represent an attempt to follow Gregory's dictum in a slightly different sphere, but it explains little if anything (the chancel of St Martin's at Canterbury excepted) of the character of the Kentish group.

The second possibility is that the type is based on Romano-British churches like that adapted by Augustine for his cathedral, and the others in Kent which he restored (*HE*, i, 26). Although nothing is known of any of these, the plan of a fourth-century church survives at Silchester.[18] It has a short nave with side chambers and an entrance vestibule ending to the west in an apse flanked by a pair of square porticus, one entered from the nave and one from one of the chambers next to the nave. It thus has much in common with a number of the early Saxon buildings to the extent that it would be foolish to deny a connection. What is not clear is whether this link was direct. On the contrary there is every reason to doubt that Augustine saw his church programme as a revival of Romano-British forms. The chief reason for entertaining this doubt is the state of relations between the Roman missionaries and the British church.

On the face of it one might have expected Augustine to make common cause with those Christians remaining in Devon, Cornwall, Wales and the west of England and to present his mission as a re-establishment rather than an importation, but this he certainly did not do. The British Christians went out of their way to be obnoxious to the missionaries and were eminently successful in engendering a similar response from the newcomers and their Anglo-Saxon successors. The few meetings organised between Augustine and the Britons were acrimonious and riddled with suspicion, giving rise, for instance, to complaints about representatives not standing up when the other side entered the room. An Irish bishop, according to another report, refused to eat not merely with the Romans present, but even in the same house as them, while a later Saxon bishop complained that members of the British Church with whom he had had a meeting threw away any food that had been touched by his party to pigs and dogs. Finally and perhaps most seriously, the Britons declined to help with the conversion of the English (*HE*, ii, 2, 4; v, 22).

It is, then, no surprise that Augustine was reluctant to acknowledge the chronological dependence of his Church on that of the Britons. This would in turn decrease the likelihood of any fundamental architectural dependence, and apart from its name the Celts appear to have bequeathed singularly little to the kingdom of Kent. Similarities between Silchester and Reculver are then likely to be fortuitous, the result of their both being related to the same body of late Roman building types, the third possible source and the tradition to which we must now turn.

In addition to the indications offered by Silchester and Stone-by-Faversham, the 'Roman' element in Kentish building is easily pointed up by a comparison between the plans of SS Peter and Paul in Canterbury and Reculver on the one hand, with plans of imperial date in the capital itself on the other, such as those of the temple of a Syrian goddess on the Janiculum (fig. 16), or the Basilica of Junius Bassus.

It is also underlined by the various forms of masonry of the two periods, as the materials used in Roman structures differ little if at all from those of the early

Anglo-Saxon period. Walling falls into two main categories, namely stone with brick levelling courses, and brick on its own. Examples of the first type at Minster-in-Sheppey and Reculver can be compared with Stone-by-Faversham, the lighthouse in Dover, and Richborough, and the all-brick church of St Pancras and the chancel of St Martin's with Roman structures in Verulamium and more nearly contemporary churches in Ravenna and in Rome itself.

There is no reason whatever to suppose that the Roman building industry survived in Kent through the sixth century, and since Augustine would not have found masons to hand on his arrival he must have imported them. As there can have been no incentive for these builders or their patrons to set about producing a conscious revival of ancient local building techniques, the similarities must be explained by the two traditions, the Romano-British and the seventh-century continental, deriving from the same over-all western Roman background.

If, then, the origins of the early architecture of the south of England and in particular of Kent are to be sought on the Continent, the Frankish kingdom at first seems the obvious place to look to. *Francia* or Gaul was a large, powerful, Christian state only separated from Kent by the English Channel. Not surprisingly it exerted an influence, in the course of the sixth century changing the cultural orientation of its smaller neighbour from one which can loosely be labelled north Germanic to one which was without doubt Frankish, a change particularly evident in the style and quality of jewellery used and eventually made in Kent. The marriage in the late sixth century of the Kentish king to a Frankish princess was merely the outcome of a long-established process and not the start of a new one.

The coming of Christianity only seems to strengthen this view. The missionaries from Rome had to traverse Gaul to get to England, using the route via Marseilles, Lyons and Burgundy, while Bede describes how many English churchmen were accustomed to go to the monasteries of the Franks 'to practice the monastic life' (*HE*, i, 2$\frac{2}{3}$–4; iv, 1; iii, 8). The institution of the double minster of both monks and nuns such as that at Lyminge was imported from Gaul, and Ethelburga, the founder of Lyminge, sent her children to the Frankish court when their lives were in danger.[19] Architectural features such as the porticus and the externally polygonal apse can also be paralleled there. The Old Minster at Winchester for example, has a layout very like that of St German in Speyer, undated but probably of the seventh century, suggesting that the Frank Agilbert might have had a hand in its genesis before he became bishop of Dorchester in 650 (figs. 20, 21).

Yet however impregnable a Frankish source may appear on *a priori* grounds, there are nonetheless good reasons for denying its validity, at least for Kent, and instead looking beyond, to Italy. Firstly, there is the corrupt state of the contemporary Frankish Church and the marked differences in organisation between it and the Church established by Augustine in England. The English mission came on the initiative of the Pope, it was staffed by churchmen from Italy, it dedicated its churches to Roman saints and, most important of all, it organised itself on a diocesan system equally foreign to the Frankish and Celtic Churches. This system, a legacy from late-Roman secular administration, had triumphed over the whole of the west by the end of the eighth century, but it did so because of the activities of Anglo-Saxon missionaries on the Continent, and in particular of Boniface who never lost an opportunity to stress his dependence on Rome, and who was primarily responsible for the reform of the Frankish hierarchy along these lines. It is for this reason that archbishoprics, a peculiarly Roman form of church organisation, were only established at Sens and Reims almost a century and a half after their counterpart at Canterbury.

Similarly, the Roman chant and liturgy brought to England by Augustine had spread all over the country by the eighth century, whereas it was only introduced into the Gaulish church in 754. The secular legal system also points in the same direction, since Ethelbert established a code of laws 'after the Roman manner' (*HE*, ii, 5). This could of course mean that the 'manner' was simply foreign or even that only the mere idea of codifying the laws, which themselves remained Germanic, was 'Roman', but Levison has argued that the Anglo-Saxon charter has an ecclesiastical origin connected with late Roman and Byzantine Italy.

Even where specific links can be established between England and Gaul, Kent remains an exception. In the first half of the seventh century many different types of monastery were founded in England. The majority, says Knowles, 'derived in one way or another from the monasticism of Iona or Gaul. Only the houses of the kingdom of Kent followed the Italian model with its Roman traditions'. To descend from the general to the particular, while Ethelburga, foundress of Lyminge, sent her children to the Frankish court, her tutor was the Roman Paulinus. Lastly, no Frankish church actually looks (or from descriptions sounds) like a Kentish one, and it is significant that the English parallel to the Frankish church of St German in Speyer should be in Wessex rather than in Kent.[20]

So much for the negative evidence. This argument would amount to no more than special pleading if there were nothing positive to support an Italian source. The polygonal apses, salient buttresses and brick masonry common in the fifth- and sixth-century churches of Ravenna are all of a distinctly Kentish type (figs 13, 14). Even closer similarities are to be found in the Italian Tyrol and Switzerland. Examples include the fifth-century church of St Peter at Altenburg in (fig. 17), with an apse preceded by a pair of porticus and a nave flanked by aisles or chambers, the fifth-century church at Sabiona with an apse, nave and two porticus, and, in Switzerland, Notre Dame at St-Maurice-d'Agaune of the sixth or seventh century, and the fifth-century church at Romainmôtier.[21] Laubendorf in Austria can also be mentioned again, with its arrangement of altar and apsidal presbytery like that at Reculver (see map, fig. 12).

To sum up, parallels with Kent can be found in Ravenna, in the Alps and (in the triple arcade and the placing of the altar) in Tunisia. Italy, via Sicily and the Po valley, is the obvious common element in these three areas, especially given the Italian origins of Augustine and his fellow missionaries.

Chapter Four

CHURCH BUILDING
IN THE KINGDOM
OF NORTHUMBRIA

After Paulinus had succeeded in converting Edwin of Northumbria in 627, the king was baptised in a church at **York** dedicated to St Peter which, as Bede says, 'he had hastily built of wood while he [Edwin] was a catechumen'. Although wood was the standard building material of the Anglo-Saxons it may have been used in this case because of the need for haste, as the church was soon rebuilt in stone. Bede describes this new building as follows:

Very soon after his baptism, he set about building a greater and more magnificent church of stone, under the instructions of Paulinus, in the midst of which the chapel which he had first built was to be enclosed. The foundations were laid and he began to build the church (*basilicam*) in squared form (*per quadrum*) surrounding (*in gyro*) the former chapel, (*HE*, ii, 14).

This building of the new church around the old may have been in order to maintain the continuity of the rites performed there, as has been proposed for building D2 at Yeavering. The question of the form of the church is more complicated. A centralized plan is suggested by the fact that the type is appropriate for baptism, the purpose for which the wooden church was built, and by the use of the terms *in gyro* and *per quadrum* in Bede's description, calling up a picture of a square structure with four similar faces. A longitudinal plan is, however, equally possible, since the idea of building 'around' something does not preclude longitudinal extension. Similarly *per quadrum* need suggest no more than that all the corners were right angles, as when a rectangular chancel is described as a square east end, or masonry shaped into rectangular blocks is referred to as squared stone (*opus quadratum*).

In other words Bede might have been saying that Paulinus's church did not have an apse, the sort of form one might have expected given that he came from Italy and Kent. This raises the possibility that St Peter's at York had the same form as the buildings that were to characterise Northumbrian church architecture in the second half of the century.

Other than the most fragmentary of remains, after the forced departure of Paulinus with the first Roman mission in 632, there is evidence at only one site from the years between the arrival of the Celtic bishop Aidan in the 630s and the victory of the Roman party in the 660s. Oswy, king of Northumbria from 654 to 670, vowed to provide land for monasteries if he should defeat Penda of Mercia, the same pagan as had been responsible for the death of his grandfather Edwin. This he duly achieved in 655, and accordingly in 657 Hilda, another of Edwin's relatives, founded a community at *Streoneshalh* which is almost certainly Whitby in Yorkshire (*HE*, iii, 24; iv, 23). The plan of the Anglo-Saxon church has not been retrieved, but a curved feature and seven or eight rectangular rooms, which may go back to the seventh century, have been unearthed.[1] If the curved element was the perimeter wall then it may owe something to the monasteries of Aidan and his followers, but there is nothing Celtic in England, Ireland, Wales or Scotland which shows anything like the degree of order and regularity of the buildings at Whitby. This is less evident when they are shown in isolation than when they are placed in the context of their paths and linking features. All the buildings are rectangular and the largest measures 19 ft by 47 ft (5.75 m by 14.25 m), whereas Celtic monastic buildings were usually circular and small, as for example at Skelling Michael or Church Island in Ireland (both in Co. Kerry), or Annait on Skye. Given that the patrons were all Northumbrians and given the regularity with which the English laid out villages and, a little later, towns, the character of the layout at Whitby can be more satisfactorily explained as Anglo-Saxon than Celtic while still leaving more questions asked than answered.

The re-arrival in Northumberland of 'Roman' missionaries from the south soon caused disagreements with the resident Celtic churchmen, no doubt to the acute confusion of the laity, especially in the passion aroused over the different ways of calculating Easter. To resolve the dispute a council was held at Whitby in 664 under the patronage of King Oswy and his son Alhfrith, at which Wilfrid, abbot of Ripon and a Northumbrian of the Roman party, defeated his Celtic adversary, Colman the bishop of Lindisfarne (*HE*, iii, 25). This was the first of two major events which were to turn the face of the kingdom firmly towards the south. The second was the fate which befell the advance of Northumbrian power into Scotland. In 685 Ecgfrith led an army across the Forth and the Tay and into the lands of the Picts, until at Nechtanesmere he was defeated and his forces annihilated by the redoubtable Brude MacBile. In the short term this meant the loss of Lothian and the bishopric at Abercorn, and over the longer term an end to Northumbrian ambitions on her northern border. The spate of church building which took place over the century and a half between 664 and the late eighth century was to show, on the contrary, how completely Northumbria, like Kent and Wessex, had become a part of western Europe. The excavated and standing remains at Monkwearmouth, Jarrow and Escomb offer an adequate illustration of this point.

In 673 a certain Benedict, who for reasons which are obscure was called Biscop, founded a monastery dedicated to St Peter on land donated by King Ecgfrith at the mouth of the Wear, now called **Monkwearmouth** (Co. Durham/Tyne and Wear). This house was destined to become famous both in its own right and through its twin at Jarrow, the home of the Venerable Bede from boyhood to old age. By the early eighth century the two together had over 600 monks, more than double the number at the royal Frankish abbey of St Riquier in the late eighth century, or that of the order of Cluny at its height in the late eleventh century. The church was begun and finished in 674, but altered and added to over the next few decades. The standing westernmost parts and the excavations suggest a nave 65 ft long by 18 ft 6 in. wide and 30 ft high internally (20 m by 5.5 m by 10 m) (fig. 22).[2] Externally these vertical proportions would not have been stressed quite as much as they are now, since originally there was nothing on the western face except the arch giving entry to the church. At some point a western porch with finely turned shafts was added in masonry very similar to that of the nave, but not bonded into it. Bede mentioned this porch and the fact that in 716 the bones of Abbot Easterwine

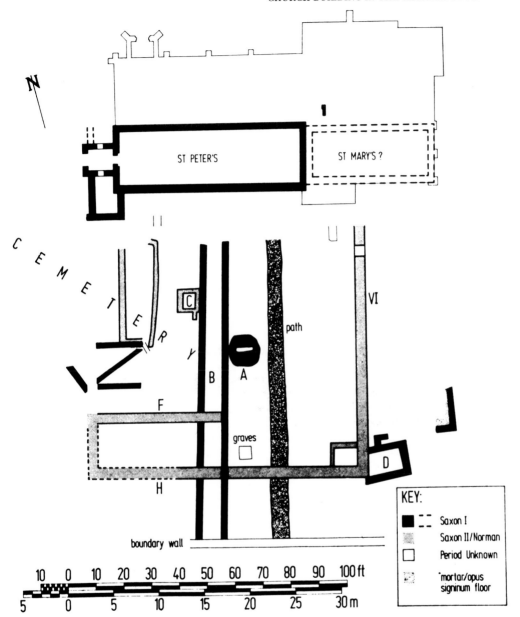

were removed from it, and as the abbot died as early as 685, the addition must have been made shortly afer the completion of the church. The upper floor has an arched opening looking into the nave. A gable-line above the porch and the partial blocking of two single-splayed arched windows in the western wall of the nave, indicate that the porch was originally of these two storeys and that it was only heightened later, probably, to judge from the decorations of the openings, in the eleventh century.

A few walls of the monastic buildings have been discovered to the south. These are on the opposite side of the church to the finds at Whitby and so are not strictly comparable, though at least one rectangular structure is of very much

22 Monkwearmouth (Co. Durham/Tyne and Wear), St Peter, late seventh century. Plan of excavations, 1:400 (Cramp, 1976)

the same type. The most interesting find is an extensive walkway running south from the church for over 100 ft (30.5 m), the southern end of which has still not been found. It had plastered and painted stone walls, glazed windows and a roof of stone tiles, with lead flashing, making it as smart as the church itself. This otherwise inexplicable structure finds a close parallel in the layout of the late eighth-century Carolingian monastery of St-Riquier in northern France, where three churches set some way apart were linked by elaborate covered walkways, one of which extended due south from the church in the same manner as the passage at Monkwearmouth.

One cannot be completely certain that the remains at Monkwearmouth are of Benedict's time, but the likelihood is increased by the extreme reluctance on the part of the Anglo-Saxons to knock down and rebuild venerable structures. All the evidence suggests that they preferred to add and enlarge piecemeal, as with the porch and the tower here. Equally, many of the characteristics of Monkwearmouth occur at **Jarrow** (Co. Durham/Tyne and Wear) where again there is nothing to prevent one from inferring that the oldest surviving fabric belongs to the same period.[3] Bede (*HA*, 364–87) describes how in 681 King Ecgfrith, delighted at what Benedict had done with the land he had given him at Wearmouth, gave him 40 more hides at Jarrow for the founding of the twin monastery of St Paul. An inscription preserved in the present building records the consecration as follows: 'Dedication of the church (*basilica*) of St Paul on the ninth of the kalends of May in the fifteenth year of Ecgfrith the king and the fourth year of Ceolfrith, abbot and founder under God of the same church'.[4] As the fifteenth year of Ecgfrith and the fourth of Ceolfrith fell in 684 or 685 the church of St Paul appears to be a closely dated building, but unfortunately what remains is only tangentially connected with this consecration.

From at least the eighth century and possibly from 685 Jarrow had two churches lying on the same axis (figs 23, 24). Of these the larger one to the west must be the church to which the inscription refers, but it was demolished in the eighteenth century. Conversely the smaller building to the east stands to its full height, but has no necessary connection with the document.

The standing building forms the chancel of the present church, but originally it stood separate, a few feet east of the larger one. It could be contemporary with the foundation, as examples exist of churches built in series, as with SS Peter and Paul and St Mary's in Canterbury. Equally it could be an addition, though not later than the late eighth century, after which the site was only sparsely occupied. In its early form it consisted of a rectangular cell approximately 40 ft by 16 ft internally and 22 ft high to the eaves (12.25 m by 5 m by 6.75 m), with a gallery at its western end entered through a door high up in the south wall. It is related to Monkwearmouth by its vertical proportions and by the character of its quoins, though the masonry is on the whole larger and better finished.

Despite the fact that the larger church is known only from drawings, excavations and fragments, it can be shown to have paralleled Monkwearmouth even more closely. The nave measured 65 ft by 18 ft 6 in. by 30 ft internally (20 m by 5.5 m by 10 m), and the western porch was some 13 ft (4 m) wide externally. The respective lengths at its twin monastery are 65 ft, 18 ft 6 in., 30 ft and 11 ft 7 in. (20 m by 5.5 m by 10 m, 3.5 m). Also similar is the two-storeyed western porch with the upper storey opening into the nave, while turned shafts preserved in the present north porch indicate the use of similar elements on jambs or on screens.

Jarrow differs in having features flanking the nave. The elevation drawing

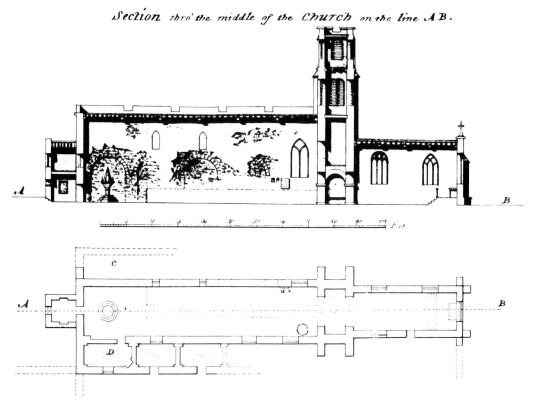

23 Jarrow (Co. Durham/ Tyne and Wear), St Paul, plan of 1769. *By permission of the British Library. (K. top. xii. 47b)*

made in the eighteenth century shows four large arches in the north wall conforming with the positions on the plan of four openings in the south wall leading to porticus beyond. One would therefore assume that the same arrangement had existed on the north side of the north wall, but this is treated as an aisle. The evidence of the drawing has been corroborated by excavations conducted in the 1960s. The result is a nave symmetrical on the interior but asymmetrical on the exterior, with a narrow aisle to the north and to the south a wider series of chambers or porticus like those in the Kentish churches, but entered through a series of arches as large and open as those of the arcade in the north wall. This layout is so odd that one is tempted to ascribe the two sides to different periods, except that no evidence has been unearthed of one system overlaying another.

The most dramatic revelation of the excavations was a pair of monastic buildings discovered underneath the standing Norman ones.[5] Two huge halls 91 ft 6 in. by 26 ft (28 m by 8 m) and 60 ft by 26 ft (18.25 m by 8 m) externally parallel the churches in both orientation and scale. They were of stone with glazed windows and covered with stone tiles and lead flashing, that is, as at Monkwearmouth they were structures of some quality. The larger may have been the refectory and the smaller, with its high seat and wall-bench, a chapter house. The contrast with a layout like that at Skelling Michael could not be more stark and underlines the difference in attitudes to monastic organisation. Whatever the significance of this for the inner life, the difference is of great import architecturally, both for the effect it must have had on what the monastery as a whole looked like, making it a veritable symbol of order, and for

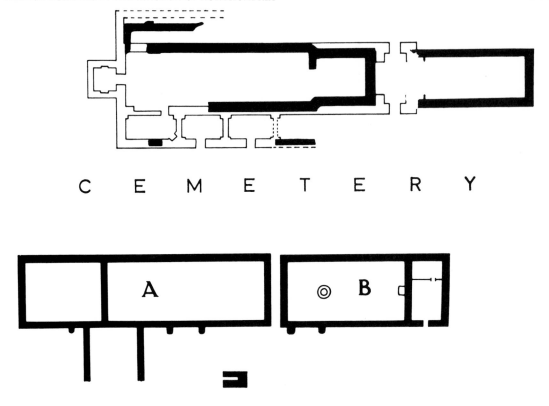

C E M E T E R Y

24 Jarrow (Co. Durham/ Tyne and Wear), St Paul, late seventh century. Plan of excavations, 1:400 (Cramp, 1976)

the clear way in which it points south to Gaul and beyond for its models.

The life of St Philibert describes how, around 650, the saint founded an abbey at Jumièges and built, among other things, a two-storey building with a refectory and cellar beneath and a dormitory above, with glass in the windows, the whole being 290 ft by 50 ft wide (88.5 m by 15.25 m)[6]. Much nearer the size of the buildings at Jarrow are the east and west ranges of the courtyard of the first monastery at Lorsch in the Rhineland. This consisted of a Roman villa which was converted to monastic use between 760 and 765 (fig. 25). The organisation which at Jarrow is expressed by setting the monastic buildings parallel to the churches is here carried a step futher, with the re-use of a central square around which the buildings are grouped. It is of course unlikely that Jarrow represents an actual step in this development since it almost certainly only reflects what was going on in Gaul, but the Northumbrian monastery is nonetheless important as the one surviving example of this stage of the process.

The seventh-century buildings at Jarrow form two sides of a rectangle, those of the eighth century at Lorsch form three sides, and the layout of the St Gall plan in the ninth century utilises all four sides (fig. 42), establishing the classic pattern of the monastic cloister, the form which was to be introduced into England at Glastonbury and Canterbury during the reform movement of the tenth century, and which was to survive almost unchanged to the end of the Middle Ages. In this way Jarrow takes its place in the mainstream of early medieval architectural development, something that need cause no surprise given the writings of Bede and the contemporary flourishing of the arts of stone sculpture and illumination.

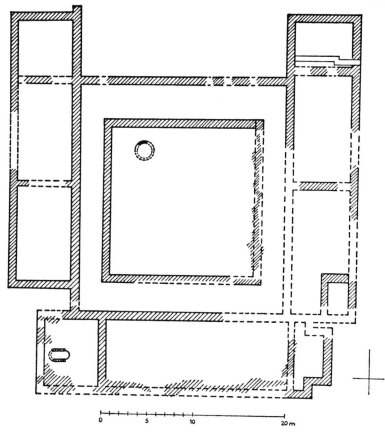

25 Lorsch (Hessen), the first monastery, *c.* 760. Plan, 1:400 (Oswald, 1966)
26 Escomb (Co. Durham), St John, seventh–eighth century. Plan and elevation, 1:400
27 Kapellenfleck (Niedersachsen), chapel, ninth century. Plan, 1:400 (Oswald, 1966)
28 Yeavering (Northumberland), hall A1b, seventh century. Plan, 1:400 (Hope-Taylor, 1977). *Crown copyright – reproduced with permission of the Controller of Her Majesty's Stationery Office*

25

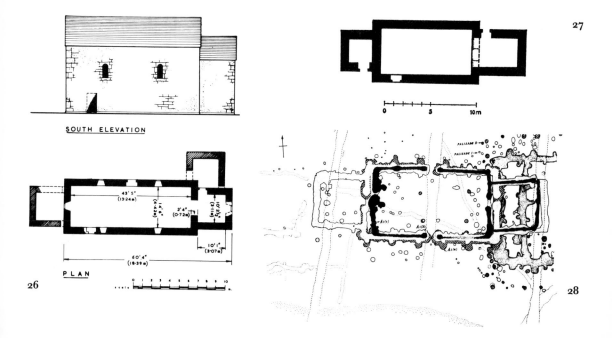

SOUTH ELEVATION

PLAN

26

27

28

Only one building of the period in Northumbria stands in its entirety, and hence despite its humble scale it is worth examining in some detail. The church of St John at **Escomb** (Co. Durham, fig. 26) consists of a nave and a square chancel entered through a tall narrow arch with radial voussoirs rising from chamfered imposts, in turn laid on jambs of through-stones set alternately vertically and horizontally, a popular technique known as jambs laid 'Escomb-fashion' (fig. 29). The windows are all single-splayed with grooves for wooden insets to receive glass, fragments of which have been found in excavations. Those in the south wall have lintels cut in the form of arches, while those in the north are left horizontal. On the outside the quoins and the well-finished masonry are of a size similar to that at Jarrow, although the biggest stones are

29 Escomb (Co. Durham), St John, seventh–eighth century. Chancel arch

much larger than anything there. There are three doorways, a mutilated one at the west end of the south wall and two rectangular-headed ones on the north side, one exactly in the middle of the north wall of the nave and the other, which is thought by some scholars to be an addition, in the chancel.

Almost everything about this building relates it to Monkwearmouth and Jarrow. The ratio of internal width to height is similar, about 1:1.5, the steep proportions being complemented by the sharp angle of the gable which, to judge from the early window at its apex, is original. The nave is very similar in size to the lesser church at Jarrow, with doorways in the same positions in the north and south walls, while the masonry, single-splayed windows both arched and rectangular, and the rectangular-headed doorways, are all closely comparable.

There is no documentation for St John's at Escomb. It is small, not even reaching the width of the smaller church at Jarrow, and it is devoid of ornament. This should be sufficient to mark it off as an unimportant village church of indeterminate purpose warranting both the label 'barbaric' which Clapham applied to Northumbrian architecture as a whole, and Taylor's surprise that glass should have been found in association with such a simple building, but instead it serves to illustrate the fact that apparently minor structures can be of some quality.[7] The masonry itself is of no mean standard. On the exterior the quoining is as good as that of the other two churches, while the walling, especially on the inside, is superior to both. The courses on the interior are much more evenly laid than those on the exterior and produce a consistent, even surface. The same precision marks the setting of the chancel arch, all elements of which are properly placed and aligned, including the radial voussoirs.

In part this quality can be attributed to the fact that most if not all of the masonry is re-used Roman work. Two blocks bear Latin inscriptions and the chancel arch may be a Roman one dismantled and re-erected.[8] Much of the stone is broached and provided with a drafted edge around each face, both of which techniques occur on Hadrian's wall, for example at Milecastle 42, while openings of both arched and linteled types can be found in the drains at Vindolanda. The walling overall, especially in its upper parts, is, like that at Jarrow, almost indistinguishable from Roman walls like those in the amphitheatre at Chester.

Considering this it may seem that praise of the masonry is misdirected in the present context, but this would be to underestimate the builder's achievement. No Roman building ever looked quite like Escomb. Thus while the chancel arch and even the windows may have been re-used, the church as a whole must have been cannibalised from parts of different buildings. This in itself would demand some skill. So too would the demolition, which would have to proceed without damage to the demounted stones, especially those forming the chancel arch, while some blocks, especially the lower quoins at the east end, are very large, reaching 4 ft (1.2 m) in length, making them correspondingly difficult to handle. Having dismantled and transported his material the mason then had the task of re-erecting it (including re-cutting some of the blocks), and in this he has acquitted himself as well as his Roman predecessor.

The care expended on the masonry is also evident in the dimensions. The external quoins all slope inwards, as do the jambs of the two complete doorways, but they do so regularly and therefore intentionally. The slope is very slight and the effect quite elegant, unlike the oddity of, for example, the sloping doorways popular in twelfth-century Ireland. The walls have a uniform thickness of about 2 ft 4 in. (0.72 m). As this was determined by the width of the single stones forming the jambs of the chancel arch, it follows that the double-skin walls of the nave and chancel have been built to this specification. The nave has an interior width of 14 ft 6 in. (4.42 m) at both its east and west ends, while the north wall at 43 ft 5 in. (13.24 m) is only two inches (0.05 m) longer than the south. In the chancel the north and south walls are both 10 ft 1 in. (3.07 m) long and those to east and west 10 ft 2½ in. (3.11 m). As the space was probably intended to be square the error is only of 1½ in. (0.04 m) or a little over one percent. As well as being executed with impressive consistency, these dimensions bear neat geometrical relationships to one another, since the diagonal of the square in the chancel equals the width of the nave, and that in turn multiplied by three equals the length of the nave[9]

As originally built and as described above, Escomb was, as has often been remarked, a classic example of a two-cell church. It did not remain so for long however, as a square adjunct very like the chancel was added to the west end of the nave and another to the north side of the chancel.[10] These two porticus are known only from their foundations and a fragment of wall, but it is clear from the way they abut the main wall that they are additions. The eastern porticus presumably functioned as a sacristy of some sort, but the western one was not, surprisingly enough, a porch, as there is no sign whatsoever of any means of access between it and the nave. The gable of the roof has left a line on the nave wall indicating that the structure was quite tall and could therefore have contained an upper floor. On the other hand it is no taller than the single-storeyed chancel, and there is no sign of an upper opening looking into the nave. Its purpose is a mystery.

Escomb is the best preserved of a number of similar buildings including Seaham, Ledsham, St Peter's at Bywell, and perhaps Corbridge, which can consequently with greater or less conviction be dated to the late seventh or the eighth century. Having established that Escomb is a church of no mean quality and that it has some representative value, we can now examine the most likely source for the ideas and techniques behind its form and those of Monkwear-mouth and Jarrow.

The first and most obvious answer is Rome, in the broadest sense. Builders have always re-used masonry, but seldom if ever with the care displayed at Escomb. In most cases re-use is motivated by economy, as when carved stones are reversed, squared off and used to build a wall. Here on the contrary the intention appears to have been to recreate if not exactly, since the plan and function are different, then in broad outline and detail a 'Roman' building. The evidence of the masonry leaves little doubt about what it was that the patrons admired, and one is entitled to see in a stone building in seventh-century Northumbria something of the glamour of a new technology. Perhaps this is not surprising considering the recent southerly orientation of the Church in the kingdom, and in this case, unlike with Kent, Gaul fulfils its role as the most likely immediate source of the Roman tradition.

In the first place Bede records that Benedict Biscop brought back with him Gaulish masons who were expecting to build according to the *morem roman-orum*.[11] Town walls of the fifth and sixth centuries in places such as Beauvais not surprisingly reveal a continuation of Roman masonry techniques, so the immigrant builders could be expected to understand the Roman material with which they were called upon to work. The yellow mortar and pink interior plaster found at Monkwearmouth can be paralleled in Gaul, for example at Angers, and the characteristic shafts of both Monkwearmouth and Jarrow occur in the fifth century at Nouaillé (Vienne) and in the ninth at Germigny on the Loire, while clear even if later parallels for the monastic buildings at both sites have been pointed to at St-Riquier and Lorsch.[12] Gaul also has a lot to offer in terms of types of plan, but here the position is a little more complicated.

The plans of the Northumbrian buildings discussed above belong to three types: the simple cell like the east church at Jarrow, the two-cell type of Escomb, and the nave flanked by porticus or aisles like the main church at Jarrow. This last type will be considered in the next chapter, with some related buildings in Mercia. The single cell has a long and illustrious history in the Christian Church, varying from tiny Irish oratories such as that on Church Island to immense buildings such as St Alban's in Mainz which have seldom been surpassed in width. Given the existence of the Irish examples and the proximity of places like Ardwall in Kirkcudbrightshire, within the sphere of the Northumbrian bishopric of Whithorn, it is unnecessary to look further afield to explain Anglo-Saxon buildings of this type. For very long examples such as Monkwearmouth and St Patrick's at Heysham, however, better parallels exist in Gaul than in Ireland. Ste-Gertrude at Nivelles, for example, probably built between 640 and 652, had a nave approximately 76 ft by 22 ft (23 m by 6.75 m) (fig. 30), a proportion of 1:3.5.

The two-cell plan is almost as common as the single cell, but examples datable before the late seventh century are very hard to find. We shall begin by examining and rejecting the case for a Gaulish source. The late eighth-century church of the monastery at Lorsch mentioned in connection with the monastic buildings at Jarrow has a nave almost three times as long as wide, and a rectangular chancel (fig. 25). That the type is much older is shown by the existence of a similar though aisled plan in the fifth-century church of SS Felix and Fortunatus in Vicenza.[13] These examples are unsatisfactory as sources, however, since in each the chancel is very shallow and lacks a wall separating it from the nave. The seventh-century church of St German at Speyer has already been suggested as a source for Cenwalh's church at Winchester (figs 20, 21) but once again it illustrates the fact that while rectangularity may be a feature of both Gaulish and Northumbrian churches, the particular layout of Escomb is more difficult to parallel.

Some simple rectangles had chancels added to them, such as that of the church of St Victor at Xanten, but there the addition was only made in 768. When she died in 659 St Gertrude was buried outside the east end of her church in Nivelles, and within a few years an extension from the church was built out over the site of the burial (fig. 30). This may sound like the perfect source for Escomb and Jarrow, especially given the parallel between the naves of Nivelles and Monkwearmouth, but this is not the case. The saint was not buried on the

30 Nivelles (Brabant), St-Gertrude. Plan, 1:400. Black: church of between 640 and 652; hatched: later seventh century addition over St Gertrude's tomb; broken lines: nave walls of ninth century church; crosses: centres of eastern piers of eleventh century church (see fig. 68).

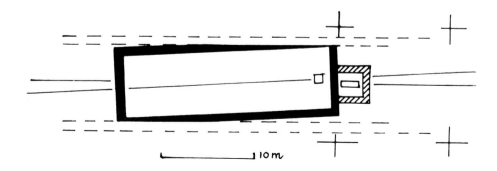

└———————┘ 10 m

axis of her church nor on the same orientation. When her tomb was enclosed these characteristics were considered of such importance that the tomb, not the church, conditioned both the axis and the orientation of the new building, giving it an extremely odd relationship with the original nave, its outer walls lying about 4 ft (1.3 m) from the south corner of the east wall of the nave and about 8 ft (1.75 m) from the north. As all the subsequent rebuildings of the church took their axis from the body and its chapel this is an extreme case of the tail wagging the dog; more importantly, the distorted result bears no resemblance to the Northumbrian buildings.

Setting aside the question of date, there are of course many plans of churches in the eastern territories of the Franks which are very similar indeed to Escomb. One of the most striking is that at Kapellenfleck which has a long nave, a rectangular chancel with a narrow chancel arch and doorway in its north wall, a main entrance at the west end of the south wall of the nave, no western doorway, and a porticus added later to the west face (fig. 27).[14] The only differences are the lack of a central doorway in the north wall of the nave and proportions of 1:2 instead of 1:3 in the main body. The church was probably built in the early ninth century and hence is too late to constitute any explanation for the English building, nor can its continental forerunners be traced back much before the middle years of the eighth century. The reason for this is that box churches such as that at Kapellenfleck are likely to have been built under the influence of the very Anglo-Saxon buildings which we are trying to explain. St Willibrord, the first of the English missionaries to the Germans, was educated at Ripon, went to Frisia in 690 and later became archbishop of the Frisians, while by the mid eighth century Boniface, another Englishman, was primate of the church in Germany (HE, iii, 13, v, 2, 24). The influences and peoples which had flowed to England from beyond the Rhine in the fifth and sixth centuries began to run in a reverse direction and with an ecclesiastical content in the seventh and eighth. The churchmen were well aware of this. The inhabitants east of the Rhine were 'our people' (gens nostra), and it was amongst the new converts that the term 'Anglo-Saxon' for the Germanic inhabitants of England was first used.[15]

But the Anglo-Saxons were not the only missionaries active in this field. The Irish were there as well and some of the buildings with which they can be connected bear some resemblance to Escomb. In 741 Büraberg near Fritzlar was selected by Boniface as the site of the first bishopric in Hesse. As there is no mention in his biography of him having built a church there, the three-cell chapel of St Brigid may pre-date his arrival, in which case it would have been built by the Irish missionaries previously active in the area, as its dedication suggests. The box church with a rectangular chancel in the Niedermünster in Regensburg also has an Irish connection. Albert the archbishop of Cashel came to Regensburg to find the Bavarian bishop Erhard, but learning on his arrival that the latter had expired, he himself died of grief and was buried next to his friend, apparently in the building in question. These events suggest that the earliest church on the site was in existence around 700. Lastly St Martin's at Pier near Cologne was a wooden church with a rectangular chancel. It may be as early as 700 and hence attributable to the Irish rather than the Anglo-Saxons in this area.[16]

A date in the early eighth century still, of course, does not get these examples back before the late seventh-century date it is reasonable to postulate for Escomb, nor are there any surviving plans of the type to which one can point in Ireland. Yet given the conservatism and apparent insularity of the Irish clergy it is unlikely that they approached their potential German converts armed with the latest in Anglo-Saxon church design. If there was an Irish tradition of buildings of this sort, then at this date they must have been built of wood. It is true that early in the fifth century St Ninian built a church in stone at Whithorn, but Bede calls this 'a method unusual among the Britons' and describes Ninian as 'a Briton who had received orthodox instruction at Rome. ...' (*HE*, iii, 4). More representative is the mid seventh-century bishop Finan who built a church at Lindesfarne 'after the Irish manner (*more scottorum*), not of stone but of hewn oak' (*HE*, iii, 25).[17]

While this may establish that Irish buildings were traditionally constructed of wood, we know nothing of what they looked like. Nevertheless, now that our attention has been turned to wooden architecture we can embark on the last leg of this rather circuitous journey in search of a convincing source for the two-cell box church. This leads us back to Northumberland and to the largest collection of wooden buildings recently excavated in the north of England, in the palace at Yeavering. Most of these buildings consist of a central rectangle with an opening in the centre of each long wall and either a variety of subdivisions to the main space or annexes attached to the end walls. One representative structure, labelled A1b by the excavator (fig. 28), bears a strong resemblance to Escomb, with a square annex at each end and the central entrances into the nave. The annexes are 16 ft 6 in. (5.03 m) (that is, a perch) square and their diagonal, 23 ft 4 in. (7.11 m), equals the width of the main body, which has a length twice this width. Except for the 'nave' of 1:2 instead of 1:3 these are the proportions of Escomb, an arcane parallel which suggests that the buildings were conceived and laid out in the same way.

The type of church represented by Escomb can probably be seen as a compromise, or more positively as a bridge, between two very different traditions, using the layout of one, the Germanic, and the masonry techniques of the other, the Roman, paralleling in some measure the carved stone crosses of the period. This suggestion throws into relief the possibilities presented by the two churches built in York by Paulinus for Edwin in the 620s, the first in wood and the second, perhaps conditioned by it, in stone.

The churches of St Andrew's at Hexham and St Peter's at Ripon stand a little apart within the Northumbrian group. Both were built by Wilfrid, one of the liveliest and most controversial ecclesiastical politicians of the second half of the seventh century. After participating successfully in the Council of Whitby he departed for Gaul to be consecrated bishop of York, returning only to find his see usurped. After taking up his position in 669, between 672 and 678 he founded and built a monastery at Hexham and at about the same time rebuilt the Celtic one at Ripon. He was twice bishop of Hexham, which had been raised to the rank of cathedral in 681, from 686 to 691 and from 702 until his death in 709.

Only the crypt survives at **Ripon** (Yorkshire). It lies under the eastern end of the present nave and is set below ground level with no windows or other sources of natural light. The walls and vaults are built of well-cut stone, including small recesses presumably for lamps. The crypt proper consists of a rectangular chamber some 11 ft (3.25 m) long lying on the central axis of the early Gothic church (fig. 31, inset). It has two entrances, one stairway coming from the west and the other from the east. Presumably the first was for the laity, coming from the nave, and the second for the clergy, coming from the sanctuary, but this would mean that pilgrims had to come and go in a single passage less than 3 ft (1 m) wide, while the monks had to walk all the way to the west end of the crypt, where they were provided with an entrance vestibule almost as large as the main chamber itself. Conversely if the laity used this hallway as an exit they would have to pass through the main chamber and finish their journey in the sanctuary.

In almost all respects the crypt at **Hexham** (Northumberland) is very like that at Ripon, in scale, location, material and in the disposition of its elements, except that confusion between the means of entry and egress appear to have been removed (fig. 31). The main chamber again lies on or near the axis of the church and there are separate passages for clergy and laity. The single passage, probably for the clergy, descends from outside the sanctuary wall and enters unobtrusively on the south side. The laity, on the other hand, have a passage from the centre of the nave in the west to take them down into the crypt and another to take them out again, emerging just to the north of the north wall of

31 Hexham (Northumberland), St Andrew, seventh century. Plan, 1:400. Crosses: centres of thirteenth century crossing piers. Inset: Ripon Cathedral, crypt

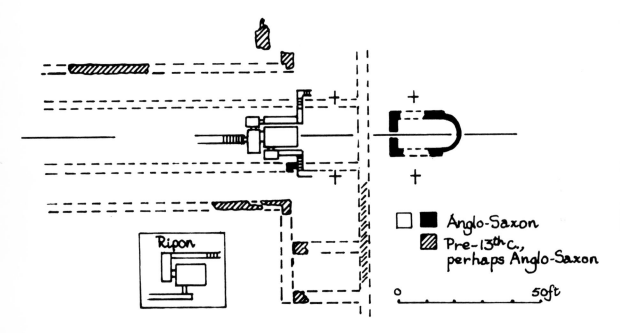

the nave. The entrance and exit passages meet underground in the vestibule set to the west of the main chamber, allowing pilgrims to stand at this point and witness whatever relics were on display beyond a separating grill. The demands of circulation and different types of access are therefore much more happily satisfied here than by the promiscuous arrangements at Ripon. Given the great similarities between the two crypts it consequently seems likely that Hexham's is a slightly later and improved version.

Apart from the crypt, the excavated remains which can with some certainty be attributed to Wilfrid's building consist of only two items, a fragment of the main wall of the church over the southern passage to the crypt, and a free-standing apsed chapel to the east, on the same axis as the crypt and surrounded with burials. The other elements, indicated in the plan by cross-hatching, can be no more securely dated than to before the rebuilding of the thirteenth century, and only possibly to before the Conquest. They suggest an aisled structure with some adjuncts flanking the east end.[18] This meagre information, however, can be fleshed out with the description by Eddius, Wilfrid's contemporary and biographer.

My feeble tongue will not permit me here to enlarge upon the depth of the foundations in the earth, and its crypts of wonderfully dressed stone, and the manifold building above ground, carried by various supports (*columnis*) and many side aisles, and adorned with walls of notable length and height, surrounded by various winding passages with spiral stairs leading up and down; for our holy bishop, being taught by the spirit of God, thought out how to construct these buildings; nor have we heard of any other house on this side of the Alps built on such a scale.[19]

The supports of the arcades must have been piers as Richard of Hexham, writing in the twelfth century, describes them as *quadratis ... columnis*, or 'squared columns'. Eddius's description of the upper parts of the church shows that they were complicated enough, but Richard again supplies the crucial clues when he says that the building was divided into three storeys and that people could stand and walk all around it in such a way that they could not be seen from below. This can only mean that there were galleries above the aisles and perhaps across the west wall of the nave as well. Access to such galleries would have been by Eddius's spiral stairs and above the galleries a clearstorey would have provided light for the nave.[20]

Eddius also says that Wilfrid built three churches at Hexham, St Andrew's, St Peter's (which may be the eastern, apsed chapel)[21] and a centralised building dedicated to the Virgin and described in the twelfth century as almost round and like a tower, with four porticus attached to it.[22] To the east of the apsed chapel lay a number of graves including one marked by a cross shaft and therefore almost certainly that of Bishop Acca, Wilfrid's successor, whom Symeon of Durham describes as having been buried in such a manner.

Much of this is already familiar. The stone blocks of the crypt and some surviving fragments of the walls of the church with their broaching, drafted edged and arched lintels bear the same pedigree as the masonry of Monkwearmouth, Jarrow and Escomb, and may of course be earlier than any of them, while the grouping of churches on an axis occurs at Canterbury. Despite these links, however, no other building of the seventh century in Northumbria, or in England for that matter, had both galleries and crypt. These features clearly put Hexham into a special category, as Eddius realised when he said that he had not heard of any other house on this side of the Alps on such a scale. He may not have been well enough informed for his judgement to be particularly impressive, but William of Malmesbury (*Gest. Pont.* p. 225), writing in the twelfth century, goes to the heart of the matter when he quotes some of his contemporaries as claiming that 'at Hexham they see the glories of Rome'. He adds that Wilfrid brought masons from Rome specifically to build the church.

Galleries flanking the nave and as wide as the aisles they stand on occur among the very earliest longitudinal churches of any architectural pretension, namely the basilica on Golgotha in Jerusalem and the first church on the site of the Hagia Sophia in Constantinople, both built for the Emperor Constantine in the first half of the fourth century, and both now known only from descriptions. In the fifth and sixth centuries the gallery is a characteristic feature in the Aegean area, as well as in Asia Minor and Egypt, but it only makes an appearance in the western Mediterranean during the sixth and seventh centuries, after the expansion of the eastern Empire in the time of Justinian. San Lorenzo (579–90) and Sant' Agnese (625–38) are representative examples from this period in Rome.[23] The galleries of the 670s at Hexham are therefore likely to have been an import from Rome at the only period when they were in use there.

Crypts in Rome are of a very particular kind. In the early seventh century Gregory the Great revolutionised the feature when he introduced a ring crypt into the apse of St Peter's (fig. 40). This consisted of a passage-way sunk slightly below ground level following the inside face of the apse, with a spur running along the axis of the church back from the apex of the apse to a chamber on the chord containing the tomb of St Peter. The curved passage provided for circulation and the straight passage for viewing the relics. The sanctuary filled the whole apse above this arrangement. In practical terms this also describes the crypt at Hexham, where the crypt lay under the sanctuary and the relic chamber was passed by a circulatory passage. The form however could hardly be more different, and it is difficult to argue that, as in the case of the columns and piers, this is simply due to the translation of a set of requirements concerning circulation into a different language. This is because the crypt at Ripon, while clearly being an experimental stage leading up to Hexham, does not satisfy those requirements. Rather than St Peter's, Gaul appears to have a convincing prototype for Ripon, in the pair of crypts at St-Étienne at Déols (Indre), described by Gregory of Tours in the sixth century, and still in existence. That on the north side of the sanctuary is nothing but a rectangle with one access stair, while that to the south has two stairs.[24] They form a neat typological sequence with the English buildings, running from the north crypt (one entrance) to the south (two), to Ripon (two entrances and a vestibule), and then to the efficient layout at Hexham. This formal pedigree does not detract from the fact that the extensive crypt at Hexham would at the time have

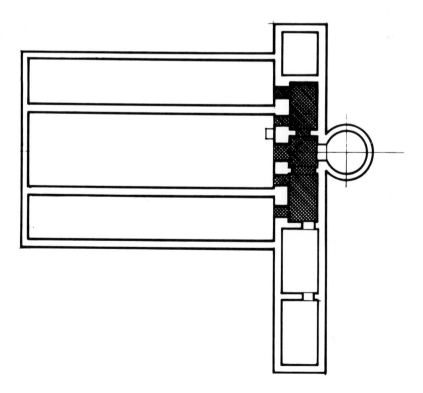

32 Cabeza del Griego (Cuenca), Cathedral. Copy of eighteenth-century plan, with crypt hatched. Not to scale

been connected quite readily with the use of crypts in the Roman basilicas.

Before leaving Hexham there is one other parallel from outside Rome that should be drawn. The bishops' church at Cabeza del Griego in the province of Cuenca in Spain was destroyed in the eighteenth century and is known today only from a plan and notes made at the time (fig. 32).[25] These describe a large aisled rectangular building with a series of chamber-like crypts under the east end arranged and extended in such a way as to create a long thin transverse element across the eastern face of the building. The church had a rectangular east end with a circular feature attached to it containing the epitaph of a bishop who died in 550, providing a date before which the church is likely to have been built. The position of the crypts, the transverse element and the flat east end all appear to find their echo at Hexham, and the eastern chamber can even be compared with the apsed chapel surrounded by, though not containing, burials.

This is not to suggest that the Spanish building was in any way a source for Hexham, but it helps, along with the crypts in Déols and the basilicas in Rome, to illustrate the sort of context in which Hexham was conceived. St Andrew's church must have been a truly extraordinary building, containing elements such as the galleries and the crypt found together in no other part of western Europe except Rome and occurring only intermittently in places across Gaul and Spain. The combination has to wait two or three centuries to become common, a distinction which sounds worthy of Wilfrid's aristocratic predilections and high assessment of his own status.

A century after Wilfrid's church at Hexham Archbishop Ethelbert (767–80) built a new church at **York**, dedicated to the Holy Wisdom (*Alma Sophia*) and placed on a different site from Edwin's church of St Peter. Recent excavations have revealed nothing of these two Anglo-Saxon buildings except that they did not stand on the same site as the present cathedral, the earliest parts of which belong to the time of the first Norman archbishop, Thomas of Bayeux. A late eighth-century poem of Alcuin of York describes the *Alma Sophia* as having round arches and solid piers (so that it probably had aisles), many porticus and upper chambers (which may suggest galleries), and no fewer than thirty altars, which is as many as the whole royal abbey of St-Riquier mentioned above, built a few years after York by Angilbert, a close relative of Charlemagne.[26] Wilfrid's ambition, not to say hubris, seems to have started a tradition.

Since little if any architectural activity is recorded in Northumbria after the late eighth century, this is the point at which to turn to the last of the great kingdoms of the early period.

Chapter Five

MERCIA AND THE ANGLO-SAXON BASILICA

Following the successes of the pagan Penda and the Christian Wulfhere in the seventh century, Ethelbald (716–56) and especially Offa (757–96) turned Mercia into the most powerful of the English kingdoms, directly controlling all the land south of the Humber and even eclipsing Northumbria. During the 820s Wessex reasserted herself, but Mercia remained in control of the Midlands until the coming of the Danes in the third quarter of the century. Given this background it is not surprising that the kingdom contains a number of important and impressive monuments about which there has been a great deal of debate.

Deehurst (Gloucestershire) lay in the territory of the Hwicce, who had lived under Mercian hegemony from an early date. The earliest parts of the surviving church of St Mary indicate a building with a nave almost three times as long as wide, no separate chancel and a porch to the west (fig. 54). The walls only survive to a height of twelve feet. The fabric above is also Anglo-Saxon but later, and as there is no evidence, either here in particular or anywhere else in general, that walls were often demolished and rebuilt, it is possible that the upper parts of the first church were finished in wood. Apart from this hypothetical detail the form of the building corresponds closely with that of Monkwearmouth in the late seventh century, and as a monastery is known to have existed at Deerhust by 804 these are probably the remains of the original church.[1]

Breedon-on-the-Hill (Leicestershire) illustrates another facet of activity in Mercia as the friezes of sculpture preserved in the present church, which may still be in their original positions, are among the finest pieces of carving produced in western Europe in the eighth and ninth centuries. Many other sites are known only from references, such as the cathedrals at Lichfield and Leicester, Offa's church at St Albans and the monastic churches at Ely and Peterborough. Recently, dates in the ninth century have been proposed for St Wystan's at Repton and the tower at Barnack, but these claims will be discussed in the context of the post-Danish period.

Conversely the smaller of the two buildings at **Much Wenlock** (Shropshire), which is normally dated to the early Anglo-Saxon period, has here been attributed to the Romans.[2] This is chiefly because the apse is so small in relation to the space in front of it, almost like a niche, and because it is set into a huge mass of masonry forming a wall almost as thick as the diameter of the apse. Such 'enclosed' apses are unknown in the Anglo-Saxon period, when walls are usually less than three feet thick and those of 4 ft (1.25 m) at Brixworth are always noted as exceptional, but they are a common feature in Roman and late antique buildings at all dates after the mid first century AD.[3] Much Wenlock is situated some ten miles from Wroxeter and twenty from Walltown, both of which have Roman remains.

Three major buildings remain to be discussed, namely those at Brixworth, Cirencester and Wing, which introduce the important subject of the Anglo-Saxon basilica. A definition of this type of building is important both for a clear understanding of the character of a number of churches and as an aid to dating them. A basilica may be defined as a building normally on a large scale with a central hall flanked on each side by a subsidiary structure of equal or nearly equal length, with the central space taller than the flanking parts and lit by windows set in the wall above them. As the examples of Anglo-Saxon churches which fit this description are not numerous it will help to list them in order of date, separating them into two categories, those with subdivisions in the flanking structures and those without, that is those with porticus and those with aisles.

Basilicas with subdivisions	*Basilicas with aisles*
Jarrow (south side)	Hexham
Brixworth	Jarrow (north side)
Cirencester	Wing
	Winchester, New Minster
	Great Paxton
	Sherborne[4]

The main body of the large church of All Saints at **Brixworth** in Northamptonshire is three times as long as it is wide (fig. 33, 34).[5] The eastern third is separated off into a square choir bay by a wall at the eastern end of the nave which originally consisted of a tall central arch flanked by areas of wall pierced by two tiers of arched openings.[6] To the east of the square bay stands the chancel, seen through a tall central arch flanked at springing height by two windows and at and below floor level by two doorways leading to an outer crypt. The resulting arrangement of the five forms would have echoed that in the wall between the nave and the choir. The crypt passage, with its floor below ground level and its roof above, was barrel-vaulted and ran round the exterior of the semi-circular apse, which was later demolished and replaced with a polygonal one. That the crypt belongs to the same date as the original apse is indicated by the fact that the apse wall stands on the barrel vault, overhanging the passage by about 1 ft (0.3 m), and by the use of the same material in both, marked by courses of brick in contrast to the coarse stone of the polygonal apse. There was probably an opening at the head of the original apse to permit access from the curved part of the crypt into a passage under the raised sanctuary.

The nave is divided into four bays by arches with double rows of brick voussoirs, those at springing level tilted inwards in a distinctive manner. These arches led into flanking spaces divided into porticus. At the west end of the nave there is a porch which provided access from the west and led to a room in its own upper storey looking onto the nave through a large arch.[7]

Hugh Candidus, a Peterborough chronicler of the twelfth century, says that Brixworth was founded from Peterborough by Cuthbald who became abbot in 675. In the absence of contrary evidence it may seem reasonable to accept this as the date of the surviving building, as has been done by most authorities.

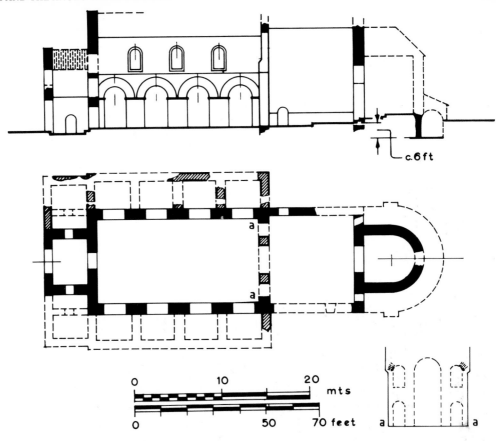

c.6ft

0   10   20
                              mts
0   50   70 feet

33 Brixworth
(Northamptonshire), All
Saints. Plan and section
of pre-Danish church,
1:400

Comparative material also appears to support this view. The brick and rubble
technique is used in late seventh-century buildings in Kent, and the non-radial
laying of the brick voussoirs occurs at Bradwell-on-Sea and in a large number of
early churches in Italy. The porch with an upper storey looking into the nave
exists at Monkwearmouth, which had flanking chambers. St Paul's at Jarrow in
the early 680s had porticus of a similar type flanking the nave.

This represents a formidable case for a date around the year 700, but it leaves
at least three questions, concerning the crypt, the choir bay and the choir arch,
unanswered. The ambulatory at Brixworth has been called a ring crypt and its
presence explained by reference to the ring crypt added to St Peter's in the early
seventh-century, and subsequently extensively copied both in Rome and
elsewhere.[8] The crypt at St Peter's, however, lies inside the wall of the apse and
hence underneath the sanctuary, while that at Brixworth lies outside (fig. 40).

Whether the passage is placed inside the wall or outside it may seem an
irrelevance, but it is nonetheless the case that all the followers of St Peter's used
the internal arrangement until the beginning of the ninth century, when
churches in the Carolingian Empire began to acquire outer crypts. One of the
earliest examples is provided by the abbey church of St-Denis, which in 832 had
an oratory added to its east end with access provided by doorways flanking the
apse, as at Brixworth. This was swiftly followed at Grandlieu after 836, Auxerre
after 841 and Corvey possibly before 844. Brixworth has a very simple version of

34 Brixworth (Northamptonshire), All Saints. From the south

this, without any eastern extensions and only the suggestion of tomb recesses in its outer walls, so that it may lie early in the development, and in addition St-Denis may not be the first. Yet even making the most generous allowances it is still extremely difficult to date an outer crypt any earlier than the early ninth century.

The square choir bay leads to the same conclusion. In all the English buildings examined so far, without exception, the nave has formed a single space with or without a room to the east to act as a sanctuary (or as a presbytery, as at Reculver). Brixworth is the first church to interpose an architecturally separate space between nave and sanctuary. When one looks for parallels to this they are found, once more, around 800 in the Carolingian Empire. One can point to what appears to be a square crossing in the church on the St Gall plan of *c*. 820 (fig. 42), or to that at Reichenau-Mittelzell in the building consecrated in 816.[9] Once again the arrangement at Brixworth is a simple version and hence may be early, but even then it is unlikely before the year 800.

The western wall of the choir bay provides a third and similar indication. It used to be thought that this consisted of a triple arcade standing on piers, paralleling the Kentish arrangement with columns. The new reconstruction, which Taylor has proposed on a closer reading of the nineteenth-century restoration reports, and which has been adopted here, produces as noted above a perforated wall, that is, a wall containing 'windows' communicating between two internal spaces. The distribution of this feature is of some interest. The earliest dated example occurs in the walls between the crossing and the arms of the centralised chapel built at Germigny-des-Prés in the Loire Valley by Bishop Theodulf in the early ninth century, while all other examples are tenth or eleventh century in date.[9a]

In this regard the church at St-Généroux in the Poitou is of particular relevance (fig. 35).[9b] It has been dated anywhere from the mid tenth century to the mid eleventh and related back to early ninth-century buildings in northern Spain. In its original form it had a large aisleless nave, an oblong choir bay separated from the nave by a perforated wall consisting of three main arches with subsidiary openings above, and apses to the east, all, *mutatis mutandis*, as at Brixworth, which once again appears to fit best in a Carolingian context.

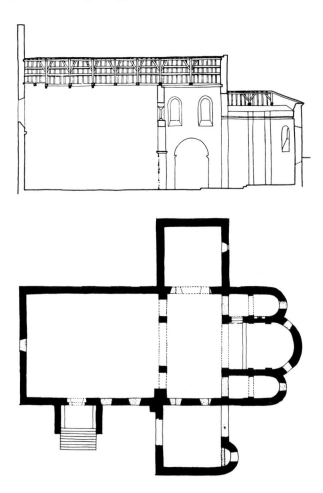

35 St-Généroux (Deux-Sèvres), church, tenth–eleventh century. Plan and elevation, 1:400 (Segretain, 1842)

It is difficult to parallel most of the characteristic features of All Saints in the tenth century; thus the start of the Danish invasions in Mercia in the third quarter of the ninth century marks the latest likely date for building, while conversely all the continental parallels suggest a date no earlier than around the year 800. The points mentioned at the start in favour of a late seventh-century date, such as the brick and rubble technique, the non-radial voussoirs and the porch with an upper storey and flanking chambers, do not present any obstacle to such a date as they can be taken as indications, not just of the early date, but of any time in the pre-Danish period.

The bracket *c.* 800–60 which comes out of all this has received surprising corroboration from a fragment of apparently original scaffold-pole recently extracted from a putlog hole in the clearstorey wall, and dated by radio-carbon tests to between 830 and 990. Hugh Candidus's documentary reference to the late seventh century has the twin disadvantages of having been written nearly five centuries after the event and of dating the institution rather than the building. It has now also to contend with a combination of stylistic and technical evidence which places the church at least a century later.[10]

According to an eighteenth-century quotation from a lost chronicle, a prebendal college was founded at **Cirencester** (Gloucestershire) in the reign of Egbert, king of Wessex from 802 to 839.[11] The church should therefore strictly speaking have been considered under Wessex, but Cirencester lies on the border between the two kingdoms and probably only fell into Egbert's hand during the expansion of Wessex in the 820s. It has consequently been included here because it makes more sense when seen in conjunction with buildings like Brixworth rather than those of seventh-century Winchester or Glastonbury.

The foundations of massive re-used Roman stone outline a most unusual, not to say mannered plan (fig. 36). The nave is about 22 ft wide and staggering 160 ft long (6.75 m by 49 m), contrasting with 65 ft (20 m) at Jarrow and Monkwearmouth. It is flanked by porticus which are also elongated, as if the stretching of the nave of Brixworth from 60 ft to 160 ft (18.25 m to 49 m) required the nearly square flanking chambers to follow suit, becoming

36 Cirencester (Gloucestershire), church, ninth century. Plan, 1:400 (Taylor, 1978)

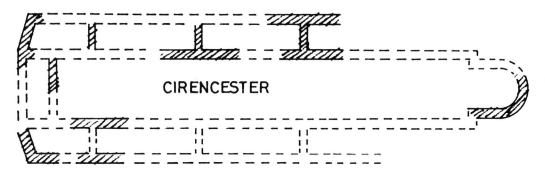

CIRENCESTER

distended rectangles 10 ft (3 m) wide and 30 or 40 ft (10 or 11.25 m) long. There was a narthex at the west end and at the east a stilted apse preceded by a crypt, giving overall external dimensions of 54 ft by 180 ft (16.5 m by 55 m). The remains are so sparse that it is difficult to offer any comment on them, but the great length can be put into context by comparing it with the church built around 650 by St Wandregisilius at Fontanella, or what is now St-Wandrille in Normandy. The *Gesta Sanctorum* of the abbey says that the church of St Peter was 37 ft wide and 290 ft long (11.25 m by 88.5 m) and even if that represents a substantial exaggeration it must still have been longer than Cirencester.[12]

Despite the fact that it is a large and well-built church, no documents survive concerning All Saints at **Wing** in Buckinghamshire.[13] In its original state it consisted of a nave three times as long as broad and flanked by side aisles entered through three arches in each wall (fig. 37). Doorways high up at the west end of the nave gave access from the exterior to a wooden gallery like that in the eastern church at Jarrow. The orginal apse, an erratic seven-sided polygon, only survives at crypt level, defining a large, unsubdivided space with three recesses to the north, south and east, of uncertain purpose as they are too small to have held bodies.

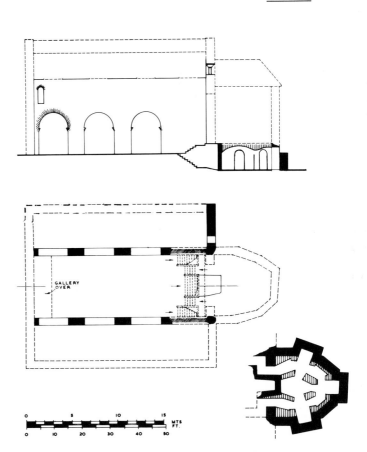

WING

37 Wing (Buckinghamshire), All Saints, eighth–tenth century. Plan and elevation, 1:400

Wing shares many features with Brixworth, such as the 1:3 proportions of the nave, the appearance of the nave arcades, the imposts of three courses, and the voussoirs set non-radially, while the practical effect of the wooden western gallery would have been like that of the room above the porch at Brixworth. These similarities suggest that the two buildings were not built at very different dates. Even the major difference, the large, unsubdivided crypt, supports this view, for two reasons in particular. Firstly, the large crypt approximating to the area of the apse is yet another invention of the Carolingian period, exemplified at Fulda shortly after 800 and in the church of St Gall around 830. Secondly, the recesses opening off the central space recall those on the mausoleum at Repton built for himself by Wiglaf, king of Mercia from 827 to 840.

Consequently these two features combine with the elements common to Wing and Brixworth to support a date for both in the first half of the ninth century.

Having introduced these three buildings, it is now possible for us to examine in greater detail the distinction drawn above between porticus and aisles. This is usually considered to be fundamental and has been debated at length with regard to Brixworth, but there are grounds for calling it into question, if for no other reason than that William of Malmesbury in a well-known quotation says that Dunstan added 'aisles or porticus' (*alas vel porticus*) to the church at Glastonbury.[14]

The argument is greatly clarified if it is acknowledged that the porticus in question, those in the left hand column of the table given above, are of a particular kind occurring only in a basilican context. They are not to be confused with the porticus at, for instance, Reculver or Deerhurst, which were added piecemeal to the sides of the nave, and which are entered through little more than a doorway (figs 13, 54). At buildings like Brixworth, on the other hand, the nave is flanked from the start by structures which create an entirely basilican profile. Even the subdividing of these may not mark a significant difference. The church on the St Gall plan, for instance, is, by common consent, intended to be read as a columnar basilica, yet each aisle contains four altars and each altar is set against a screen blocking the passage-way along the aisle for all but a gap of two or three feet (fig. 42).

The same applies to the openings in the nave walls. At Brixworth the arches are wide and evenly, not to say majestically, spaced along the wall, forming a series by virtue of the fact that the outer face of each arch touches those of its two neighbours at the springing point. The same was true of Jarrow (figs 23, 24). This is not to deny that the supports at Brixworth are elongated and appear less as individual vertical elements and more as sections of the wall. But that after all is how a pier can be defined in opposition to a column,[15] and the piers at Wing are hardly less elongated than those at Brixworth, despite the unambiguous aisles behind them. Even the proportion of pier length to opening does not permit a hard and fast distinction, for while it is true that at Brixworth the arches are only 7 ft (2.1 m) wide and the piers 8 ft (2.4 m) across and at Wing they are 10 ft and 6 ft (3 m and 2 m) respectively, at Jarrow, which had subdivisions, the arches are 13 ft (4 m) wide and the piers only 6 ft (2 m).

A final indication of the functional irrelevance of the question 'aisles or porticus?' in this type of church is provided by the plan of the abbey church at Werden in the Rhineland, as built in the mid ninth century and consecrated in 875 (fig. 51). The foundations of the nave and aisle walls are lined by four transverse foundations dividing the aisle into four or five sections, almost exactly as at Brixworth. Only a tiny fragment of wall remains standing on any of these foundations, but by great good fortune it happens to lie at the juncture between one of the transverse sections and the foundations of the aisle wall. Since it is a pilaster attached to the aisle wall and acts as a respond for an arch aross the aisle, the transverse foundations must be seen as sleeper walls and not as walls creating porticus.

The weakening of the distinction between the porticus basilica and the aisled basilica must call into question any dating sequence which depends on that distinction. Taylor has proposed that basilicas with porticus and those with aisles are respectively early and late Anglo-Saxon types, and that there are no aisled buildings securely dated in the early period.[16] The evidence for piers at Hexham, however, appears to be sound, as does a date in the time of Wilfrid. If one accepts the date proposed above for Wing, it is possible to cite Hexham,

Wing and Great Paxton as aisled basilicas of the seventh, ninth and eleventh centuries, spanning the whole Christian Anglo-Saxon period. On the other hand, it may be possible to claim that the porticus type is not used in the late period, though that depends on the assessment one puts on the evidence for Lady St Mary at Wareham.

It remains to enquire after the sources of the Anglo-Saxon basilica, in so far as these differ from the sources of other buildings. This enquiry primarily involves an examination of supports. The Roman basilica, in both its secular and its Christian forms, is first and foremost a columnar building type (fig. 40). From Rome to Trier and Corinth the main spaces of the giant halls and churches of the first five centuries AD were flanked by columns. Piers are much less common. The Augustan Basilica Julia in Rome is supported on double rows of piers, but it is very unusual and finds no echo in Christian buildings. The Pythagorean cult basilica at the Porta Maggiore in Rome of the first century AD has a nave with massive piers, but as it was 'built' in large part by being excavated, like a catacomb, it is hardly representative.[17] Christian basilicas with piers are the rule only in the easternmost provinces of the Empire, and even then only away from the metropolitan centres, in areas such as Anatolia, Syria and Armenia. In the west examples are hard to find at any date, the tiny mid-sixth century Frankish church at Glanfeuil (Maine-et-Loire), with aisles less than 3 ft wide, being the exception which proves the rule.

One of the best instances of a Roman basilica with piers survives in this country, at **Lydd** in Kent. This small building, with a central area only 16 ft by 30 ft (5 m by 9 m), has been dated both late and early in the Anglo-Saxon period, but excavations undertaken in the 1960s revealed a plan unlike anything Saxon and hence probably of Romano-British date (fig. 38).[18] Particularly telling are the large vestibule and the way in which the apse springs from within the line of the eastern walls of the aisles, a feature which it shares with Silchester, where it is less obvious, with apsed baths buildings in the Rhineland such as those at Badenweiler and Trier, and, as first cousin, with examples of enclosed apses like that at Much Wenlock. Roman buildings of the small kind represented by Lydd may lie behind churches like that at Glanfeuil, but whether they can also be used to explain structures like Hexham is another matter. All that can safely be said is that Roman basilicas with piers were available in some form as models in the western parts of the Empire, and that in the form of Christian churches they were common in the Middle East and not unknown in Gaul.

In any summary of the history of church architecture over the whole country in the two and a half centuries between the arrival of Augustine and the arrival of the Danes, two kinds of building stand out. One is the basilican, which has just been discussed. The other and more common one consists of a simple rectangular nave with or without adjuncts to east, west, north or south. The box with no attachments occurs at Heysham and probably in the east church at Jarrow. As a type it is so widespread that it is impossible to say with certainty whether it was introduced by the Celts from the north or the Roman missionaries from the south. The rectangle is provided with a western porch at Monkwearmouth and at Deerhurst, and in the first of these at least the porch has an upper storey, paralleling in masonry the wooden gallery at the west end of the east church at Jarrow, and probably performing the same function. The nave with a room to the east and the possibility of others to the north, south and west is by far the most numerous version, since the description fits Escomb as well as it does Bradwell-on-Sea.

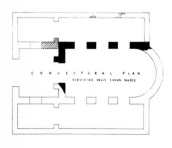

38 Lydd (Kent), basilica. Plan, 1:400 (Jackson and Fletcher, 1968)

Despite these features held in common by Anglo-Saxon buildings of the early period, the Kentish group retains its individuality. This is chiefly due to the combination of the apse and the triple arcade, features which, although not as widely attested as previously thought, nonetheless represent the commonest forms in the kingdom. Escomb and St Pancras may both have had rooms added to their west ends, but that simple statement hides more differences than similarities. Equally the form and indeed the function of the north porticus at Escomb may be indistinguishable from that at Reculver, yet Reculver could never be mistaken for Escomb, nor SS Peter and Paul in Canterbury for the church of the same dedication in Winchester. The distinctive Roman masonry techniques of the Kentish churches may be due to nothing more than what was available for re-use, but the sources of the group help to mark it off more clearly than anything else. All the indicators point to Italy via related areas in the Alps and North Africa.

Conversely Gaul is the most obvious influence on the buildings of Northumbria, Wessex and Mercia, in the form of plan types such as those of Monkwearmouth and Deerhurst, the monastic buildings at Jarrow and in the skills of masonry, plastering, glazing, roofing and turning on a lathe. Only the box church of the Escomb type might owe its configuration to indigenous Germanic or Celtic wooden buildings, a possibility which could have contributed to the popularity of the type in those parts of Germanic Europe which were christianized from England and Ireland in the course of the eighth century.

All of these statements, as well as those about basilicas and such things as the uniqueness of Hexham, must however be seen, as has already been noted, against the backdrop of the extensive losses of buildings from the period. One of the chief explanations for this loss of monuments is of course the destructiveness of the Danish wars which in one way or another lasted the whole of the ninth century and the early part of the tenth. By the same token, after that period, standing remains of many more buildings survive, providing a much clearer picture. Equally, in contrast to the paucity of buildings remaining from sixth- and seventh-century Gaul, the study of the later period is helped by our knowledge of church architecture on the Continent in the Carolingian and Ottonian Empires and in the growth of the Romanesque style. Before turning to the later Anglo-Saxon period it will therefore be useful to examine the broad developments represented by this continental material.

Chapter Six

EARLY ROMANESQUE ARCHITECTURE IN NORTHERN EUROPE

The church architecture of late Antiquity, especially in the western Mediterranean, is characterised by its spatial simplicity. In almost every case, whether the building is large or small, the nave forms a simple rectangular volume flanked by rows of closely set, undifferentiated columns. Without resorting to counting from one end it is nearly impossible to determine which supports stand opposite one another, with the result that they offer no more than a minimal subdivision of the nave space they help to define, as for example in Old St Peter's in Rome and Sant' Apollinare in Classe in Ravenna, of the fourth and fifth centuries respectively (figs 40, 41). Architectural adornment is restricted almost entirely to capitals and bases, leaving large areas of unbroken wall-surface and clean, uncluttered edges to jambs and soffits, which serves to stress the fact that the nave is a single space. Side aisles are treated in the same way, and in the two or three cases where there is a transept this is handled as if it were another volume placed at right angles at the end of the nave, free from any need to acknowledge its presence. Richness and invention are restricted to capital sculpture, paintings and mosaics.

After the end of the fifth century church design develops very differently in the two halves of the empire, the Greek east embarking on a series of experiments which, along with its forms of government, were to make of the term 'Byzantine' a synonym for tortuous complexity. In the west, as we have had reason to discover in the two preceding chapters, the sixth and seventh centuries are somewhat obscure, but by the second half of the eighth century the main characteristics of late antique architecture were apparently revived to become the basic features of church building in the Carolingian state.

The new church at St-Denis, begun by Pepin in the 750s and completed by Charlemagne in 775, illustrates this late antique revival as it is characterised by a nave separated from the aisles by rows of columns in the standard Early Christian manner, and a transept which was probably uninterrupted, like that of St Peter's.[1a]

Yet while columnar basilicas of the type of St-Denis were common enough in northern Europe in the eighth and ninth centuries, there is another more innovative side to the Carolingian renaissance. Churches become much more complicated with the invention of the three large features of (1) the westwork,

39 Church sites in continental Europe, fourth–eleventh century

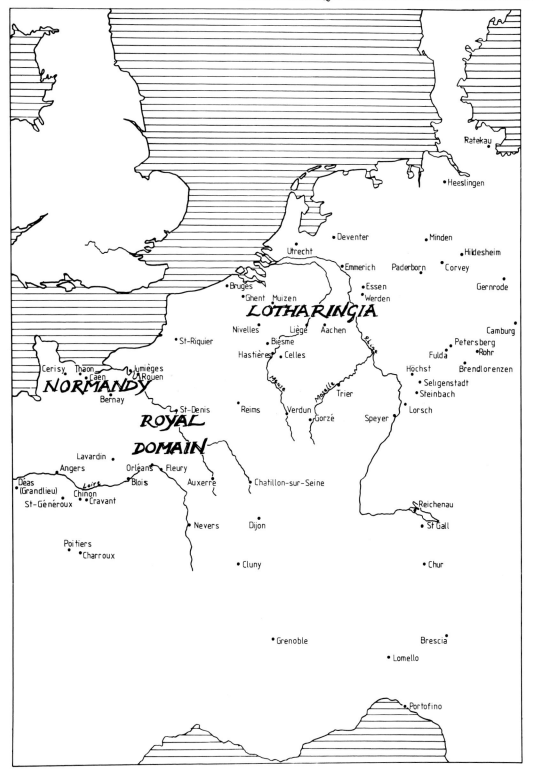

Ratekau

•Heeslingen

•Deventer   •Minden

Utrecht   •Hildesheim
•Emmerich   Paderborn •Corvey

Bruges   •Essen   Gernrode
•Ghent Muizen   •Werden

LOTHARINGIA

Nivelles   Liège   Aachen   Camburg
•St-Riquier   •Biesme   •Petersberg
            Hastières •Celles   Fulda •Rohr
Cerisy Thaon   •Jumièges   Höchst   Brendlorenzen
        Caen   Rouen   •Seligenstadt
NORMANDY   •Steinbach
    Bernay
            •St-Denis   Lorsch
ROYAL   •Reims   Verdun   Trier
                          Gorzé   Speyer
DOMAIN

        Lavardin
    Angers   Orléans Fleury
Déas   Chinon Blois   Auxerre   •Chatillon-sur-Seine
(Grandlieu) •Cravant
St-Généroux   •Reichenau
                    •Nevers   Dijon   •St Gall
Poitiers
    •Charroux   •Cluny   •Chur

                    •Grenoble   Brescia
                      •Lomello

                              •Portofino

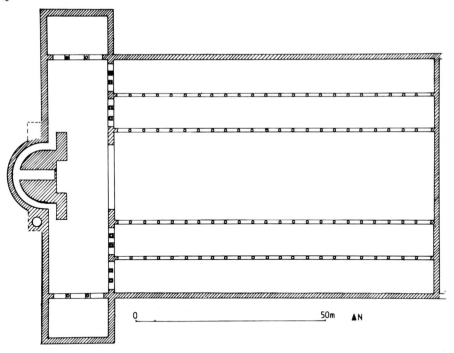

0 _____ 50m   ▲N

40 Rome, St Peter, fourth century with seventh-century crypt. Plan, 1:1000

(2) the eastern tower and (3) the outer crypt, with the result that the more progressive designs often appear somewhat disorganised, or composed of two, three or even four self-contained buildings.

The history of church building in western Europe from the ninth century to the eleventh can be described as the steps by which these elements were organised into a new architectural language, that which is now called Romanesque.[1b] When this term was first coined in the first half of the nineteenth century it meant what it appears to mean, namely Roman-ish, and by implication sub-Roman, covering all the centuries and styles between Antiquity and the Gothic, the sense in which it was still used in the titles of Clapham's two-volume work on architecture in England between the fifth century and the thirteenth. Over the last 50 years, however, its meaning has been restricted to a set of stylistic criteria characterising buildings of the tenth, eleventh and twelfth centuries, growing out of but separate from those of the first millennium. Despite these diffuse origins, the Romanesque in this restricted sense can take its place alongside the Gothic, the Renaissance and the Modern Movement as a major revolution which radically altered the course of architectural history.

Not the least extraordinary thing about the Romanesque style is the way in which it came about, in marked contrast to those movements which preceded and followed it. The style identifiable as Carolingian was, it can be argued, invented by a small group of individuals forming or connected with the court of Charlemagne and his father and successors, beginning in the Frankish centre of the kingdom and spreading to the Alps, Saxony and other areas. Similarly, it is only being mildly provocative to attribute the invention of Gothic to Abbot Suger's architect at St-Denis, but, whatever one thinks of that particular claim, the style certainly arose in the restricted areas of the Ile-de-France, Picardy and perhaps Flanders between 1120 and 1150 and spread outwards in identifiable

41 Ravenna (Emilia), Sant'Apollinare in Classe, mid sixth century. Interior to east

steps over almost the whole of Europe. When finally challenged, it was by the revival of Roman and medieval classicism known as the Renaissance, which itself was initiated by a circle of Florentine literati, artists, architects and patrons in the early years of the fifteenth century.

By contrast, the origins of the Romanesque cannot be dated more precisely than to between the first half the tenth century and the first half of the eleventh, and even then the signs appear, with an amazing consistency in their variety, in Lombardy, Catalonia, Burgundy, the Rhineland, Saxony and the Loire Valley, that is across most of western Europe. To an unreconstructed empiricist with, one might almost say, Anglo-Saxon prejudices, the concept of the *Zeitgeist* or 'spirit of the age' is of little use in the study of history, but at least for the time being it has to be admitted that no satisfactory diffusionist explanation for this phenomenon has yet been proposed.

Such wide-spread origins suggest a close dependence on a surviving Roman vernacular, but Saxony, which lies outside the boundaries of the Roman Empire, is one of the most important areas. Thus, while the presence of a readily accessible Roman background can help to explain some of the regional differences, it offers no explanation for the whole.

Leaving this question unanswered, we can turn to the one period and four regions of most relevance to an understanding of the style in its formative phases in northern Europe, namely the Carolingian renaissance and, deriving from it, the architecture of, on the one hand, the Ottonian Empire including Lotharingia, and, on the other, Capetian France and Normandy.

The prominence given to the western end of the church represents the most dramatic of the three major changes introduced during the Carolingian period. Although the abbey of St-Riquier in Picardy, built in the 790s by Angilbert, Charlemagne's son-in-law, survives only in engravings, partial excavations and descriptions of its liturgy, it had what was probably the earlist example of a westwork, that is a centralised building, almost like a church on its own, attached to the western end of the nave (fig. 56a).[2] The form of the interior can only be reconstructed from its effect on the exterior and from what is known of the liturgical requirements, but it appears to have been substantially the same as the standing westwork added to the church at Corvey between 873 and 885 (fig. 52). This has a low, vaulted ground floor supporting the main storey which consists of a square central core rising the full height of the building and flanked on at least three sides by aisles, galleries and clearstorey windows. At both buildings, on the exterior the core registers as a dominating central tower while the stair-turrets rise above the roofs to the west of it, creating a striking silhouette.

St-Riquier also appears to exemplify the second innovation, namely an eastern tower and the crossing which is normally assumed to accompany it, but, as with most Carolingian instances of the crossing, the form is ambiguous. Not only is little known of the internal arrangements, but two pieces of evidence on the engravings tell against there being a fully developed crossing of the eleventh-century type of, for example, St Michael's at Hildesheim. Firstly, the eastern block, though slightly narrower and longer than the western one, consists of exactly the same elements distributed in the same way, implying similar internal subdivisions, probably without the first-floor platform, but with a central space flanked by various storeys, preventing a transverse axis between the arms across the nave (fig. 56a). Secondly, the roofs have a single slope, instead of the double one with a horizontal ridge which one would expect with a transeptal space.

The equivalent 'crossing' area of the church on the St Gall plan is similarly unclear, both because of the draughtsman's conventions and because the layout of the liturgical furniture suggests a pair of chapels with axes to east and west rather than arms running north and south (fig. 42). The cathedral at Cologne had a square bay at both ends of the nave, but it is not clear whether the plan in question belongs to the late ninth century or the late tenth.[3] Similar uncertainties surround the other Carolingian examples of this feature at Reichenau-Mittelzell, Höchst and Grandlieu, from which it appears that the crossing is a Carolingian invention, but in imperfect form.

Finally there is the outer crypt. As already noted with regard to Brixworth, the ring crypt introduced by St Gregory into St Peter's in the early seventh century was copied at numerous places, including St-Denis, in the eighth and ninth centuries, but in all cases the passage remained inside the apse. In the ninth century the new type was introduced which followed the exterior curve of the wall and extended eastwards from it into a variety of shapes. The earliest instance may be the simple one added to St-Denis in time for a ceremony in 832, while by the 850s in St Germain at Auxerre there are half-a-dozen chapels and

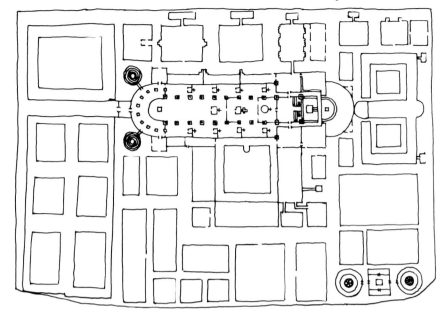

42 St Gall (Switzerland), plan of monastery, *c.* 820

an axial rotunda possibly with an upper storey.[4]

A less obvious change occurs in the supports. While most basilicas use columns, a number, like those at Steinbach and Seligenstadt, have arcades or piers, while at Reichenau-Mittelzell, Werden and the cathedral at Hildesheim, there is some evidence for an alteration of columns and piers, establishing a slower rhythm than is possible with either kind of support on its own, and creating an articulation which stands in sharp contrast to the undifferentiated rhythm characteristic of the late antique basilica (contrast figs 41, 91). In a similar way the piers of the palace chapel at Aachen successfully divide the ambulatory into a series of separately digestible bays, and some of the piers in the crypt at Soissons have pilasters each supporting its own arch. In summary, it can be said that, with all three innovations, the Carolingians set the problems and pointed the way to some of the solutions.

Even as early as the Treaty of Verdun of 843 the Carolingian Empire began to divide into the two parts which were eventually to become France and Germany. While in the western part the Carolingian dynasty survived in an increasingly weakened condition until the late tenth century, in the eastern the vigorous Saxon or Ottonian house came to the throne in 919, and over the next century turned the kingdom into 'the Roman Empire of the German Nation' and the most powerful state in western Europe.

In many respects Ottonian architecture is a continuation of the Carolingian tradition and some of its greatest buildings differ little from those of the ninth century.[5] Others, however, like the abbeys at Gernrode and Hildesheim, introduce important changes. St Cyriakus at Gernrode, begun between 959 and 963, has, along with its continuous transept and alternating piers and columns, a gallery above each aisle, inserted into what would otherwise be an unbroken area of wall, producing an effect of articulation similar to that of the alternation. Whatever their liturgical function may have been, the galleries at Gernrode are odd in that they are not used again, in Saxony at least, for over a century. It is instead in the transept that the next important step is taken.

The monastery of St Michael's at Hildesheim was founded in 996 by Bishop Bernward and the foundation stone of the present church laid in 1010.[5a] The crypt was consecrated in 1015 and the church in 1022 just before Bernward's death, and again in 1026 and 1033 (fig. 43). It provides an almost perfect illustration of what is meant by the label 'Romanesque'. The nave is longer than that at Gernrode and has alternation of two columns to each pier, dividing the space into three equal blocks. The transept is not of the St Peter's type like those at Gernrode and St-Denis, but consists of two arms flanking a crossing which represents the intersection of the two axes of transept and nave. Unlike

43 Hildesheim (Niedersachsen), St Michael, 1010–33. Plan and reconstruction, 1:600 (Oswald, 1966)

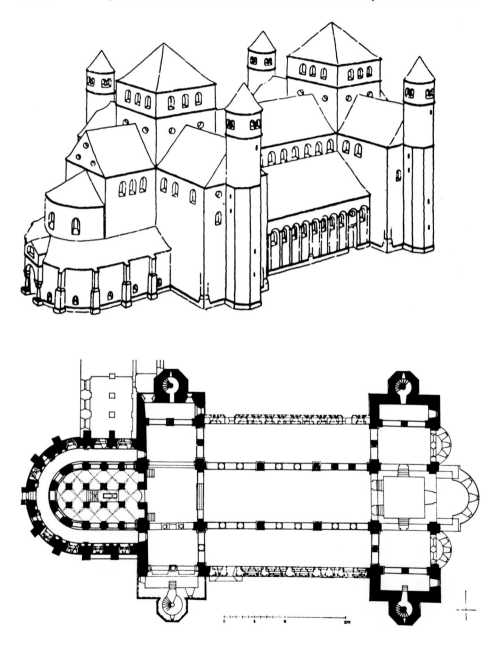

the ambiguous Carolingians examples, this crossing is directly related to the nave by being the same size as one of the blocks of space defined by the piers. To the east, the crossing is separated from the apse by a rectangular bay which can again be seen as intended to clarify the relationship between two volumes. volume can be easily identified and visually detached from its place (fig. 43).

The western transept is identical to the eastern, an arrangement which can be traced back through Cologne Cathedral to the internal uncertainties of St-Riquier. The western sanctuary on the other hand is much more elaborate than that to the east since it is raised on a crypt and surrounded by an ambulatory, and has a square choir bay between the apse and the crossing. The bay and the ambulatory can be paralleled on the St Gall plan of two centuries earlier, but the open arcading between the passage and the crypt is new, and would be important in the present context if it were not for the fact that, as with the galleries at Gernrode, the idea was still-born in Germany. In France, by contrast, it was to become the controlling element in the designing of sanctuaries through both the Romanesque and Gothic periods.

Only one decorative feature at St Michael's requires special attention, and that is the cushion capital which helps support the arcades in the nave and transepts. This misleading label, summoning up an image of soft, pneumatic forms like the doric capitals at Paestum, is used to describe the most geometrical and architectonic of all capital types. In ideal terms its shape arises from an interpenetration of a spherical form representing the curved form of the shaft below and a cube representing the rectangular section of the springing of the arcades above. The geometry is exactly the same as that of the dome on pendentives, but inverted with the shaft for the dome and the curved parts of the capital for the pendentives.

To judge by the examples which crop up in late Antiquity at a variety of disparate times and places from Italy to Armenia, the Romans must have experimented with this form, but, just as they never bothered to work out the geometry of the dome on pendentives, so here too there is something wrong with all the early examples, which are either on a small and decorative scale, or paired and with segmental lunettes. The first instance in northern Europe is on a ninth-century capital from Viernheim in the museum at Lorsch, but this too, while the right shape, has an incongrouous corinthian volute on each corner. At St Michael's it is possible to arrange the capitals in a sequence from a sort of sub-cushion to the fully formed type as if one were witnessing its genesis, as may well be the case.

It is not fanciful to suggest that the same attitude lies behind the cushion capital and the layout of St Michael's as a whole. Even though the parts of the building bear a complex intersecting relationship with one another, every volume can be easily identified and visually detached from its place (fig. 43). Four ranges of equal height and width, the nave, the transept arms and the choir bay, abut the four equal faces of each crossing tower. Against the choir bay in turn sits the curve of the apse, independent of the section of a cone forming the roof above it. Finally the four octagonal stair-turrets look like huge pins intended to keep the building blocks in place. St Michael's, as has been said above, fulfils almost every requirement of a definition of the Romanesque style.[5b] It lacks only the half-column.

The half-column was extensively employed by the Romans, decorating what became some of their most famous monuments such as the Colosseum and the Maison Carrée, but it fell into disuse in western Europe between the fifth century and the eleventh, with the single exception of the gatehouse at Lorsch, normally dated to the late eighth century. Of greater relevance here is the chapel of St Bartholomew in Paderborn built, according to the Life of Bishop Meinwerk, in 1017 by 'Greek workmen'. As there are no known earlier Byzantine examples, the phrase probably refers to Italy, where half-columns occur in the late tenth-century cloister of San Fruttuoso di Capodimonte at Portofino near Genoa and the nave at Lomello, begun shortly after 1018.[5c]

The half-column adds, literally as well as figuratively, a new dimension to the play-of-elements available to the designer. In Roman buildings it remained an applied piece of decoration, but in the eleventh century it becomes an architectonic device. Already at Paderborn it supports the vaults of the chapel, while at the cathedral of Speyer it takes on a major role in the elevation of the nave. Begun around 1030 and consecrated in 1061, Speyer has half-columns on the inner faces of the piers of the nave arcade, rising to carry arches over the clearstorey windows. Although there is no alternation, the combination of massive piers and strong vertical elements serves equally effectively to achieve a series of independently identifiable bays.

The most old-fashioned aspect of St Michael's at Hildesheim is the lack of articulation on the wall surfaces. It is true that there is some blind arcading on the exterior of the aisle walls, but there is nothing anywhere else, especially beneath the eaves where one might most expect it. At Speyer on the other hand all the surviving exterior surfaces are divided up by panels formed of pilaster strips and arched corbel tables. The presence of these elements in this building and not at Hildesheim can be attributed to its location in the Rhine valley, for the following reason. Most of the characteristics of Speyer can be explained in a Carolingian or Ottonian context, either as a legacy or a development, with the exception of the half-column and the arched corbel table. Both of these features derive ultimately from Italy, where the formation of the table out of decorative blind arcading can be traced, if one is lucky, in the ninth and tenth centuries in the Po Valley. This is one of the clearest examples of an architectural feature following trade, in this case up the Rhône or across the Alps, then down the Rhine to Speyer and, finally, beyond to Lotharingia, the region to which we must now turn.

When in the ninth century the Empire was divided into its eastern and western parts, a third kingdom, that of Lothair, was established in the lands between, extending from the mouth of the Rhine in the north to Italy in the south. Although it soon lost its independence to the stronger eastern kingdom, the name Lotharingia remained attached to the uppermost third of the original area, namely the valley of the Meuse and that of the Rhine below the Moselle, which is broadly speaking in ecclesiastical terms the archdioceses of Cologne and Trier, and in modern terms Belgium, Holland, Luxemburg, Lorraine and the contiguous parts of north-west Germany.

The architecture of this area in the tenth and eleventh centuries is marked by its conservatism, for which reason it has received little attention in discussions of Romanesque architecture as a whole, but its inclusion here is justified by its relevance to contemporary and perhaps equally conservative work in Anglo-Saxon England.[6] This traditionalism can be illustrated by the fact that, although the crossing makes an early appearance, it seldom if ever carries a lantern tower, producing a characteristic silhouette with a westen massif of more or less complexity, a long, low nave usually with aisles, and a pair of transept arms lower than the main body, so that the outline of Nivelles in the eleventh century was probably little different from that of Essen in the ninth.

It is unfortunate that little remains from the tenth century, the most serious losses being buildings in places like Gorzé, Verdun and (on the border between Lotharingia and Flanders) Ghent, the centres, along with Cluny and Fleury, of the monastic reform movement which swept northern Europe from the second quarter of the century. Though the conservatism makes it likely that the buildings of the tenth century were like those of the ninth and the eleventh, one must make do with only two partially surviving monuments, at Werden and Cologne, in order to illustrate this intermediary period.

The large fore-building added to the ninth-century church of St Saviour at Werden and consecrated in 943 has almost exactly the same plan and elevation as the Carolingian westwork at Corvey of the 870s (figs 51, 52), with one major difference. The vaulted ground floor has been done away with, leaving the core as a single space from ground level to the top of the lantern, reducing the independence of the westwork and making it more a part of the nave.

The same formula was adopted in the second of the buildings, St Panteleon in Cologne, begun by Archbishop Bruno in 964 and consecrated by his successor in 980, except that, instead of the aisle-like features surrounding the central square at Corvey and Werden, an arm extends from each face, one for the entrance porch and those to north and south which, as indicated by the shallow niches in their eastern walls, were used for separate chapels (fig. 53). Each arm has a gallery the arcades of which define the form of the central square at this upper level. Two more chambers flanked the eastern end of the now destroyed aisleless nave, but as there were no transverse arches forming a crossing on the main axis they are more like porticus than transept arms. In plan it creates the impression of having double transepts, both sets of which on investigation turn out to be something different. On the exterior all the walls of the westwork are divided into panels by stripwork and arched corbel tables like those used later at Speyer.

Churches datable to the first half of the eleventh century are much more numerous and fall in a number of ways into two groups corresponding to the valleys of the Rhine and the Meuse. The first is characterised by arched corbel tables, cushion capitals and the occasional inventive pier form, and the second by blind arcading and rectangular piers.

At Utrecht near the mouth of the Rhine, the church of St Peter, consecrated in 1048, is a simple columnar basilica with cushion capitals, but the crypt is graced with column shafts bearing spiral and zig-zag patterns laid out in pairs (fig. 66). At St Martin's at Emmerich of about the same date, the supports in the crypt verge on the fantastic, while each in a different way retains the basic shape of a rectangular block or a cylinder (fig. 75, centre).

Higher up the river, in Cologne, Sta Maria im Kapitol, consecrated in 1049 and again in 1065, uses the cushion capital and rectangular pier throughout. The arrangement of the three apses of the trilobe plan, the crossing and the aisles is a model of clarity, with none of the ambiguity of the plan of St Pantaleon. The western gallery provides an exception to the use of cushion capitals since it copies one bay of Charlemagne's octagonal palace chapel, serving as a reminder that Aachen lies in the middle of Lotharingia. In this respect, and even though the chapel must be the most copied north European building of the Middle Ages, it may be significant that the most inventive of all these copies is that added to the Minster at Essen between 1039 and 1058, reproducing three-eighths of the original in the form of a western apse topped by an octagonal tower also based on the imperial model.

In the Meuse Valley from the documentation available for its less complete twin at nearby Hastière, St-Hadelin at Celles can be dated to the 1030s. It has a three-apse east end, a crossing without a tower, arms lower than the nave, a western gallery and tower, external blind arcading and nave arcades on unadorned piers (fig. 55). The much larger church of Ste-Gertrude at Nivelles, consecrated in 1046, can be described in the same terms except that the eastern chapels are rectangular, the western massif includes a second transept and the central pier of each arcade is cross-shaped to enable it to carry a transverse arch, dividing the nave length in two and providing some articulation (fig. 68). Numerous buildings at places like Liège, Lobbes, Echternach, Susteren, Ghent and Verdun belong, with their own variations, in the same category.

Although the Carolingian Empire extended as far as Spain and Italy, buildings of a recognisably Carolingian type are almost wholly restricted to the area between the Loire and the Elbe. While the eastern regions, as just described, developed their version of early Romanesque architecture under the aegis of the Saxon and Salian emperors, the Capetian dynasty provided the equivalent catalyst in the west. For well over half a century after the accession of Hugh Capet in 987 the French kings' powers were effectively confined to the royal lands between Paris and Orléans, but, for whatever reason, the neighbouring counties and dukedoms espoused the architectural pretensions of the monarchy much more readily than their largely formal acknowledgement of feudal dependency might have led one to expect.[7]

The cathedral of St-Croix in Orléans, if we knew more about it, might be seen to stand in the same relation to early north French Romanesque as Suger's St-Denis does to the Gothic (fig. 44). After a fire in 989 which devastated the city, bishop Arnoul rebuilt the church on a grand scale with a fully developed crossing, a nave with double aisles and an aisled transept. All the arcade piers are cruciform in section suggesting that the pilasters on the aisle face supported the transverse arches of the groin vaults, those on the main axis of the wall

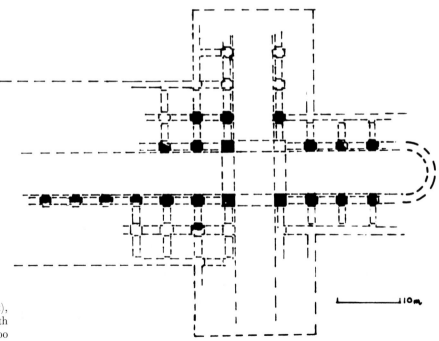

44 Orléans (Loiret), Cathedral, early eleventh century. Plan, 1:600

supported the arcade arches and those facing the main space rose to the ceiling or carried blind arcading like Speyer. The forms of the ends of the transepts and the sanctuary are lost, but St-Aignan, also rebuilt with royal funds after the fire of 989 and consecrated in 1029, had an ambulatory with radiating chapels and an aisle on three sides of each arm of the transept, so that whether the cathedral employed this arrangement or not, all these elements were available in Orléans in the early eleventh century.[8] The ambulatory can be derived directly from the outer crypt with a plausible genealogy from St-Philibert-de-Grandlieu at Déas in the ninth century via the cathedrals of Clermont-Ferrand and Thérouanne in the mid tenth to Orléans at the end of the century. Like the compound pier it illustrates a desire for the clarification of interdependent architectural forms.

Outside the royal domain the most interesting developments occur in places related in one way or another to the valley of the Loire. In the county of Blois, for instance, the late Carolingian cathedral of St-Solenne in Blois itself, possibly of between 975 and 988 or considerably earlier, appears to have had a non-projecting transept filled with galleries or upper chambers supported on compound piers (fig. 56b)[9], while further north the cathedral of Chartres was rebuilt after a fire in 1020 with an ambulatory and radiating chapels and, to judge from the surviving crypt, numerous pilasters and double orders. For standing buildings in the same area one has to go to St-Mesme at Chinon, rebuilt between 980 and 1007, and Cravant of the same period. The simplicity of the volumes of these buildings is enlivened by string courses which divide the wall surface horizontally and form blind arches, triangles, and hood-mouldings.

St-Genest at Lavardin, of the second quarter of the eleventh century, has a three-apse east end like St-Solenne, which may be because it is old fashioned or, more probably, because the ambulatory is unsuited to smaller buildings. In other respects it is experimental, with attached half-shafts in the sanctuary and, in the western porch, perhaps the earliest surviving dated barrel vault in northern France. At St-Philibert at Déas on the mouth of the river, the nave was rebuilt at about the same time with compound piers carrying arches of two orders. Apart from the odd forms on the gallery arches at Aachen and the inevitable examples in Armenia, this last feature does not occur anywhere before the late tenth century, even in Antiquity.

At the opposite end of this region, on the southern border of Champagne, the church of St-Vorles built at Chatillon-sur-Seine by Bishop Bruno of Langres between 980 and 1015 has a fully developed crossing with a lantern tower, an aisled nave with half-columns on the piers, a western massif carrying a second tower, and an exterior divided up by pilasters and arched corbel tables, the last two features probably indicating influence from Italy (fig. 62). At Auxerre, just to the east of the royal domain, the piers and arches in the crypt of the cathedral, rebuilt after a fire in 1023, represent a major advance. Their compound shape is formed by half-columns around a square core, paralleling the responds and piers at Paderborn, Speyer and Chatillon. They differ, however, in carrying, in the central aisle, semi-cylindrical rolls on the soffits of the transverse arches, echoing the half-columns below (fig. 45). At St-Remi in Reims in the north of the Champagne, the church consecrated in 1049 has, among many other features, arcade arches in two orders and compound piers of surprising complexity (figs 75, 77).

Taken together these buildings represent an architectural transformation between the late tenth century and the early eleventh in every way as profound as that in Germany. By the middle of the century their vocabulary constitutes

45 Auxerre (Yonne), Cathedral, crypt, after 1023

normal practice over the whole of northern France, from Berry and the Champagne, to Maine and Normandy.

In the course of the tenth century the new and still semi-pagan duchy of Normandy was gradually absorbed into the French body politic, so successfully that by 1066 the Norman invaders of England thought of themselves as French and spoke the language as their own. The monastic reform movement was introduced in the 960s by Duke Richard I, but of this period nothing remains, unless it is the small church of St-Pierre at Jumièges, which has been related both to documentary references of 934 and 946 and to stylistic parallels of the early eleventh century. For our purposes its importance lies in the fact that it is entirely pre-Romanesque, with flat nave walls, arches open to the aisles above the arcades, through-stone supports, and a large gallery over the western entrance, all features reminiscent of the Carolingian period.[10]

The cathedral at Rouen begun by Archbishop Robert between 989 and 1037 belongs to a different world. Only the crypt remains, with a spacious ambulatory and radiating chapels comparable to those at St-Aignan at Orléans and the cathedral at Chartres. These parallels and the fact that the vaults were carried on both attached and detached shafts suggest that work was begun fairly late in Robert's period of office.

A great deal more survives of the church of the abbey founded in 1013 at Bernay by Judith, wife of Duke Richard II (fig. 46). It has or had a three-apse east end, half-shafts rising the full height of the wall in the presbytery, a regular crossing and transepts, soffit rolls on half-shafts under most of the arches, and a passage in the thickness of the transept wall giving access to the crossing tower. Most authorities agree that these features make it difficult to date the church to the founding of the institution and have proposed alternatives ranging from the 1020s to the 1060s.

In addition, two theories have been produced to reconcile the documents and the material evidence.[10a] The first sees the half-shafts as additions to plain rectangular piers because of the lack of bonding, but this lack does not continue up the full height of each pier, and is in any case a technique sometimes used where shafts and piers are indubitably of the same date. The second theory contrasts the crudity of the western bays of the nave with the sophistication and polish of the eastern parts, placing the west end in Judith's lifetime and the rest two or three decades later. Aristocratic patrons do not, however, normally force their newest beneficiaries to build in what is little better than undressed rubble in a manner which would be judged poor by any standards, regardless of period. It seems more likely that the contrast is due to an optimistic beginning at the east end, at whatever date, and a wish to treat the sanctuary in a special way, with a falling off in interest and funds to the west. The likely sequence of three sets of capital types which can be distinguished in, respectively, the presbytery, the transepts, and the crossing and nave, support such a building programme.

Most if not all of the features at Bernay can be derived from the Capetian territories and related areas in the Loire Valley, such as the three-apse east end from Blois and Lavardin, and the shafts and soffit rolls from Auxerre. Since the wall passage is more utilitarian and less integrated than that of Notre Dame at Jumièges with a documented starting date around 1040, Bernay may be earlier, but there are contrary indications and a date anywhere from the thirties to the fifties is possible.

Abbot Robert of Jumièges began the building of a new abbey church shortly before his translation to the see of London in 1044, and the fabric was consecrated complete in 1067 (fig. 56d).[11] In its main outlines Notre-Dame is a large wood-roofed basilica with a western gallery and two-tower façade in the Carolingian tradition, as that was later developed in the Loire valley by the addition of the ambulatory, nave galleries, wall shafts and double orders to the arch. One new feature is the nook-shaft which appears on the jambs of the windows in the lantern tower, but what most distinguishes Jumièges from all the French buildings so far examined is the alternation of supports in the nave arcade, in the same way as at Gernrode in the previous century. Though this suggests an imperial link, the piers have four attached columns or shafts like those at Auxerre and unlike the German examples. In addition each side of the sanctuary of St-Genest at Lavardin has two compound piers flanking a column, and the alternation surviving in St-Hilaire at Poitiers south of the Loire may belong to the church begun around 1029 and consecrated in 1049.

The last Norman building to be discussed is St-Étienne in Caen. In 1050 or 1051 William duke of Normandy married Mathilda, daughter of the Count of

46 Bernay (Eure), Abbey, *c.* 1030–60. Nave to west

Flanders, in defiance of a prohibition issued by Pope Leo IX at the Council of Reims in 1049.[12] Papal sanction for the union was acquired in 1059 apparently on condition that two abbeys were founded by way of penance, in partial fulfilment of which William built the church in question. Work could have begun at any time between 1059 and 1066 when Lanfranc became abbot, but at any rate there was a consecration in 1077 and another probably final one in

1081. This surprising building is both a classic statement of the mature Norman Romanesque, traditional, considered and safe, and at the same time the occasion for a major increase in the Norman decorative repertoire which puts it a generation ahead of its time. These new elements are all to do with the piers and the arch profiles.

At Bernay and Jumièges, as indeed at Auxerre and Speyer, only a simple shaft was placed on any one face of a pier. At St-Étienne the inner order of each arch is carried on a large half-shaft and each of the flanking outer orders on a smaller half-shaft, the three in parallel forming a rich but controlled profile. In the arches of the nave arcade the outer order has an angle roll which looks as if it fills a nook or step cut for it into the leading edge. This interest in linearity increases dramatically in the arches of the crossing. Firstly, each of the flanking half-shafts on the inner face carries two orders instead of one, each with its angle roll, and secondly the inner and larger order, which in the arcades has a simple rectangular section, has a roll on its soffit and another on each of its faces (figs 89:6, 97). Finally, on the entrance arches the angle roll is accompanied by a hollow roll which creates an undulating and variegated surface while retaining the planes of the orders.

To summarise this chapter, in the two kingdoms which grow out of the Frankish Empire, Germany and France, the possibilities and problems presented by the three Carolingian features of the westwork, the eastern tower and the outer crypt are worked into the main elements of what is recognisably a new style, the Romanesque. In Saxony and in Lotharingia this is characterized by a simplicity of masses and volumes, as in St Michael's at Hildesheim and Ste-Gertrude at Nivelles, while in the Loire Valley and Normandy there is a greater complexity in the use of such features as the ambulatory and the half-shaft, as exemplified at St-Croix at Orléans and Jumièges in Normandy. This provides a stylistic framework against which it should be possible to measure the buildings of the tenth and eleventh centuries in Anglo-Saxon England, whether with a view to assessing their date, their sophistication, their indebtedness, or, for that matter, their influence.

Chapter Seven

FROM ALFRED TO THE MONASTIC REVIVAL

Anglo-Saxon architecture of the post-Danish period can, for convenience, be divided into two main stages of activity, firstly, the late ninth and tenth centuries, including the reigns of Alfred and his successors and the great age of monastic reform from the 940s to the 990s, and secondly, the reign of Edward the Confessor in the middle years of the eleventh century. These two phases are considered separately here and in chapter ten, with a stress on, respectively, the Carolingian parallels offered by the buildings of the ninth and tenth centuries on the Continent, and the Romanesque parallels offered by those of the mid eleventh. The two intervening chapters deal with the material in a different, thematic way, examining the crossing between nave and transepts in chapter eight, and architectural decoration in chapter nine, as an index of the growth of the Romanesque style in England in the late tenth and eleventh centuries. As a consequence, what follows in the present chapter is almost entirely backward looking in continental terms, relating to the Carolingian rather than the Romanesque material discussed in the preceding chapter.

The history of Anglo-Saxon church architecture has conventionally been divided into three periods, the Taylors following Baldwin Brown in labelling them A, B and C for, respectively, the years 600 to 800, 800 to 950, and 950 to 1100. This system seems to be more complicated than is necessary, so that there is every reason for abandoning period B, and instead following Clapham with an early and late period separated by the Danish invasions. This move is supported both by the nature of period B itself and by the unfortunate effects which it has on the centuries before and after it.

In the first place the Viking wars really do represent a violent hiatus during which one should expect a decline in building activity.[1] It is quite wrong to assume, as has on occasion been done, that few churches survive from the ninth century because many others were ravaged by the Danes. The invaders are unlikely to have selected new churches to plunder in preference to old and, on the contrary, the small number surviving must be a reflection of the small number built.

Out of 400 entries in the Taylors' catalogue less than a dozen are attributed to period B, and all for reasons which are either uncertain or negative. Tichfield for instance is so dated because it lacks features characteristic of period A or

47 Sites of churches built, enlarged or reformed *c.* 850–1066

CHURCHES c850-1066
○ DOCUMENTED
◉ EXCAVATED
● STANDING

Chester-le-Street
Durham   Norton

Kirkdale

York

Barton-on-Humber

Stow

Repton

North Elmham

Lichfield

Barnack
Peterborough
Brigstock

St Benet of
Hulme

Brixworth
Wooton Wawen
Worcester   Earls Barton
Evesham   Tredington
Hereford

Ramsey
Ely
Great Paxton
Cambridge
Bury St Edmunds

Deerhurst

Wing

Gloucester

Greensted

Abingdon   Dorchester
Waltham
London
Westminster

Bradford-on-Avon   Ramsbury
Potterne

Rochester
Canterbury

Wells
Glastonbury   Wilton   Britford   Winchester
Athelney   Shaftesbury
Worth
Dover

Sherborne   Breamore

Crediton
Exeter   Wareham   Selsey

period C. Considering the enormous losses suffered by both those periods this approach runs the risk of turning B into a wastepaper basket category or, to vary the metaphor, a vacuum which will attract more than it should, as may be the case with the recent proposed re-dating of Repton and Barnack.

In addition, ending the early period at 800 obscures the fact that building still going on in the first half of the ninth century, especially in Mercia, groups itself most naturally with the early schools of Kent and Northumbria. Similarly, period B artificially divides building in Wessex in the first half of the tenth from the era of monastic reform after 950. Lastly, period B may have been instrumental in forming the view that late Anglo-Saxon architecture was essentially Carolingian and marked by a preference for the out-of-date, which in turn obscures the extent to which England in the tenth and eleventh centuries can be seen as a part of the early growth of the Romanesque style in Europe.

The achievements of Alfred, king of Wessex from 871 to 899, are too well known to need elaboration here. From an apparently hopeless position in the face of the Danish invaders he left the English if anything in a stronger position than before the arrival of the Scandinavians, since within fifty years of his death the country was a single kingdom in a way it had never been under the successive *Bretwaldan* of the early period. This and the success of the system of *burhs* introduced and developed by Alfred and his heirs Edward the Elder and Aethelflaed, give no grounds for assuming that buildings erected at this time would be second-rate and even though the evidence is sparse it suggests results worthy of a highly successful royal house. Links with the Continent were plentiful and often at the highest level. The Frankish king Louis IV spent his exile in England in 936, and those of Edward's daughters who did not become nuns were married well in Europe, one of them to Otto I, the German Emperor, another to Charles the Simple, the Frankish king, and a third to Hugh the Great, *dux Francorum*.[2]

Whatever his interest in buildings, Alfred's architectural activity has left only one trace, and that a faint and ambiguous one. In fulfilment of a vow Alfred built a church at **Athelney** in Somerset. This is known only through the writings of the twelfth-century historian William of Malmesbury who describes it as small because of the restrictions of the site, but built in a new fashion. 'For four posts (*postes*) fixed in the ground carry the whole erection (*machinam*), with four separate areas (*cancellis*) of curved form placed round the edge (*in circuitu ductis*)'.[3] The building was almost certainly of wood. *Postes* is not a word used for columns or piers of stone, and they are spoken of as 'fixed in the ground', like stakes. Again *machina*, although sometimes used to describe a masonry structure, in both classical and medieval usage normally means a scaffold or a machine like a windlass or catapult, that is something contrived out of wood.[4] Seen in this light the result is a square with each corner marked by a post and each side opening into an apse.

It may therefore have been small and simple, but its size was due to the site and it was apparently novel. Wilfrid's church dedicated to the Virgin at Hexham may have been similar, though as the attached rooms are referred to as porticus they sound rectangular, like those of the tenth-century wooden church at Potterne. Apart from that there are no parallels for Alfred's building in either wood or stone in the whole of northern Europe, but the form was a popular one for chapels between the ninth century and the twelfth in the Byzantine Empire. The westernmost examples of this taste are a ninth-century reliquary in the form of a square building with an apse on each face, now in the treasury of St

Mark's in Venice, and the ninth-century church of St Nicholas at Nin on the Dalmatian coast. These may seem rather exotic parallels, but since Alfred modelled his coins on Byzantine originals, why not his chapels?[5]

In order to help him re-establish the monastic life in England, around the year 886 Alfred invited the monk Grimbald to his court from Flanders. Between Alfred's death in 899 and Grimbald's in 901 Edward the Elder, probably at Grimbald's behest, founded a new monastery at Winchester alongside the old or cathedral minster. This **New Minster** was consecrated in 903 and became the burial place of King Alfred. Sufficient remains have been excavated to show that it was an impressive structure consisting of a nave and aisles with the surprising width of 68 ft (20.75 m), and in all likelihood a transept.[6] The contrast with the Old Minster, lacking both aisles and transept, must have been marked. The obvious parallels are with ninth-century transeptal basilicas in the Carolingian Empire such as those at Steinbach or Seligenstadt, but the link provided by Grimbald suggests that the immediate source might be in the Low Countries.

In the year 909 the relics of Oswald, king and saint, were brought from Bardney in Lincolnshire to **Gloucester**. The church built to receive them by Alfred's daughter Aethelflaed had an aisleless nave 28 ft (8.5 m) wide, an apse at the west end and, in all probability, one at the east end as well.[7] There is good reason to doubt the claim that Heane's seventh-century church at Abingdon had such a double-ended plan and the form here is almost certainly an import from the Continent, where it occurs, among many other examples, on the St Gall plan of about 820, in the cathedral at Fulda consecrated in 819 and, geographically closest to Gloucester, at Alet in Brittany of the ninth or tenth century. In the same way as the New Minster in Winchester, this royal foundation illustrates the close dependence of church building around the year 900 on the architectural traditions of the Carolingian Empire.

Despite all this effort Alfred, Edward and Aethelflaed did not succeed in re-awakening the religious life of the country, but when it came, in the middle of the century, the revival was spectacular. It was chiefly, if not entirely, the work of three great churchmen, Dunstan, Ethelwold and Oswald, in conjunction with the crown. Their lives are closely interwoven.[8] Dunstan grew up as a well-connected young man who studied and took the tonsure at Glastonbury. After becoming chaplain to the bishop of Winchester he was consecrated a priest, on the same day as Ethelwold, and shortly thereafter in 939 King Edmund made him abbot of Glastonbury. This appointment marks the start of the reform movement. In 955 he was banished by King Edwig, spending the next two fruitful years at the monastery of St Peter at Ghent in Flanders. Returning in 957 at the invitation of King Edgar, he became in short succession bishop of Worcester, bishop of London and archbishop of Canterbury. Apart from Glastonbury he founded or refounded monasteries at Athelney (which had collapsed as an institution after Alfred's experiment), Malmesbury, Bath, Muchelney and Westminster, and in 978 he re-consecrated SS Peter and Paul in Canterbury, adding the new dedication to Augustine.

Oswald also experienced the reform movement in Europe at first hand, attending the monastery at Fleury on the Loire between about 950 and 958, where he became a monk. In 961 Dunstan persuaded Edgar to make him bishop of Worcester, a position which he retained to the end of his life in 992 along with the archbishopric of York. He was responsible for the founding or reforming of the monasteries at Worcester, Westbury-on Trym, Winchcombe, Evesham, Pershore and Ramsey.

Ethelwold was perhaps the most influential of the three, and because of his abilities in the designing and making of such things as buildings, bells, organs and retables, he is of particular interest in the present context. Born at Winchester, he worked under Dunstan at Glastonbury until in 954 he was made abbot of Abingdon by King Edred, where he acted as tutor to the young Edgar. In 963 he became bishop of Winchester where he substituted monks for the canons in the Old and New Minsters. Apart from Abingdon and the Old Minster he was responsible for the monasteries at Peterborough, Ely, Thorney and, probably, Crowland. In 973, in conjunction with Dunstan and Edgar, he convened the Council of Winchester to codify the reforms of the preceding decades.

The Council, held under the patronage of the king and queen, drew up a set of liturgical customs, the *Regularis Concordia*, which the heads of all the monastic houses present undertook to observe. These customs represent the importation into England of the monastic reform movement which had grown on the Continent throughout the tenth century, especially at Fleury and in the north at Ghent and at Gorzé near Metz. Abbo of Fleury, one of the most learned men of his time, was in England in the early 970s and may have attended the Council; Oswald was trained at Fleury and Ethelwold sent there for help and information; Dunstan spent his exile in Ghent, and the *Regularis Concordia* has been described as the purest surviving monastic customary of the Gorzé reform movement.

One might expect that churches built to fulfil a particular function would take their form at least in part from that function, but attempts to link liturgical practice and permanent architectural arrangement (as opposed to screens and barriers) have proved notoriously difficult. The architecture of the English monastic reform movement should stand a better chance than most of showing a correspondence because the reforming of the monasteries, the drawing up of the liturgical formulae, and the patronage of the buildings were all so heavily concentrated in the hands of a small group of individuals. Even given this set of circumstances the results are disappointingly meagre, yet they cannot be ignored.

The *Regularis Concordia* names three liturgical areas each with its own altar, *oratorium, ecclesia* and *chorus*, situated respectively at the west end, in the nave and at the east end of the church. Given only one altar in each case, the three are likely to have been placed axially and, since a centrally placed altar on ground level at the west end would have interfered with entry and exit, the western *oratorium* was probably in an upper chamber or gallery. In addition, pairs of choir boys singing responses needed to be placed to north, south and west of those singing in the choir. Those to the west could have been accommodated in the nave or in the *oratorium* just mentioned, but those to north and south, unless they were to stand hidden behind the choir stalls, would need upper chambers looking into the choir from above flanking porticus. [9]

The impact of the reform movement can be gauged from the fact that by the end of the tenth century most of the great Benedictine houses of the future were already in existence. Odericus Vitalis writing in the twelfth century claimed that between them the three prelates founded or reformed 26 monasteries, a total which has now risen above 30. Despite this impressive number, no part of any of these establishments remains standing and only a handful are known from excavations and descriptions. Perhaps because of this the following examples, at Glastonbury, Canterbury, Winchester, Deerhust, Brixworth, Peterborough and Abingdon, are characterised by variety and diversity.

When Dunstan became abbot of **Glastonbury** in 944 the seventh- or eighth-century church of King Ine consisted, with its additions, of a long nave flanked by porticus joined to the wooden *Vetusta Ecclesia* to the west by a courtyard, and with a square chancel to the east set over a mausoleum. He entirely re-worked the east end of this building (fig. 48). In his life of the saint William of Malmesbury he says that Dunstan 'added a tower to this [Ine's] church, considerably lengthened it and, so that it might form a square in length and breadth, he added aisles or porticus as they call them'.[10] The excavated evidence corroborates this, showing that he thickened the walls of the old chancel to enable it to carry a tower (in the process partially destroying and therefore presumably abandoning the mausoleum), flanked it to north and south with a pair of porticus and built a new chancel to the east. In 1083, during the violent term of office of the Norman abbot Turstin, armed men ascended into a gallery in order to shoot arrows at the Anglo-Saxon monks cowering around the altar. It is not clear where this gallery was, but it may have been one of a pair flanking the choir.

Of greater importance is the much clearer evidence for a rectangular cloister attributable to Dunstan, measuring 180 ft by 120 ft (55 m by 36.5 m) and defined by ranges of buildings 20 ft to 26 ft (6 m to 8 m) wide. Although it did not touch the church at any point its eastern range lay on the same alignment as the porticus to the south of the central tower, in the same way as the eastern

48 Glastonbury (Somerset), Abbey, tenth century. Plan, 1:600

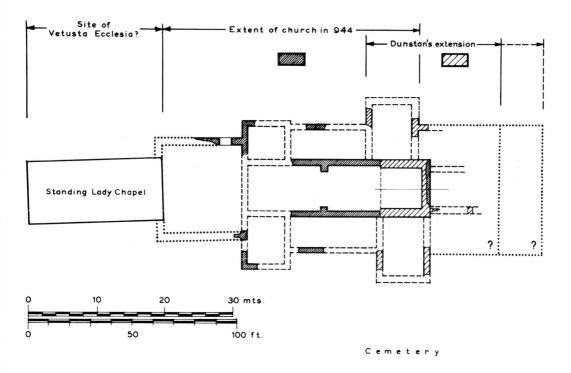

range relates to the transept in the later standard arrangement. The regular layout of the claustral buildings around a courtyard is one of the clearest indications of the influence of continental reform. Monastic buildings had already of course been laid out in relation to the church at Jarrow in the seventh century, but Glastonbury appears to have the first cloister in England. It derives from the Carolingian type first used at Lorsch in the 760s, adumbrated in the St Gall plan of *c.* 820 and used again at Cluny between 955 and 994 in the layout attributable to Mayeul.[11] While he was archbishop of Canterbury (960–88) Dunstan reformed St Augustine's and was probably repsonsible for the cloister there, doubtless modelled on the one at Glastonbury. According to the eleventh-century description the Anglo-Saxon cathedral at Canterbury had a cloister, and it is tempting to ascribe this too to Dunstan.

The pre-Norman **Cathedral** at **Canterbury**, which must rank as one of the most important of all Anglo-Saxon ecclesiastical buildings, is known from only two pieces of evidence, a description by Eadmer, an eleventh-century Canterbury monk, and, as has recently been pointed out, the building depicted on the first seal of the cathedral, in use before 1107 and almost certainly purporting to represent the church as it was before the Conquest (fig. 49).[12] Because of the lack of material remains, the building has become the subject of a number of conflicting views as to its form and date, or rather dates. There is

49 Canterbury (Kent), Cathedral, first seal, pre-1107

agreement on the following. Augustine took over and restored a Romano-British church to serve as the first cathedral. After undergoing various alterations, by the late tenth century this church had reached the form in which

Eadmer saw it before it was destroyed firstly by the fire of 1067 and secondly by Lanfranc's rebuilding of 1070 to 1077. In its late tenth-century state the cathedral had an eastern apse containing a crypt like that of St Peter's in Rome, on top of which stood the main sanctuary accessible from the choir by a series of steps. Between these steps and the choir altar lay the body of Dunstan, whose resting place was connected to the crypt by a passage. The choir extended westward into the body of the church and was separated from the lay area by an enclosure. This lay part was flanked by two towers, the southern of which provided the main entrance. At the west end was a raised sanctuary with an altar dedicated to the Virgin and behind it the bishop's throne set against the wall at the westernmost extremity of the church.

The permutations of the possible forms of the crypt, the flanking towers and the western sanctuary are numberless, each suggesting a different chronology, so that all that need be attempted here is a few comments on these three parts of the church.

Concerning the crypt, Canterbury Cathedral received a consecration in 990 which should have been occasioned by some building activity, and since Dunstan died in 988 it is possible that his cult was responsible for the development. On the other hand Eadmer's silence on any building activity at this date casts doubt on it.

On the second point, Eadmer describes the towers flanking the nave as *prominentes ultra aecclesiae alas*, which has been translated both as 'projecting *above* the aisles', and as 'projecting [in plan] *beyond* the aisles'. The representation on the seal makes it clear that the first reading is the correct one, providing as it does a two storeyed entrance porch rising above the aisle but not the nave, an arrangement which also existed at Lady St Mary in Wareham, possibly also of the tenth century.

Before leaving this question account should be taken of two objections to this reading which, while they may be overruled by the seal, nonetheless require an answer. Eadmer describes the north tower as having cloisters 'about it' (*hinc et inde*),[13] suggesting it projected northwards, but, as the arrangement on both the seal and St Mary at Wareham appear to project slightly, this need not create any difficulties. The other objection is more semantic, noting that it is tautological to speak of towers rising above anything, since if they did not do so they would not be towers. This, however, assumes a scientific rigour in Eadmer's writing which it does not possess. Too many people, architectural historians among them, have described towers 'rising above' the building of which they form a part for this to be a valid criticism. An example of just such a phrase occurs in the medieval description of Ramsey Abbey discussed in the next chapter.

The third element, the western sanctuary, has been reconstructed in two very different ways, as an apse very like the eastern one, and as an upper chamber in a western porch or tower like that at Brixworth. Once again the seal settles the issue firmly in favour of the first alternative. It is supported in this by Eadmer's description of the priest celebrating at the altar in this sanctuary facing east 'towards the people who stood below'.[14] In an upper chamber like that at Brixworth he would have been all but invisible.

The church built at **Winchester** by Cenwalh in the 640s and which became the cathedral in the 660s remained almost unaltered until Ethelwold's day. At some time, probably in the eighth century, a tower was built about 65 ft to the west of the facade, and in 862 St Swithin was buried in the open between the two buildings on the axis of the church. In 971 he was translated into the

cathedral and a structure raised over his tomb, linking church and tower and
leading to a consecration in 980. Next the eastern parts were extended, the work
being completed and consecrated by 994 by Alphege, Ethelwold's successor.

Ethelwold's western building is known both from a contemporary
description by the monk Wulfstan brilliantly analysed by Quirk in 1957 and
from complicated excavations equally successfully conducted by Biddle
throughout the 1960s (fig. 50).[15] According to Wulfstan Ethelwold

50 Winchester
(Hampshire), Old
Minster, tenth century.
Plan, 1:600
51 Werden (Nordrhein-
Westfalen), St Saviour,
ninth–tenth century.
Plan, 1:600

added many chapels with sacred altars which keep the entry of the threshold doubtful, so
that whoever walks in these courts with unfamiliar tread, cannot tell whence he comes or
wither to return, since open doors are seen on every hand, nor does any certain path of a

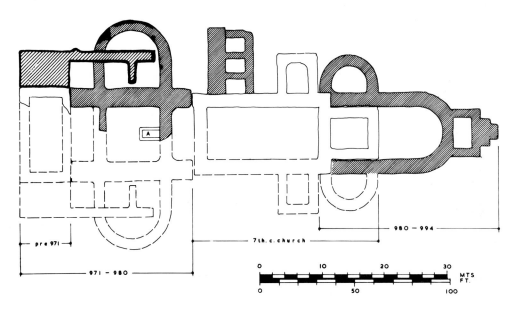

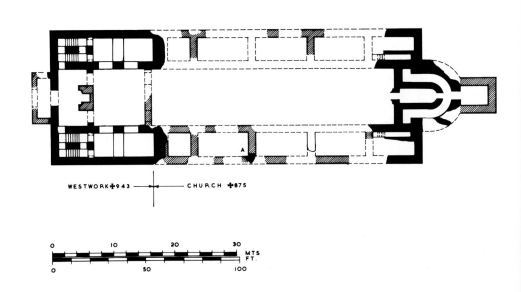

way appear. Standing, he turns his wandering gaze hither and thither and is amazed at the Attic roofs of the Daedalian floor, until a better informed guide appears and leads him to the threshold of the farthest vestibule. Here wondering in himself he crosses himself and cannot know in his astonished breast from what place he is to get out.

Biddle interprets the excavated evidence to mean that between 971 and 984 two plans were tried, the first one with large, apse-like features to north and south being abandoned and replaced with a square building closely comparable with Carolingian westworks such as those at Corvey consecrated n 885, and Werden of 943 (figs 51, 52), as Quirk had suggested from his analysis of the documents. This assumption may however be wrong. In order to argue that the foundations represent a single building it is necessary to examine the excavations in some detail.

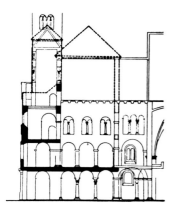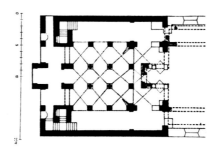

52 Corvey (Niedersachsen), Abbey, westwork, 873. Plan and section, 1:600 (Oswald, 1966)

The foundations of the north apse (the south lies hidden under the Norman Cathedral) and the central square consist of rammed chalk with wooden beams for reinforcement, while those of the outer wall of the square part of the building (marked in heavy outline and sparser shading on the plan) have been entirely robbed and hence can be assumed to have been of masonry. The difference in material itself suggests a difference in date, which is supported by the fact that at one point the robbed founds cut through the chalk founds. This evidence is incontrovertible, but the introduction of a new type of foundation does not necessitate the abandoning of any part of the original design. The central square and the eastern wall of the finished building stood on the chalk foundations, therefore there is no reason why the apses need not have been built as well. Further, the robbed foundations lie on the chord of the surviving curved wall. If a square building had been designed to replace the one with apses this would constitute an odd coincidence, but it would be entirely to the point if they formed part of one building.

The finished structure was on a magnificent scale, with apses 29 ft (8.8 m) wide internally, a north-south length of 112 ft (34 m) between their apexes, and a square element (as represented by the robbed founds) 79 ft (22.9 m) wide, which greatly exceeds the 62 ft (19 m) width of Corvey. The central space containing the tomb probably rose the full height of the building like a lantern tower, surrounded on three if not four sides by aisles and galleries, with stairwells and the incorporated old tower to the west. The result enables one to understand the confusion of Wulfstan's newcomer.

The Carolingian westwork must in large measure explain the character of this building. In its fully developed form it occurs from the late eighth century at St-Riquier through the ninth century at Corvey to the mid-tenth at Minden, while the reduced version, without a platform creating a first-floor level in the central well, remained popular throughout the tenth century, as at Werden and at St Pantaleon in Cologne (fig. 53). Westworks were used primarily for the cult of the Saviour, providing a place at the west end of the church for choirs and altars and, as we have seen, it is likely that the *Regularis Concordia* required some such space at the west end (though not necessarily on this scale) which, combined with the continental sources of the customs in the *Concordia*, adds weight to a derivation of Ethelwold's building from the westwork.[16]

53 Cologne (Nordrhein-Westfalen), St Pantaleon, late tenth century. Plan, 1:600 (Oswald, 1966)

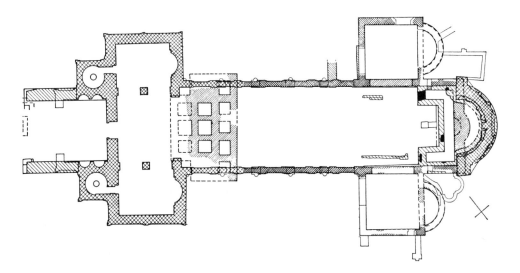

On the other hand westworks can explain neither the north and south-facing apses, nor the importance of St Swithin's tomb. After the body had been translated into the church in 971 the site of the burial became the pivot of the new building, set against the eastern wall of the central space in the same position as the altar at Werden. It remained a site of pilgrimage and structural elaboration through the tenth and eleventh centuries, and continued as such even after the Old Minster had been demolished to make way for the new Norman cathedral in the late eleventh century. Many functions have been claimed for westworks, from imperial chapel to baptistery, but acting as a martyrium is not prominent among them.

It is almost as difficult to find parallels for Winchester among martyria as among westworks. In a number of cases a burial chamber originally lying beyond the east end of a chancel has subsequently been incorporated into the church by building the east end out over it. This happened in the eighth century at Glastonbury and in the tenth or eleventh at Repton. Frankish and Carolingian churches frequently set rotundas in a similar position east of the apse, as at St-Pierre in Geneva, St-Germain in Auxerre or the cathedral at Hildesheim, most of them with funerary connotations. Rotundas at the east end are however rather different from flanking exedrae at the west.

The best formal parallel to the arrangement at Winchester is provided by the Nea Moni on Chios in the Aegean. As it dates from between 1042 and 1056 it is considerably later than the English building, but it was built under the direction of the emperor and belongs to a tradition of church building in Constantinople, where a number of tenth-century churches have narthexes flanked to north and south by apses. The western end of the church consists of a central square flanked to north and south by oblong areas which lead in turn into apses. There is a separate space between the central square and the church, and to the west a double entrance porch, all as at Winchester, though the connection between the two buildings, if there is one, is obscure.[17]

This formula goes back to imperial tombs of the late Antique period. The church of Sta Costanza in Rome, built as an imperial mausoleum in the early fourth century, and the tombs of the Honorian dynasty of a century later attached to St Peter's, represent a common type with entrance blocks flanked by apses. Closer both in time and space is the small trefoil building of around the year 800 in Grenoble which has at its west end a square room with apses to north and south, and to the west a chamber containing tombs.[18]

These examples do not add up to a very satisfactory explanation, but two connotations, the funerary and the imperial, stand out more clearly from them than any others. The idea that the Carolingian westwork was a chapel for the use of the emperor has long been discredited, but that does not rule out such a function here. In the first place the building at Winchester is not a westwork, or at least not just a westwork, and in the second, unlike Corvey, Werden, Reims and the other westworks, but like Aachen, it stood only a few yards from the palace to the north-west (fig. 8). Since Charlemagne had a throne in the western tribune at Aachen it is possible that Edgar intended something similar at Winchester. The building may then have had a number of uses, acting as a separate western sanctuary, as a martyrium and, on occasions, as a tribune for the king and his retinue.

The new eastern arm built between 980 and 994 raised the floor of the old easten porticus above a crypt and flanked it with a pair of semi-circular chambers. Further east was the main apse with beyond it a small crypt containing an altar. This evidence is even more difficult to interpret than that at the west end, but it implies a series of altars set on the axis of the church, at the west end, in the nave, in the sanctuary and in the outer crypt. There may also have been one over the central crypt, but this area is as likely to have housed the choir. These arrangements can be related to the *Regularis Concordia* and through it to buildings with similar functions such as St Pantaleon in Cologne, which was rebuilt between 964 and 980 and then enlarged to east and west between 980 and the end of the century (fig. 53). It shares with Winchester not only its dates but also the distinction of being a major church without aisles, and of having a major fore-building to the west and at the east a choir flanked by chambers and an apse with a small crypt. In addition its liturgical requirements were almost identical to those contained in the Winchester book. Similarly, the Minster at Essen, rebuilt after a fire in 946, had a westwork, a choir at the east end flanked by chapels in two storeys, and a raised crypt, while the usages of the Essen *Liber Ordinarius* are again very much of the same type.[19] Lastly Werden, like Winchester, had a rectangular outer crypt off its eastern end, giving it a relationship to the latter in overall dimensions, as surprisingly close as that evident in the scale and disposition of the core of the western massif (figs 50, 51).

There is no documentary evidence for any building at **Deerhurst** in the tenth century, but it is likely that Oswald reformed the monastery around 970 and that the church was modernised at the same time. St Mary's ceased to be an abbey at some date before the Conquest, perhaps as early as in the antimonastic reaction following Edgar's death in 975, though from the fabric it is clear that additions and alterations must have continued well into the eleventh century. The dating and sequence of the various parts of this building are unusually complicated, especially since the excavations and stripping of plaster undertaken in the 1970s, with the result that any discussion of the subject requires extensive detailed argument.[20] The précis which follows is presented in the knowledge that it obscures a number of difficulties and ignores others.

At the time of the reform the nave of the pre-Danish church was raised to its present height of about 40 ft (12 m) and its east end made into a square choir bay by the insertion of a cross-wall (fig. 54, W). Two double-storeyed porticus were attached to the north and south of this choir, each upper chamber looking inwards through a large arched opening (S). At an indeterminate date between the original foundation and these tenth-century alterations a semi-circular apse had been added to the original apse-less nave, rising from a level considerably below that of the rest of the church, even though it had no crypt either inside or outside the apse. In the late tenth century this apse was rebuilt in polygonal form with stripwork marking the angles and forming pedimental shapes. There seems to have been a chamber above the sanctuary, since looking into the choir from above the chancel arch is an opening which, from its size and apparent

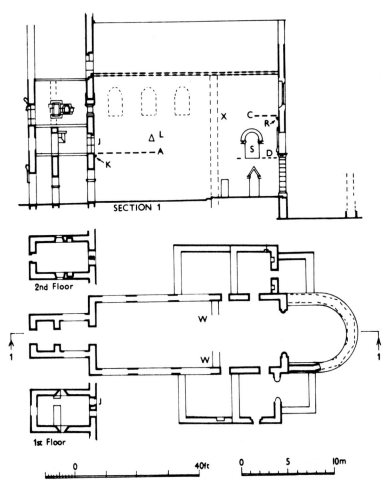

54 Deerhurst (Glourcestershire), St Mary, eighth–eleventh century. Plan and section, 1:400 (Taylor, 1975)

position, is unlikely to have been a window.[21] A pair of surviving corbels (R) supported a wooden gallery (C) running immediately in front of this opening.

The western porch was given three upper storeys and either at the same time or a little later was extended further into a tower. The eastern wall of the first-floor chamber has at its north end a doorway (J) which led onto a narrow wooden gallery supported, as with the eastern gallery, on two surviving corbels (K). The placing of the door off-centre suggests that an altar stood on the axis of the chamber, with a small triangular opening permitting the celebrant to see into the nave, though only for the most restricted and utilitarian of purposes. The second-floor chamber is more impressive, being taller and having openings on both axial walls. That to the east consists of a pair of small triangular-headed arches carried on stubby fluted pilasters and set in the middle of the wall space. Although subsequently cut away to form a doorway, this paired opening was

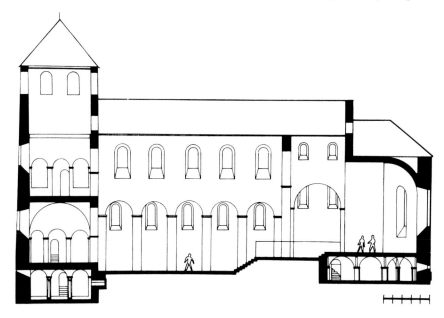

55 Celles (Namur), St-Hadelin, *c.* 1040. Section, 1:400 (Genicot, 1972)

designed and built only to be used as a means of viewing the nave, albeit in a more impressive manner than from the triangular hole in the room below. The opening in the west wall of this chamber is a doorway with its sill on the level of the floor, which presumably led onto an external wooden balcony. On the third floor a final doorway in the east wall gave access to the interior of the roof, the gable line of which remains on the eastern face of the tower. As the sill is badly worn it must have been heavily used. On the exterior of the nave a large stringcourse with a complex moulding marked the base of the clearstorey 25 ft (7.5 m) above the ground. During the years between the remodelling and the Conquest extra porticus were added at different times, running westward from the pair flanking the choir until they clasped even the western porch.[21a]

St Mary's at Deerhurst is not a large church, but since every available space appears to have been called upon to perform some function it can be described as a veritable machine for worshipping in. Attention has already been drawn to the three timber balconies or galleries: that over the chancel arch could have served as a rood-loft, that at the west end of the nave as a singers' gallery and that on the tower as an external but secure means of displaying relics.[22] The space of

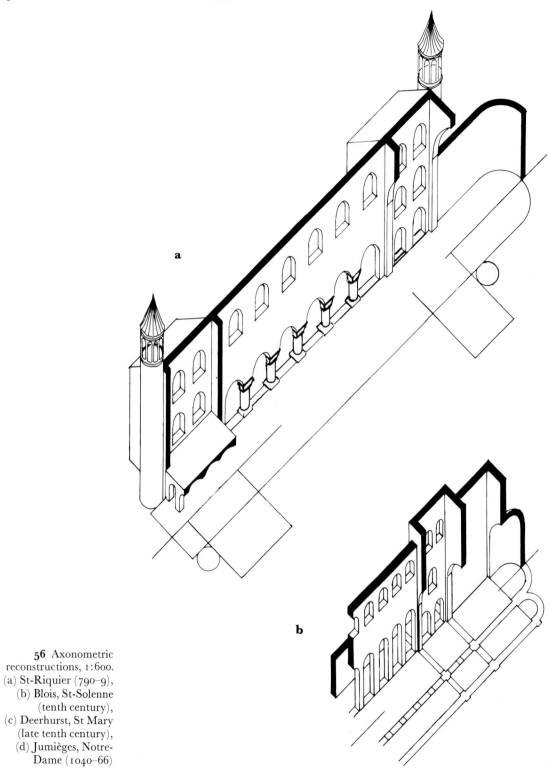

56 Axonometric
reconstructions, 1:600.
(a) St-Riquier (790–9),
(b) Blois, St-Solenne
(tenth century),
(c) Deerhurst, St Mary
(late tenth century),
(d) Jumièges, Notre-
Dame (1040–66)

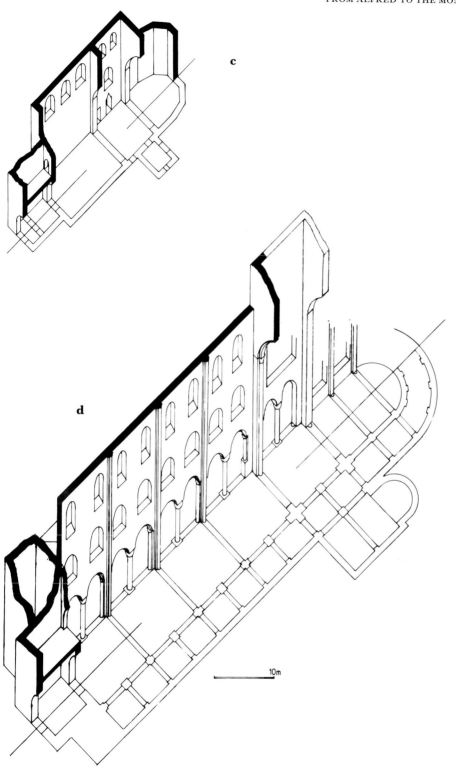

c

d

10m

the nave roof could have been used as a treasury and the chamber above the sanctuary for theatrical purposes. All this is so much speculation, but the functions of the main parts of the building can be gauged and paralleled with more certainty. If we assume the presence of an altar in the first-floor chamber above the porch, another in the nave before the entrance to the choir and a third in the sanctuary, then we would have the three liturgical focuses required by the *Regularis Concordia*, as well as a choir with flanking upper chambers or galleries for the singing of responses. Deerhurst would then take its place in a sequence of churches extending from, for example, St-Riquier in the late eighth century, with its three altars on axis (the western in an upper chamber) and a choir flanked by galleries (fig. 56), to St-Solenne at Blois in the tenth century, with its transept arms entirely filled with the platforms flanking the choir, and lastly to the abbey church at Jumièges begun about 1040, with all the features of St-Riquier in a more Romanesque form. Its silhouette also bears a noteworthy similarity to that standard in Lotharingia at, for example, Celles (fig. 55).

One detail remains to be discussed, involving the size of the wooden gallery at the west end of the nave and a similar gallery proposed for the church at Tredington in Warwickshire. In an elevation of Deerhust published in 1975 (see fig. 54) Taylor reconstructed the western gallery as extending over half the length of the nave (A), on the grounds that the pair of small triangular openings (L) in the nave walls were intended to light a space considerably closer to them than the floor of the nave. As a parallel he refers to the nave at Tredington at the west end of which there is a pair of windows set higher than the others to the east, which is a sure indication of the former existence of a gallery at this point. About half way along the nave there is a pair of large arched openings which Taylor takes as the entrances to the gallery, which therefore as at Deerhurst would have extended half way along the nave.[23]

This analysis can be called into question at both buildings. At Deerhust the surviving corbels are unsuited for anything other than a narrow gallery so that in order to accommodate an extended one it is necessary to postulate a series of lost supports. Secondly, as is indicated by their small size and lack of splay, the triangular openings are not windows since both factors would render them very inefficient at providing light. They are peepholes or squints, by analogy with the exactly comparable opening in the west wall looking into the nave from the first-floor chamber above the porch. Their presence requires not an extended gallery but an upper chapel on each of the porticus over which they lie.

At Tredington the evidence of the pair of raised windows suggests only an ordinary gallery of modest width such as those postulated for the smaller church at Jarrow and for Wing. The openings half way along the nave are in this case not too small to be windows, as at Deerhurst, but on the other hand they are too large to be doorways. With a width of some 4 ft they would represent the largest doorway in an upper storey in any Anglo-Saxon' building. What they are comparable with at Deerhurst is not the triangular holes but the arches of the upper chapels flanking the choir (S). The nave at Tredington originally had porticus which are now lost. The large openings require one pair to have been double-storeyed, like those on the nave of St Mary's at Wareham and perhaps like those described by Eadmer as flanking the entrance to the choir at Canterbury Cathedral.

Among the many alterations undergone by the pre-Danish church at **Brixworth** two stand out as likely to belong to the same period as the changes at Deerhurst here attributed to the time of Oswald. The apse was re-built on top of its semi-circular predecessor in a form curved on the interior and seven-sided on the exterior with pilasters at the angles and a surviving single-splayed window, as at Deerhurst except that there the apse was polygonal on the interior as well. At the west end the floor of the original upper chamber of the porch was raised and its opening to the nave blocked to make way for a new chamber higher up the facade and with a higher ceiling. The triple arcade looking into the nave is supported on turned stone shafts with capitals (or rather 'ends' since the bases are little different) which attempt a transition from the cylindrical, if bulbous, form of the shaft to the square section of the arch springers. Access to this chamber, to the tower-like structure above and to the roof space is provided by an ambitious spiral staircase on the western face. This is built of the same type of coarse stone as that used in the apse window indicating that the two additions at the east and west ends are probably of the same date. The triple opening can be compared to the double opening in the second-floor chamber at Deerhurst.

The seventh-century foundation at *Medeshamstede*, now **Peterborough**, was revived by Ethelwold around the year 966.[24] Parts of the east end of what

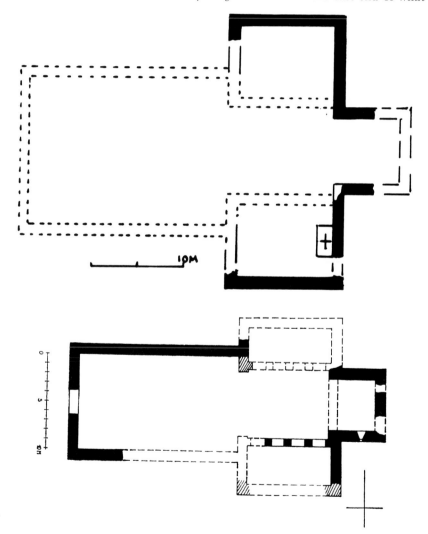

57 Peterborough (Northamptonshire/ Cambridgeshire), Abbey, late tenth century. Plan, 1:400

58 Camburg (Thüringen), St Cyriakus, tenth century. Plan, 1:400 (Oswald, 1966)

appears to be the tenth-century church have been excavated under the south transept of the twelfth-century building, consisting of a rectangular chancel and two arms which have been interpreted as the remains of a continuous transept like that at Old St Peter's or the Carolingian basilica at Fulda (fig. 57). Such a form would be an interesting occurrence in England at this date, but the dimensions make the reconstruction extremely unlikely. The chancel is 22 ft (7 m) across, which is neither very broad nor very narrow, but the proposed transept would be 34 ft (10.4 m) wide, greater than any other known space in an Anglo-Saxon church and wider than all but the very widest of Norman naves. This, as well as the meagre 2 ft 9 in. (.8 m) thickness, of the walls, suggests that each arm was a chapel with its axis running east-west rather than north-south, and permits a reconstruction along the lines of the tenth-century churches of St Cyriakus at Camburg and St John at Brendlorenzen in central Germany, where the chancels are approximately 17 ft (5.2 m) wide and the flanking chapels 30 ft (9 m) long (fig. 58). The resulting spaces at Peterborough would be nearly the same width as the chancel.

Nothing remains standing of any church building on the site of the abbey at **Abingdon** and the documentary and excavated evidence is meagre and conflicting, yet because of its close association with Ethelwold, the crown and the reform movement it cannot be ommitted. It will be argued below that the four churches known to have existed on the site had the following forms. The church of Heane, the founding abbot, of about 675, was probably a small rectangular building set with numerous separate dwellings and chapels in a circular enclosure of the Celtic type. Ethelwold rebuilt this church along the lines of the palace chapel at Aachen or one of its copies. There are no material remains of either of these buildings. When Ethelwold's church collapsed in the late eleventh century abbot Rainald moved the site a few score yards to the north and constructed a longitudinal building of Norman type with an apse, crossing, transept and nave, which abbot Hugh and his successors rebuilt in stages after the late twelfth century. Parts of both of these buildings have been excavated (fig. 59).[25]

Working backwards through these phases, dimensions of the then standing building taken by William of Worcester in the fifteenth century are compatible with the later of the two plans uncovered by archaeological investigation. The few traces of robber trenches indicate a rectangular chancel, a transept and a long nave. Both Clapham, who helped with the excavations in the 1920s, and Biddle, who published the first interpretation of them in 1968, consider that this building represents Rainald's Norman church as later enlarged by Hugh. Beneath this level, and hence earlier, are the remains of an apse and the north-west corner of what might be a nave which, if taken together, produce a building about 200 ft (61 m) long. Following the dictates of stratigraphy Clapham accepted the apse as part of Ethelwold's church, but because the Abingdon Chronicle describes this as centralised he dissociated the fragment of nave to the west. Biddle also takes these remains to be Saxon but accepts both fragments as belonging to the same building. He overcomes the problem posed by the description by proposing that this is not Ethelwold's church but Heane's.

None of the problems created by these two solutions arises if the apsed building (labelled III on the plan in fig. 59) is attributed to Rainald in the late eleventh century. Its scale and apse are compatible with such a date and the location of the apse permits the reconstruction of a transept in the same position as that of the larger church. Hugh's enlargement would then have become a complete re-building in the course of the thirteenth and fourteenth centuries. If

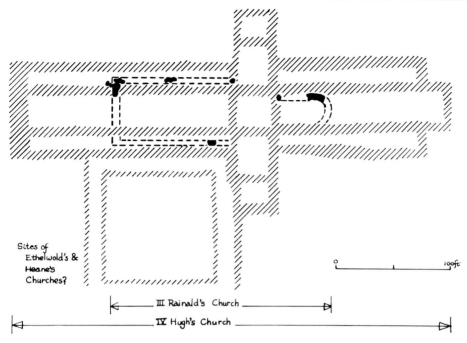

Sites of
Ethelwold's &
Heane's
Churches?

0   100ft

III Rainald's Church

IV Hugh's Church

this view is accepted then there are no excavated remains of either of the Anglo-Saxon churches, which is not surprising since the Chronicle says that they were on a different site, Heane's monastery having stood 'where now is the monks' cellar' (*Chron.* ii, 272).

The church built by Ethelwold between his inception as abbot in 954 and its consecration in 963 is described in the Abingdon Chronicle as having 'a round chancel, a round nave twice the length of the chancel, and a tower which was also round' (*Chron.* ii, 277–8). In 1091 Rainald, before embarking on the complete rebuilding on a different site, first tried to enlarge the east end of this church, but having taken down the chancel on the east side of its 'old tower' he provided inadequate buttressing with the result that the tower collapsed (*Chron.* ii, 23–4). From this it can be deduced that the 'tower' was the centralised nave itself rising above an ambulatory, and not something attached or separate at the west end.

The most popular centralised building in ninth-, tenth- and eleventh-century Europe was without doubt Charlemagne's palace chapel at Aachen. As this has an octagonal core or nave and a rectangular chancel it appears to be very different from Ethelwold's Abingdon, but polygons are frequently described as round in medieval accounts of buildings, and the copies of Aachen themselves offer a wide variety of chancels, including round ones.[26] At Muizen in Brabant, for example, the church perhaps attributable to Notker, bishop of Liège from 972 to 1008, had a polygonal nave and ambulatory with a semi-circular chancel. At both Aachen and Muizen the length of the chancel is about half the diameter of the nave, which fits the description of Abingdon.[27] There may also be some significance for a link with Aachen in the fact that King Edred took such a close interest in the building of the monastery, visiting it every day and even measuring the foundations with his own hand (*Chron.* ii 258).

Of the earliest work, that of Heane, the Chronicle says that the *monasterium* 'had a length of 120 ft (36.5 m) and was round as much in the western part as in

59 Abingdon
(Berkshire), Abbey.
Excavated plans, 1:1000

the eastern' (ii, 272). This has generally been taken to mean a longitudinal double-ended church, with an apse at the west end as well as the east, like the church on the St Gall plan of the early ninth century or St Oswald's at Gloucester of the early tenth.[28] Heane's church would then be the first north of the Alps to adopt the form, an outcome which, while certainly not impossible, is sufficiently striking to warrant a re-assessment.

Monasterium is an ambiguous term in that it can mean both 'monastery' and 'church', but when the above quotation is set in context there can be no doubt that here it means the whole monastery.

The monastery of Abingdon, which Heane the first abbot of this place built, was thus: it had a length of 120 ft (36.5 m) and was round as much in the western part as in the eastern. This monastery was founded in the place where now is the monks' cellar, in such a way that the altar stood where now is the lavatory. Around the circumference of this monastery there were twelve little dwellings and as many chapels, twelve monks eating, drinking and sleeping in the same place in the little dwellings; nor did they have a cloister such as they have now, but they were surrounded by a high wall which acted as a cloister for them. . . . On Sundays and on principal feast days they would gather together at the same time and celebrate Mass in the church (*ecclesia*) and eat together.[29]

In the first place the church is separately mentioned and designated by the term *ecclesia*, which must distinguish it from the *monasterium*. Secondly, the phrase 'around the circumference of the monastery' suggests, rather than a church, a circular enclosure after the manner of Celtic foundations with their separate dwellings for the monks. The figure of 120 ft (36.5 m) is also compatible with this interpretation, since Patrick's foundation at Armagh is described as being in an enclosure measuring 140 ft (43 m) and Cuthbert's at Lindisfarne as 'almost round' and four or five poles (between 48 ft and 100 ft, 14.6 m and 30.5 m) across. Abingdon did not lack Celtic links since Heane's successor as abbot was called Conan.[30]

To conclude these remarks on Abingdon, however one reads this enigmatic documantary evidence, it seems likely that all the surviving material evidence is post-Conquest.

To sum up the period of reform, from the descriptions and remains of these tenth-century English buildings it emerges that towers, apparently unknown before the Danish invasions, become popular, occurring in a variety of positions at Glastonbury, Canterbury, Abingdon, Winchester, Deerhurst and Brixworth. Those at the last three mark or stand on top of a western sanctuary, which also existed at Canterbury. Glastonbury, Winchester and Deerhurst acquire a separately identifiable choir bay (while Brixworth retains one from its earlier plan). Chapels flank this bay at ground level at all three sites, while Deerhurst and perhaps Glastonbury had upper chambers as well. At Glastonbury and Winchester the east end is extended and at Deerhurst and Brixworth it is rebuilt. Only Winchester can be said to have acquired new crypts as that at Canterbury has a very uncertain date, and cloisters are added at Glastonbury and the two Canterbury churches. This adds up to the elaboration of the east and west ends plus towers and cloisters, which is what liturgical and architectural developments on the Continent during the ninth and tenth centuries would lead one to expect.

The claustral square is no help in any attempt to localise the continental area of most importance for England in these developments, because early instances are so widely scattered at for example, Lorsch in the Rhineland in the eighth century, St-Wandrille in Normandy in the ninth, and Cluny in Burgundy in the tenth. The documentary evidence points clearly to Fleury as a potential candidate as a source in general, but as no architectural remains are available at present the lead cannot be explored.[31] The same shortcoming affects the other centres of the reform movement, but at least in Lotharingia it is possible to identify a school of churches which used liturgies similar to those in England, involving such features as three axial sanctuaries the westernmost of which is raised and surmounted by a tower. All of the 14 houses of those reformed from Gorzé with parts surviving from before 1050 have or had western axial towers, western galleries and chambers on two levels flanking the choir, and some impression of what the type was like can be gained from Werden and St Pantaleon. Similarly the Mosan silhouette of the eleventh century which is so like Deerhurst is, as already noted, likely to be a continuation of earlier practice.

Chapter Eight

ANGLO-SAXON ROMANESQUE: THE CROSSING

The adjective 'Romanesque' in the title of this chapter might have been enclosed in quotation marks to indicate that the usage is somewhat novel, as Anglo-Saxon architecture is usually specifically contrasted with the Romanesque style, particularly as it developed in Normandy. The term has been used here to describe any building manifesting a tendency to the articulated formalism of the new style as described in chapter six, whether or not the building in question has affinities with Norman work. This approach not only makes some sense in its own right, but also serves as a contrast to, on the one hand, that of Baldwin Brown and Clapham who saw late Anglo-Saxon building as primarily Carolingian and, on the other, Taylor's thesis of a slow, indigenous development from before the Danish invasions with few if any continental contacts.[1a]

An awareness of Romanesque design shows itself most clearly in an Anglo-Saxon context in two areas, the crossing square and the architectural decoration used to articulate the spaces and elements of the building. The simplest type of crossing is that represented by Breamore, Dover, Wooton Wawen and Repton, and perhaps, from documentary evidence, by Ramsey and Ely. In this type the eastern end of the main body of the church is divided off into a square choir or crossing bay with porticus to north and south and a chancel to the east. No examples of this type attain the status of a full Romanesque crossing created by the intersection of two similar masses on the two main axes, since the arms are always much narrower than the crossing. A peculiarly English variant of this, as at Stow and Sherborne, makes the nave as well as the other three arms narrower than the crossing, leaving the latter with four salient angles. Finally only Great Paxton has arms as wide as the crossing and arches to match, yet even here the height of the transept arches and roofs is much lower than that of the nave. These three types will now be examined.

The 'Breamore' type of crossing can be traced in embryo back to the early period, through Winchester, Brixworth and Deerhurst (figs 20, 34, 54). At Cenwalh's seventh-century church in Winchester the east end of the nave is not divided off from the rest of the space by any architectural feature, but it achieves a separate status by being the place where the altar and its canopy are located and by the three porticus leading from it to east, north and south. Brixworth, which may belong to the first half of the ninth century, has a square area between the nave and the chancel, clearly defined, unlike Winchester, but lacking any rooms to north and south and therefore in no sense forming a crossing.

The simple unsubdivided nave of the pre-Danish church at Deerhurst was re-ordered, as we have seen probably during the monastic reform movement around 970, by the insertion of a wall creating a square choir bay between the nave and the chancel, and the construction of a two-storeyed porticus to each side. There was little if any communication between this choir square and the ground-floor room of each porticus, but the upper chambers opened inwards through large arches, creating a species of crossing with arms. It is significant however that at Brixworth and Deerhurst the walls of the square bay rose no higher than those of the nave so that, apart from the possibility that they each had a separate roof system, they were not picked out from the nave on the exterior. The interior of Deerhurst in the second half of the tenth century, with all its subdivisions, upper openings, galleries and porticus, is in fact a good example of pre-Romanesque informality and clutter.

At St Mary's at **Breamore** in Hampshire the eastern end of the main body forms a square bay with a chancel beyond and single-storeyed porticus to north and south, each much narrower than the crossing and, in the case of the porticus, entered through arches which are narrower still (fig. 60). Despite their narrowness, however, they are not doorways but arched openings given great prominence by robust imposts each of which protrudes on all three faces, in the church, under the soffit and in the porticus, and by an inscription on the southern one of bold design if opaque intention. The status of the square as a crossing is enhanced by the fact that its walls rise above those of the nave into a tower-like structure. Its present two-stage stepped roof is fifteenth-century, but if it reflects the original arrangement then the height of this part of the church would have exceeded that of the nave by an even greater amount.

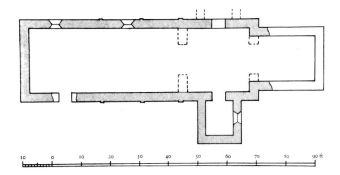

60 Breamore (Hampshire), St Mary, c. 1000. Plan, 1:400 (Taylor and Taylor, 1965)

On the exterior the nave is divided into bays by pilaster strips, three to each side, the easternmost pair of which mark the western corners of the crossing square. This may be an attempt to emphasize the independence and verticality of the tower bay, masked as it is in part by the nave and crossing having the same width. The effect, intended or not, is enhanced by the fact that the westernmost pair of strips divides the nave into two squares each the same size as the crossing.

There is no documentary or archaeological evidence for either the date or the status of this church so that attempts to place it must rely on stylistic analysis. The lettering on the south arch contains a number of peculiarities which are thought to indicate the early eleventh century, a date which is by no means incompatible with the architectural evidence.[1b] Breamore is arranged as if the flanking chambers at Deerhurst had been made single-storeyed in order to simplify and articulate the design. Of course there may have been differences between the liturgical requirements of the two buildings, but no such requirement can explain the placing of the porticus at Breamore exactly in the centre of the side of the crossing square, whereas at Deerhurst they lie to the east of it. It is this sense of control which marks the Hampshire church off, regardless of functional considerations, and which suggests that it is later than Deerhurst. Typology is a clumsy tool when the sample is a small one, and many factors other than stylistic development, such as availability of money and the status of the foundation, can explain the position of a building in a sequence.[2] Even though, therefore, Breamore should on the face of it be dated shortly after Deerhurst, there is nothing to prevent it having been built at any time in the fifty years after 970, including the second decade of the eleventh century proposed on palaeographic grounds. By the same token there may be churches more fully developed than Breamore, which can be dated as early as the late tenth century.

A case in point may be the church which Oswald built at **Ramsey**, the description of which makes it clear that a crossing of more articulated form than that at Breamore existed at the height of the reform movement and not just in its aftermath. Oswald's church was consecrated in 974, but the structure proved faulty and was repaired and reconsecrated in 991. According to the chronicle of the abbey and the Life of St Oswald the building had two axial towers, one at the west end, probably containing a gallery for an organ and singers, and another larger one at the east end. Three porticus led off the eastern tower to the north, south and east in the form of a cross. Thus far one can reconstruct the design along the lines of Breamore, but the text goes on to say that the tower was supported on four arches and four piers (*columnas quattuor*).[3] The arches to the porticus at Breamore are too small to excite anyone to describe them as supporting the tower as they are nothing more than holes punched in the wall. Equally, the walls running from the corners of the square are far too prominent as surfaces to submit to being described as piers. Finally as there were no aisles at Ramsey the corners of the crossing could not have looked free-standing for that reason. The best explanation for this description is that the arches on all four faces were so wide that the sections of wall in the corners between them read as single identifiable upright members. This in turn implies that the porticus themselves were more nearly of the width of the crossing than they are at Breamore.

It is possible that Ethelwold's church at **Ely** had a form as advanced as that at Ramsey, but this is by no means certain. Clapham reconstructs the late tenth-century church with both an eastern and a western transept, and, if not in Ethelwold's day then by the early eleventh century, with a pair of aisles to the nave as well.[4] This reading of the documents is supported by a number of curious parallels between the Norman and Saxon establishments at Winchester and Ely. Walkelin's late eleventh-century cathedral at Winchester had prominent aisled transept arms and a crossing at the east end, and a large massif at the west, probably comprising a central tower flanked by two arms. The contemporary Norman church at Ely was begun by Abbot Simeon who had previously been prior at Winchester, and it too has an aisled transept to the east and at the west a central tower with flanking arms. This dependence repeats that of the previous century, as the Old Minster provides a forerunner for the western massif in the Norman cathedral at Winchester, while Ethelwold selected his prior Brihtnoth to be first abbot of the reformed house at Ely.

This constitutes a formidable and attractive case which may very well be right, but it must be noted that the texts are equivocal. The Anglo-Saxon Chronicle describes how Alfred Aetheling was buried at Ely in 1036 low in the sacred earth 'to the steeple full nigh in the south aisle to lie of the transept west'. This is Clapham's rendering of the original phrase 'aet tham west ende/tham styple ful gehende/on tham suth portice',[5] which might be put more straightforwardly as 'at the west end/near the tower (or steeple)/in the south porticus'. Read in this way the arrangement sounds more like the west end of Deerhurst or Brixworth as re-modelled in the tenth and eleventh centuries than a fore-runner of the Norman abbey. Again Clapham's belief that between 981 and 1016 one Leofwin 'rebuilt and enlarged the south aisle' is based on the statement in the *Liber Eliensis* that 'he began to extend the walls of the church and to enlarge them towards the south, and joining them to the other work he completed them at his own expense', which says nothing about the building of a new aisle or the enlarging of a previous one.[6] Finally, neither of the two texts makes it clear that there was an eastern tower. In sum, the form of Ely before the Conquest remains an open question.

The most dramatic surviving remains of a church with two axial towers are those of St Mary-in-Castro at **Dover** (fig. 61). The plan is a larger version of Breamore, with a nave twice as long as broad followed to the east by a square crossing with a narrower chancel and narrower still porticus to north and south, the rectangular end of the chancel perhaps giving an indication of the original form at Breamore. On the other hand, conversely to Breamore the eastern and western arches of the crossing remain while those to north and south have been removed. It is therefore impossible to say whether the arms were more integrated, but an indication that they were not is afforded by their position slightly east of the centre of the side of the square, that is in a less 'organised' position than at Breamore.

Another difference is that the tower is much more prominent, rising about twice the 34 ft (10.4 m) size of its square base, while the nave is externally about the same height as its breadth. This large scale is carried into the nave windows which are over 7 ft (2.1 m) high and nearly 4 ft (1.2 m) wide, into the massive plinth which runs around the whole building, and into the only surviving doorway, which has jambs of massive through-stones laid Escomb-fashion and an arch of two rows of brick voussoirs like the arcade arches at Brixworth, though here laid radially.

As a western axial tower St Mary's has incorporated the Roman lighthouse already mentioned in connection with Kentish architecture. The church has been placed so that there is only a narrow gap between its façade and the tower, and, although oddly enough the two structures do not lie on the same axis, a doorway at first-floor level in the façade wall indicates a link with the tower in much the same way as the nave at Deerhurst communicates with the chamber above the western porch. Inside the church the doorway led onto a wooden gallery. This is known to have existed from the holes for timber beams found by the restorers, and from the fact that the windows lighting the western end of the nave are lower and smaller than the others, and have rectangular heads to enable them to fit as neatly as possible under the gallery floor.

There are no relevant documentary references for St Mary-in-Castro, but its affinities with Ramsey and Breamore make the date in the late tenth or early eleventh century traditionally ascribed to it entirely acceptable.

Since neither of the two standing buildings so far discussed has a complete set of crossing arches it will be useful to note the arrangements at one church where all of them survive.

61 Dover (Kent), St Mary-in-Castro, *c.* 1000. From the north-west

The four arches leading out of the crossing of St Peter's at **Wooton Wawen** are of no fewer than three different sizes.[7] The smallest are those to north and south, the next that to the chancel and the largest that into the nave. The flanking entrances, like the arms themselves, are off-set to the east, while all the arches are so low and narrow that the spaces are compartmentalised, making them relate in a severely utilitarian manner.

St Wystan's at **Repton** in Derbyshire, a building probably of the Breamore type, requires special attention since over the last few years it has attained a position of pivotal importance in the history of Anglo-Saxon architecture. With immaculate reasoning and minute attention to detail Harold Taylor has re-written the sequence of events revealed in the eastern parts of the church. The relative chronology thereby established appears to be incontrovertible and will be described as such below, but the absolute chronology proposed by Taylor is more open to question, and as he dates the monument before the Danish invasions, some two centuries earlier than the date previously attributed to it, the question is clearly of some importance.[8]

The *earliest parts* of the remaining fabric are the four walls of the square crypt which originally formed a free-standing structure largely sunk below ground level, probably standing just to the east of a church. There was a small recess in the centre of each wall, that to the north giving onto the access stair and the others rising to ground level, at which point they were probably covered by the heavy triple plinth which still runs round part of the exterior. In the *second phase* this room was incorporated into the church by the chancel built over it with walls of brown stone no thicker than those of the structure below (fig. 63). In the *third phase* four spiral columns were set in a square in the centre of what had now become the crypt, with a pair of pilasters as responds attached to each wall, all twelve supports carrying a series of nine vaults of ambiguous form. The top of

62 Chatillon-sur-Seine (Côte d'Or), St Vorles, between 980 and 1015. From the south-west

each of the north, south and east recesses was provided with an arch broken through the plinth and intended to allow daylight into the interior. The walls of the chancel were rebuilt in their upper parts in a white stone and thickened in their lower so as to rest on the haunches of the vaults, indicating that they are either contemporary with the vaults or later than them, and the rest of the church to the west was rebuilt. *Fourthly* and finally, steps were cut diagonally down from the flanking porticus into the north-west and south-west corners of the crypt.

Taylor dates all four of these phases to the eighth and ninth centuries. He identifies the *original building* as a mausoleum and attributes it to King Ethelbald of Mercia who, according to the Anglo-Saxon Chronicle, was buried at Repton in 757. The *second phase*, the incorporation of the mausoleum into a chancel with thin walls, is not attached to any events or particular years but must be later than the building of the mausoleum and earlier than the changes made in the next phase. According to the twelfth-century text of Florence of Worcester, Wystan, the grandson of King Wiglaf (827–40), was murdered in 850 and buried in his grandfather's mausoleum.[9] On this basis Taylor dates the *third phase* (the vaulting of the crypt and the rebuilding of the chancel) to Wiglaf's time, the king smartening up Ethelbald's building to use as his own burial place, and the *fourth phase*, the insertion of the diagonal stairs, to the years following 850, in the wake of Wystan's death and his growing saintly reputation.

This interpretation is open to a number of objections. While the Anglo-Saxon Chronicle records that Ethelbald was buried at Repton it does not say where in the town this took place, nor that he built himself a mausoleum. Conversely Florence of Worcester clearly says that Wystan was buried 'in the mausoleum of his grandfather Wiglaf'. A combination of the silence of the Anglo-Saxon

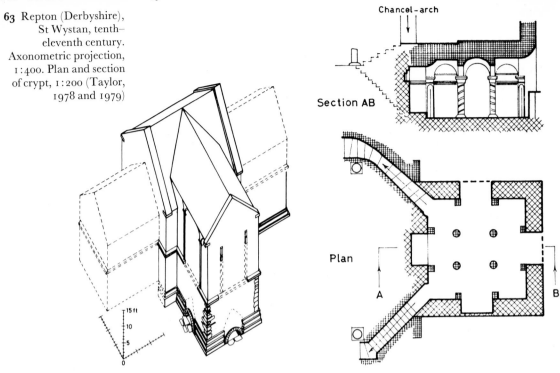

63 Repton (Derbyshire), St Wystan, tenth–eleventh century. Axonometric projection, 1:400. Plan and section of crypt, 1:200 (Taylor, 1978 and 1979)

Chancel-arch

Section AB

Plan

A

B

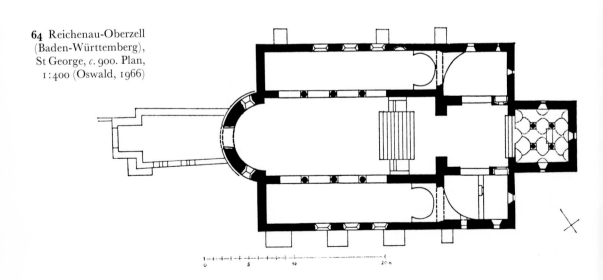

64 Reichenau-Oberzell (Baden-Württemberg), St George, c. 900. Plan, 1:400 (Oswald, 1966)

Chronicle with the literal meaning of Florence's words suggests that it was Wiglaf who built the mausoleum (*phase one*) and that a few years later Wystan was buried in it while it was still in its original form.

An examination of the nature of *phase two*, the extension of the chancel, also supports the contention that the mausoleum was only incorporated into the church after Wystan's death. There was a monastery at Repton at least by the late seventh century when St Guthlac became a monk there,[10] and although there is nothing to prove it, the subsequent relationship between Wiglaf's mausoleum and the church suggests that when it was built the mausoleum stood immediately to the east of the first church. The placing of a tomb in such a position is attested by the burial chamber of King Sigismund built between 513 and 516 and attached to the apse of the church of St-Pierre at Geneva (fig. 65).

As we have seen in discussing Kentish buildings, burial in church had been largely conceded by the ninth century, but the building of a chancel over a mausoleum housing either Ethelbert or Wiglaf, while not impossible, would be surprising, placing these secular rulers beneath the sanctuary in the same relationship to the altar above as, for example, that of the body of St Peter in the

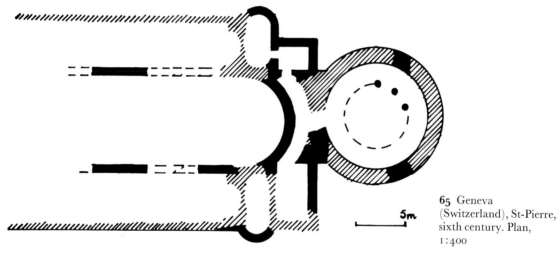

65 Geneva (Switzerland), St-Pierre, sixth century. Plan, 1:400

Vatican basilica in Rome, or that of St Gertrude at Nivelles discussed in chapter four (fig. 30). It is extremely difficult to see Ethelbald's burial place treated in this way by even the most admiring of his progeny, or Wiglaf adorning and rebuilding for his own purposes what had become a crypt under a sanctuary. Such behaviour is only conceivable in a Constantine or a Malatesta, and should be contrasted with that of Pepin who had himself buried face down at the west door of St-Denis, in order that those entering might tread him underfoot. The conclusion seems inescapable that the extension of the chancel over the mausoleum at Repton would only have occurred once the mausoleum had acquired an odour of sanctity after the establishing of the cult of St Wystan.[11]

The use of columns with spiral shafts in *phase three* only serves to reinforce this, as from the fourth century to the eleventh these appear to have enjoyed a special status as markers for places of particular holiness. The columns connected with the tomb of St Peter in Rome set the fashion, occasioning numerous copies including the ninth-century altar canopy of Sant'Apollinare in Classe, near Ravenna. But the closest parallels to Repton are to be found in the series of

66 Utrecht (Netherlands), St Peter, c. 1048. Crypt

eleventh-century crypts including St Peter's at Utrecht (fig. 66) and St Lebuinus' at Deventer, and culminating in the sanctuary of the Virgin in the crypt of Anselm's extension to Canterbury Cathedral. In these three cases spiral columns help to concentrate the attention on the centre of the crypt, and to define, at Canterbury for instance, the sanctuary for the altar.[12] Wiglaf is therefore most unlikely to have built them for his own aggrandisement at Repton, whereas conversely they would be highly appropriate as markers for Wystan's body after it had achieved a certain saintly status.

If this analysis is correct then phase two, and with it phases three and four, must be dated after 850. The question is, how long after? The pressure of the Danish invaders on the Midlands increased steadily during the middle years of the ninth century until in 874 they established winter quarters at Repton itself.[13] The preceding 24 years hardly seems a sufficient or auspicious enough time for the establishing of a cult of the saint and the subsequent provision of at first a simple then a more elaborate architectural setting. If phase two (or at least phase three) does not belong before 874 then it must be placed well into the tenth century, after the reconquest of the Danelaw.

It is not clear what happened to the foundation in this period. The abbey may not have been re-established as, according to Domesday, at the time of the Conquest the church at Repton was served by two priests, with no mention of any monks. The Evesham Chronicle records that Cnut (1016–35) 'caused that glorious martyr Wystan to be moved from Repton to Evesham'. This shows that no architectural work in connection with the shrine can be dated later than some point in Cnut's reign, but it also indicates that the cult was flourishing at the time.[14] Phases two, three and four must all then be accommodated between 850 and 1035, and probably between about 920 and 1020.

The available architectural parallels support these date brackets. The square crypt subdivided by four columns is a common feature in the ninth and tenth centuries, but one building bears a much stronger relationship than any other to Repton as a whole, namely St George's at Reichenau-Oberzell, where a rectangular chancel contains a sanctuary set over a crypt with four columns supporting the vaults (fig. 64). To the west stands a square crossing flanked to north and south by transept arms entered through openings considerably narrower than the full width available, all as at Repton. The church used to be ascribed to Abbot Heito around 822, but as a result of recent excavations it has been re-dated to the time of the third abbot of that name, who held office between 888 and 913, and was probably built to honour the relics of St George which arrived in 896.[15] It is not possible to prove any causal relationship between Reichenau-Oberzell and Repton, but if there was one then the relevant English building would belong in the tenth century. The capitals in the crypt and on the columns in the crossing find their best parallels in the crypt of St-Avit in Orléans, probably of the tenth century, in the late eleventh-century undercroft of Lanfranc's dormitory at Canterbury and in the contemporary crypt of Rochester Cathedral. These, like the spiral columns at Utrecht, Deventer and Canterbury, again help to pull the shrine at Repton, albeit gently, out of the pre-Danish period.

The same conclusion is suggested when the church as a whole is considered in an English context. The closest thing to a crossing which can be dated before the Danish invasions is the choir at Brixworth, but that has no porticus to north and south and hence does not really fit the definition. Repton on the other hand has a distinctive and familiar form closely related to the eastern ends of Breamore and Dover, even sharing with the latter the displacing of the arms slightly to the east. It differs however in that those very arms are as large as the chancel, whereas at the other two buildings they are considerably smaller. In this at least, Repton is less *ad hoc*, more articulated and hence closer to the full Romanesque crossing. In other words it would be difficult, to put it no more strongly, to place phase three at Repton much earlier than Breamore or Dover, so that a date after 970 seems reasonable.

A similar date is suggested by the alterations carried out at **Wing**, where the large open crypt of the first building was, at a later date, subdivided by the insertion of four piers forming a central space surrounded by a species of ambulatory, the whole covered by vaults carried on the piers and on responds attached to the walls (fig. 37). The similarity of this procedure to that adopted at Repton suggests that the insertion had a similar function, but nothing is known of the relics held at Wing. An approximate date for the operation can, however, be arrived at from the fact that, at the same time as the alterations to the crypt, the apse was rebuilt.[16] The external decorations on this apse can be related to similar alterations at Deerhurst and, less closely, Brixworth, both of which are likely to belong to the late tenth century.

The second type of crossing is that in which the two western corners are left salient, like the two eastern ones in the Breamore type. Recent work at **Sherborne** Abbey represents one of the most attractive aspects of Anglo-Saxon studies. Through the 1960s and early 1970s James Gibb and John Leach, two masters at Sherborne School, aided by a number of pupils, excavated parts of the site, drew up elevations and interpreted a mass of evidence until, with the help of Richard Gem on the documentary material, they were able to reconstruct almost in its entirety the eleventh-century Anglo-Saxon cathedral. The building is as important in its way as the Old Minster at Winchester and has the advantage of still being available for study.[17]

In 705 King Ine established a see at Sherborne with Aldhelm as bishop. Wulfsin or Wulfsige, who around 990 became the third bishop of that name, introduced a monastic community and with it Dunstan's reforms. Within a few years of his death in 1001 miracles began to occur at his tomb, and the cult grew until Bishop Aelfwold II (1045–58) decided to provide the saint with a worthy setting and rebuilt the old church, or, perhaps, built the new one next to it.

From the exterior the present church appears to be a structure of the late Middle Ages, but it conceals within its fabric a major rebuilding of the early twelfth century, which in turn in large measure follows the outline of the Saxon church. This was between 200 ft and 220 ft (61 m and 67 m) long depending on how one reconstructs the chancel, and consisted of an eastern crossing with the peculiar characteristic of being larger than any of the four arms attached to it, leaving its four corners standing proud (fig. 67). At the western end of the aisled nave stood another crossing, smaller than the first and indeed smaller than the nave, but with transept arms and a western adjunct, again all narrower than itself. Claustral ranges ran north from each of the two transepts and doubtless had a cloister between them.

The evidence for this reconstruction is worth setting out in detail. Because of the distribution of the surviving parts it is advisable to begin a description at the west end, where the present façade marks the eastern side of the western crossing. A large square platform lying on the axis of the church has been excavated at this point, with a shallow projection to the west and two arms to north and south. The north and east walls of the north arms survive to some height, with long-and-short quoins at the north-east corner and a double plinth along the base the upper member of which is chamfered. A contemporary

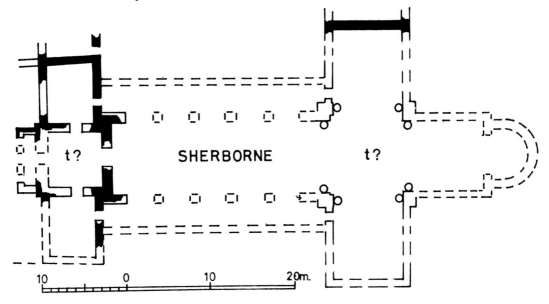

67 Sherborne (Dorset),
Cathedral, after 1045.
Plan, 1:400 (Taylor,
1978)

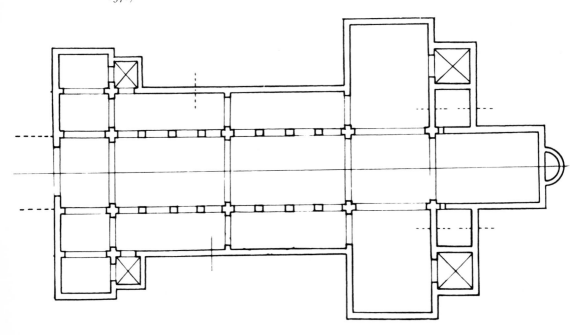

68 Nivelles (Brabant),
St-Gertrude,
consecrated 1046. Plan,
1:600 (Genicot, 1972)

doorway with stripwork and chamfered imposts leads eastwards from the north arm into the north aisle of the nave (fig. 69). Much of the wall of the present façade belongs to this building, and before 1849 it also included, according to the restorer, a 'double row of small pillars of early date' in the place now occupied by the lower half of the traceried window. This implies an upper chamber in the western tower with an opening looking east into the nave.

An early eastern transept can be extricated from the north wall of the present one, where the lowest of three gable lines indicates a pre-Norman transept 33 ft (10 m) wide, 21 ft (6.4 m) high to the eaves and 37 ft (11.25 m) to the gable. The lower part of this wall is decorated with five blind arches which mark the passage running through the eastern claustral range and which imply, since they may have served as seats, that the space also functioned as a room for meetings. It is possible that these arches also belong to the Saxon church, since they differ from the Norman arcading, but resemble the north-western doorway, and because the centre of the central arch lies much nearer to the line of the Saxon gable-head than to either of the other two gables. The eastern crossing is now entirely Norman, but one can argue that it probably follows an earlier arrangement, because of the comparable form of the western crossing, because the north arm of the Norman transept exactly follows its Saxon predecessor, and because the salient form is antithetical to the standard Norman handling of the crossing.

Sherborne Cathedral as rebuilt under Aelfwold between 1045 and 1058 is one of the handful of dated Anglo-Saxon churches and as such is extremely useful as a point of reference for the features it contains, including the salient crossing, stripwork and chamfered imposts. It is also the latest building so far encountered, but this is not the explanation for its large size. Its scale is what one would expect for a cathedral, and between them Sherborne and Winchester have demolished the notion that Anglo-Saxon buildings were as a rule undersized and uninspiring. Winchester may in fact have provided the impetus for the new church, since Aelfwold had been a monk there and he could easily have seen Wulfsige as a local Swithun, an earlier saintly bishop for whom architectural provision was required. But if Winchester supplied the idea it was not responsible for the form, as the Old Minster had no transepts and no aisles.

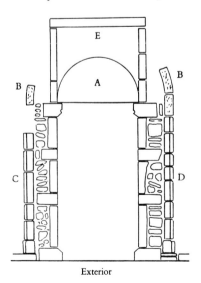

Exterior

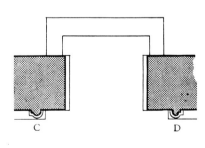

69 Sherborne (Dorset), Cathedral, after 1045. West doorway from the north aisle. Plan and elevation, 1:50 (Taylor and Taylor, 1965)

Of course the half century and more separating the two buildings must be taken into account, but Aelfwold's church cannot in any sense be explained as a development out of Ethelwold's.

The salient crossing occurs in at least four Anglo-Saxon churches, in five more of post-Conquest or uncertain date but with strong signs of Anglo-Saxon survival in their design, and in none where the context is purely Norman. The other three Anglo-Saxon examples can best be examined in series and the rest discussed in the chapter on the overlap.

The church of St Mary at **Stow** in Lincolnshire is one of the most imposing and interesting buildings of the late Saxon period. As it stands it comprises a central crossing some 35 ft (10.7 m) square externally, two narrower transept arms, a nave and chancel of more nearly full width, and a tower supported on piers inside the corners of the crossing (fig. 70). It is possible to discern four or perhaps five separate phases in the fabric, and, as the documentary evidence is equally complicated and unclear, Stow presents an unusually large number of problems and opportunities.

The earliest parts are the walls of the crossing up to the imposts, and the lower half of the transept arms. The four piers stand on massive plinths of one square and four chamfered stages, while each jamb is decorated with a pilaster strip and a half-shaft rising from ungainly bases (fig. 71). The walls of the arms are bonded to the crossing, making them contemporary. In the west wall of the north arm there is an arched opening (D in fig. 72) with non-radial voussoirs on chamfered imposts, and jambs laid Escomb-fashion (fig. 72).

There are signs of severe fire damage on some of the piers, especially on the unrestored parts of the faces towards the nave, and on most of the external quoins up to some 9 ft (3 m) from the ground at the ends of the arms and considerably higher on the crossing itself. Above this line the walls seem to have been rebuilt, as not only is there a lack of fire damage but in some cases the quoins have been differently cut, three for instance having a pilaster strip below the break but not above. There are remains of four windows in these upper

BELOW
70 Stow (Lincolnshire), St Mary, mid eleventh century. Plan, 1:400 (Taylor and Taylor, 1965)
OPPOSITE
71 Stow (Lincolnshire), St Mary, mid eleventh century. Crossing to east

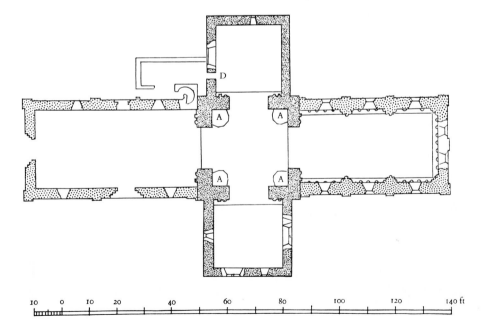

72 Stow (Lincolnshire), St Mary, mid eleventh century. Archway in north transept

sections, that in the south wall having a hood-moulding decorated with a form sometimes called the Jew's harp motif. The arches of the crossing have a completely different profile from the piers supporting them and from the doorway in the north transept, and as the hood-moulding on the western arch bears the Jew's harp motif, it appears that the second phase consists of these crossing arches and the upper parts of the transept walls.

The chancel and the nave are marked as additions by their undeniably Norman style and by the fact that they are not bonded to the crossing. None of the mouldings or orders on any of the windows or doorways bears any resemblance to those of the crossing arches and transept windows, indicating that they form part of a third and perhaps a fourth period of building. Finally the crossing tower is a later medieval structure standing on arches set within the Anglo-Saxon crossing (marked A in fig. 70), minimising the impact of the salient corners on the exterior, which would have been much more prominent with their original tower, whether it was of stone or wood.

The documentary references permit one to say little more than that Eadnoth bishop of Dorchester may have been responsible for building a church at Stow, but this is by no means certain, and it is equally unclear which of the two bishops of that name is intended, the first of c. 1006–16 or the second of c. 1034–49. Support for the foundation was forthcoming from Bishop Wulfwig (1053–67) and through him from Leofric Earl of Mercia and his wife Godiva, whose gifts are listed in a charter of 1055. In the early 1070s Remigius, the first Norman bishop (1067–92), moved the see from Dorchester to Lincoln, and on turning his attention to Stow found it in a ruinous state. He returned it to good order and in 1091 or possibly before introduced monks from Eynsham. Lastly Bishop Bloet (1093–1123) moved the monks back to Eynsham and appropriated Stow to the bishopric.[18]

Opinions diverge widely on how this evidence should be accommodated to the phases described above, but there are good reasons for believing that the earliest parts are no earlier than the second quarter of the eleventh century. The large half-shafts on the jambs, over a foot (.3 m) in diameter and nearly 20 ft (6 m) in height, immediately recall similar features on a large and architectural scale on the Continent as discussed in chapter six, such as those at Paderborn and Speyer of between 1017 and 1030, and at Auxerre, of the 1020s (fig. 45). Unless the half-shafts at Stow are to stand out as extraordinary in a European setting, completely isolated from what is happening in imperial and royal circles in Germany and France, they should be accorded a similar date.

This would suggest that we are dealing with the second Eadnoth, placing the first phase between 1034 and 1049, and paralleling Aelfwold's work at Sherborne between 1045 and 1058, which has an external plinth using both the square and the chamfered profile and, in the opening to the north aisle, stripwork of half-shafts as well as chamfered imposts and non-radial voussoirs comparable with those in the archway in the north transept at Stow.

Phase two can then be attributed either to Wulfwig around 1055 or to Remigius around 1090, but the relationship between the crossing arches at Stow and the profiles of the niches on the façade of Remigius's cathedral at Lincoln makes the later date more likely. The particular link is provided by an oddity in the position of the angle roll which at both places, contrary to standard Norman practice, does not fit symmetrically within the leading edge of the order, but is set back from its front face and followed by a large hollow. The popularity and indeed the invention of complex mouldings belongs to the middle of the eleventh century, in both England and Normandy, and examples like those at Stow and Lincoln, whatever specific date they are to be assigned, should be seen in a Saxo-Norman context (fig. 89: 8, 9,). Finally, if Remigius was responsible for the crossing arches then the nave and chancel must both belong in the twelfth century as their chevron decoration would suggest, whether or not they were added at the same time.[19]

St Mary's at **Norton** in County Durham is of particular interest because of its similarity to aspects of Stow. Exactly the same parts survive, a salient crossing flanked by two square transept arms, and evidence that both nave and chancel were also narrower than the central body. In relation to the size of the crossing the transept arches are as large as those at Stow, but they differ in that their entrances are off-set to the east. Four openings in the upper part of the tower appear to have led to the roof-spaces and indicate that all four arms were of the same height, lending support to the reconstruction of an arrangement at Stow parallel to the surviving Norman one. There was probably a corbelled timber gallery linking these openings around the inside faces of the tower, access to which was achieved by a fifth doorway lower down and tucked into the corner of the south wall, well placed to take a staircase from the south transept.

The only documentary mention of even partial relevance occurs in the Durham *Liber Vitae* which records that 'I Ulfcytel, Osulf's son, give Northtun, with all that belongs to it, unto St Cuthbert', a reference which the editor ascribes to the years between 966 and 992.[20] In style Norton is an earlier building than Stow. Its transept arches have a simple profile and the off-setting of the north and south arches to the east, like the whole of each porticus at Dover, suggests that utility, whatever it was, took precedence over appearance. Of course, these characteristics could be due to a difference in status rather than date, and even if Norton is earlier than Stow it is unlikely to be so by more than fifty years, considering conditions in the north of England in the tenth century. Apart from the possibility of some work at Chester-le-Street only one new church is recorded north of the Humber, namely Aldhun's cathedral at Durham, in the light of which Ulfcytel's bequest may not be directly relevant to the date of the church.

With examples at Sherborne, Stow and Norton, and probably at Tamworth and Bakewell in addition, the salient crossing is a well-established form in the late Saxon period.[21] There are three ways in which it might be explained, namely as the result of influence from contemporary building on the Continent, as the revival of an Early Christian type of centralized martyrium, or as a development out of earlier English buildings. The first of these can be ruled out because there are no similar examples. The second possibility provides at least one close parallel. The martyrium-church of St Babylas, built near Antioch in the late fourth century, has a central square with four arms of lesser width leading off it leaving salient angles on the exterior, while the arches into these arms are all the same size and are sufficiently narrow to leave the walls in the corners to read as prominent responds.[22] The parallels with Stow are striking, but as St Babylas was almost certainly destroyed many centuries before Stow was built, the possibilities suggested by this exotic parallel must be set aside for the more mundane, though more satisfying, explanations available in England.

It is only a short step from the plan of Breamore to the salient crossing. Because the chancel and the transept arms there are narrower than the central square the north-east and south-east angles are already salient, while the western angles, although disguised by the nave, are marked by pilaster strips which set the tower off as something separate from the ground up. All that is needed is the narrowing of the nave in the same way as the three other arms. The ease of a possible transition from one type to the other can also be illustrated by the fact that Repton has in the past been reconstructed in both ways. In addition the same variety in the placing and size of arches and arms is evident in both types. Thus in typological terms Wooton Wawen stands first in a sequence which proceeds to Norton with its much larger but still off-set side arches, and then to Stow which has a large, centrally placed arch in each face of the crossing. The conclusion seems inescapable that the salient crossing is an indigenous invention.

The last type of crossing and the one which comes closest to the fully developed Romanesque form is represented by only one building, but it is a special monument which bears close examination for its own sake. The mid eleventh-century church of the Holy Trinity at **Great Paxton** in Huntingdonshire is not only a fine example of architectural design, but its Anglo-Saxon parts have the distinction of all belonging to one date. One is therefore confronted not with a chronological puzzle, useful though that may often be, but with something worth assessing in the form which the architect or builder intended it to have.

Great Paxton is the only English building so far discussed in which the crossing is defined by the intersection of the nave and transepts (fig. 73), but even so it is not of the full, regular type as defined by Hildesheim, because the lateral arches indicate that the arms were originally lower than the main body, with gables probably rising no higher than the top of the wall, an arrangement usually referred to as a dwarf transept. Despite the standard definition of a full

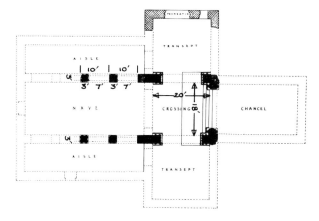

73 Great Paxton (Huntingdonshire/ Cambridgeshire), Holy Trinity, mid eleventh century. Plan, 1:400 (Dickinson, 1971)

Romanesque crossing as a square resulting from the intersection of two ranges of equal width, in many and perhaps most examples the greater importance of the east-west axis is made clear by one means or another. In many cases the arms are simply made narrower than the nave, on the same principle as that applied more vigorously at Breamore and Dover. At Great Paxton the greater importance of the main axis is clearly established by the nave being taller than the arms, but this precedence is called into question by the odd fact that the transept is considerably wider than the nave and would, if given its head, cut the east-west axis and divide the nave from the chancel. Yet by his handling of the crossing piers the designer has prevented this from happening, as the following description may indicate.

Although the western arch of the crossing is now missing, the western wall of the transept indicates that the crossing was 20 ft (6 m) long from the east to west, while the nave is only 18 ft (5.5 m) wide. The responds to the opening into the arms, however, protrude more than those of the chancel arch, so that the latter is only a few inches narrower than the arches to north and south.

The same end, of subordinating the arms to the nave and chancel, is achieved not only by the dimensions of the responds but also by what they look like figs 74, 76). The shafts, pilaster strips and areas of wall are so arranged that, while the eye moves easily through the crossing from nave to chancel, its passage from north to south is interupted and uneven. This is achieved in the following way. The plane of the nave wall re-appears on the inner face of the respond of the transept arch, helped if anything by the flat face of the pilaster and barely disturbed by the corner shaft. This is repeated on the opposite, eastern, respond from where the eye is led easily onto the soffit face of the chancel respond by the shallowness of the respond itself and the gentle curve on which its shafts are set. Conversely, on the north-south axis the eye moving along the eastern wall of the transept encounters the outer face of the deep transept respond as a barrier to its progress. After negotiating this, with no curving transitions on the soffit face, it is then confronted with a section of wall which is too short to establish any identity with the plane of the transept wall, and then by the protruding edge of the chancel respond. After crossing the chancel opening the process begins again on the opposite respond.

There can be no liturgical or practical advantage in the wider transept since there are only two extra feet, which forces one to the conclusion that the greater width of the subsidiary axis is a deliberate indulgence on the part of the architect, intended to provide him with a problem at the crossing which he can then solve with great ingenuity. This interpretation is obviously subjective,

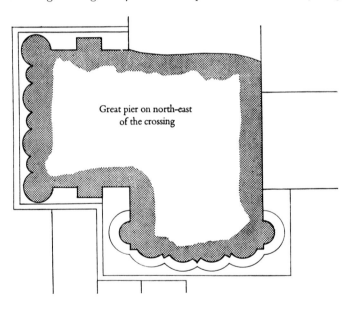

Great pier on north-east
of the crossing

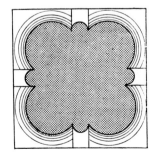

74 Great Paxton (Huntingdonshire/ Cambridgeshire), Holy Trinity, mid eleventh century. Plans of north-east crossing pier (top) and west (left) and east (right) nave piers, 1:25 (Taylor and Taylor, 1965)

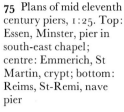

75 Plans of mid eleventh century piers, 1:25. Top: Essen, Minster, pier in south-east chapel; centre: Emmerich, St Martin, crypt; bottom: Reims, St-Remi, nave pier

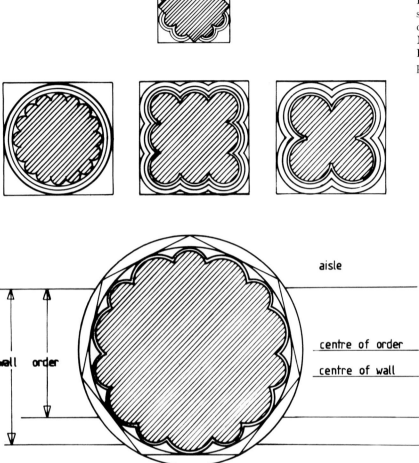

but the physical arrangements all exist as described, and in any case the same mastery is evident in the nave.

The piers of the arcade have a highly distinctive form, consisting in plan of a quatrefoil set diagonally on a square base (figs 74, 78). Between each of the lobes there is a small vertical moulding, semi-circular on the eastern pier and forming a ridge on the western. The curved one has a rectangular base and the rectangular one a curved base, illustrating the almost playful manner in which elements are alternated and juxtaposed. The base of the rectangular feature is in addition in some instances carved into a human or animal head or an abstract shape, while at the upper end of the pier each lobe has a neatly cut semi-circular necking ring and a bulbous almost pneumatic capital, the smaller elements ending in a leaf nestling between the curves of the flanking forms.

Given all this attention to detail it is not surprising to find that the building is laid out using a small number of repeated and interrelated lengths which, interestingly enough, imply the use of the English foot at this early date. Each

76 Great Paxton
(Huntingdonshire/
Cambridgeshire), Holy
Trinity, mid eleventh
century. South-east pier
of crossing
77 Reims (Haut-
Marne), St-Remi, mid
eleventh century. Nave
pier

bay is 10 ft long and 10 ft (3 m) high to the springing point of the arcade arch. The openings are 7 ft (2.1 m) across and the piers 3 ft (1 m) wide, forming a square base with the 3 ft (1 m) thickness of the wall, while at 20 ft (6 m) the crossing is twice the length of an arcade bay. The nave is 18 ft (5.5 m) wide internally and 18 ft (5.5 m) high to the stringcourse above the arcade, while the 24 ft (7.3 m) height of the sills of the clearstorey windows is the same as the external width of the nave. Finally the full height of 38 ft (11.6 m) can be seen as a combination of the 20 ft and 18 ft (6 and 5.5 m) lengths.

There are no documentary references by which Holy Trinity can be dated, but comparative material in other buildings, the high quality of the design and execution, and the fact that Edward the Confessor (1042–66) held the major part of the estate all conspire to make this a church worthy of royal patronage erected in the middle years of the eleventh century.[23]

In so far as they are not English, sources and parallels point firmly to Lotharingia, dwarf transepts, for instance, occurring in the Mosan region, as at Celles in the 1030s (fig. 55), or at nearby Biesme. Similarly the piers can be paralleled in mid eleventh-century Rhenish churches, especially at the Minster in Essen, in the south-western chapel of the church built by Theophanu during her period as abbess from 1039 to 1058 (fig. 75), at St Lucius in Werden, consecrated in 1063, and in the crypt of St Martin's at Emmerich of around 1050 (fig. 75). This last example has three pier types, the easternmost a quadrilobe with proportions very similar to those at Great Paxton, the middle

78 Great Paxton (Huntingdonshire/Cambridgeshire), Holy Trinity, mid eleventh century. Nave to west

one of eight shafts, the central shaft on each face standing in the place of the vertical strip in the English building, and the westernmost a bundle of 16 shafts, continuing the doubling progression, under a gigantic cushion capital. This third type has no equivalent at Great Paxton, but it underlines the inventive variety which characterises both buildings.

Something similar occurs in the arcade piers of St-Remi at Reims, where one large shaft and two smaller ones adorn each face of a polygon which, because it is seven-sided, is completely asymmetrical on its east and west faces. The responds of the chancel and transept arches at Great Paxton look like a segment of such piers, which also support arcade arches in two orders (figs 75, 77).[24]

St-Remi was consecrated in 1049 in the presence of a number of Englishmen including Abbot Wulfric of St Augustine's, so that there is no difficulty in assuming a channel of influence.[25]

The bulbous capitals have a wider chronological distribution than any other feature in the building and hence cannot help with dating it, but they serve to illustrate the presence of a strong indigenous element alongside influence from the Continent. Examples occur in the scene of a bishop blessing in the benedictional made for Ethelwold of Winchester in the late tenth century, in the scene of the three Marys at the tomb on folio 13v of Cotton Tiberius C., VI, and on folio 22 of Wadham College manuscript A10. They also turn up in a German context, like the bulbous bases in the Fulda Evangelistary of the second quarter of the eleventh century, where one suspects that the influence is flowing from England to Germany. The profile of the imposts at the east end of the nave of Great Paxton may also be a wide-spread one of Roman origin, occurring as it does in the corridors of the Colosseum, and is therefore as likely to find its source in England as analogous, though more accurate, examples at Aachen, Essen and Werden are to find theirs in Roman Germany.

The picture that emerges from this is of a church whose affiliations, in so far as they are not English, lie in Lotharingia, at its heart in the Rhineland and on its edge at Reims. Apart from a dubious piece of billet on an impost of the rebuilt chancel arch there is not a Norman element in the building, while its aggressively Anglo-Saxon character is underlined by the sizes of the blocks forming the Escomb-fashion responds of the crossing, some of which are almost 4 ft (1.3 m) square.

To summarize this discussion on the crossing, the Breamore type has transept arms and a chancel which are much narrower than the crossing. The palaeographic evidence at Breamore, the fact that the latest possible date for Repton lies in Cnut's reign, and the existence of a crossing of some form at Ramsey in the 970s or 990s all combine to suggest that at least the earliest members of this group belong in the late tenth century. There are no continental examples of the type, but what parallels there are point to a similar period. For example, the form of church represented by Ramsey and Dover with an eastern crossing, tower and arms, and a smaller western tower, can be found (with the proviso that the arms are never narrower than the crossing) in churches like the nunnery at Essen in the third quarter of the ninth century, Petersberg near Fulda in the first quarter of the tenth, and in eastern France at Chatillon-sur-Seine between 980 and 1015 (figs 61, 62). Similarly the plan and crossing arches at Dover can be compared with St-Martin at Angers in its early eleventh-century state.[26] Lastly, the nave of Breamore offers a slightly different comparison as it consists in plan of two squares each equivalent to the crossing, and is marked as such by pilaster strips on the exterior. This shows essentially the same attitude to the articulation of volumes as that evident in St Michael's at Hildesheim of 1010–33, where the nave, through the alternation of supports, approximates to three crossing-squares (fig. 43).

The salient form lies only a short step beyond the Breamore type. Given this and the numbers of lost churches, it is hazardous to assume that it is not another product of the reform movement. Nonetheless the only dated example is the western crossing at Sherborne (provided that is not part of an earlier building), while Stow is arguably of a similar date in the 1040s. As for Norton in County Durham, which looks simpler and hence earlier than the other two, it is hardly well placed to be a centre of architectural innovation at a time like the tenth century, when monastic activity in the north of England was almost non-existent.

There may have been double transepts at Ethelwold's Ely, but there is insufficient evidence to warrant the claim. Apart from St-Riquier and Cologne Cathedral, doubtful respectively on grounds of form and of date, the earliest examples on the Continent are Aschaffenburg, with continuous transepts and hence no crossings, around 970, St Michael's at Hildesheim with crossings and lantern towers, and Ste-Gertrude at Nivelles consecrated in 1046.[27] The last building is of particular interest in relation to Sherborne, the only English church of this type, as both have a western transept smaller than the eastern (figs 67, 68).

A crossing need not always carry a tower, as for example at Repton and Great Paxton, but the two features occur together so often that it is convenient in concluding this chapter to examine the subject of towers as such. Towers make such a frequent appearance on buildings of the late Saxon period (as has already been noted at the end of the preceeding chapter) that they can be seen as characteristic of it. Clapham went even further than this, denying that any are earlier than the late tenth century, on the grounds that the bell-towers of Italy and France could be traced no further back than the ninth and tenth centuries respectively.[28] Yet the origins of the practice of hanging bells in towers are shrouded in mystery, or at least ignorance. Whether or not churches were occasionally built with towers between the fourth century and the eighth in the Christian west, there is no doubt that they became popular immediately thereafter, in the Carolingian period. The reasons for this development may have been practical, liturgical, symbolic or aesthetic, or even the result of a realisation of the romantic possibilities of the silhouette, an awareness of which was indicated already in the sixth century by Venantius Fortunatus, but, whatever the cause, from the time of the building of St-Riquier in the 790s the tower was available as part of the western architectural repertoire.[29] If one adds to this the fact that bells were used at St-Riquier from the beginning and that in the tenth century the *Regularis Concordia* stresses the peculiar importance accorded to bells in the English church, there can be no objection in principle to a ninth-century date for the earliest Anglo-Saxon towers.[30]

Such a date has been proposed by Taylor for the western tower at Barnack, primarily on the basis of a classification of bell openings, as follows.[31] These are of four types, one with a single opening, and three with double openings which can be arranged from the simplest to the most complicated and identified with the three periods 950–1000, 1000–50 and 1050–1100. As the whole development from the first type to the fourth should not be crowded into the one hundred and fifty years available between 950 and 1100, the earliest type can be dated to the ninth century. Finally, since Barnack has single bell openings it should therefore be dated in the ninth century.

There are a number of objections to this reasoning. Architectural development seldom if ever follows the even, measured tenor of the kind that Darwin claimed for natural evolution, but is more often characterised by explosions of new forms appearing over a short period of time, like outer crypts in the ninth century, compound piers in the eleventh or rib vaults in the late eleventh and twelfth. In addition doubt is easily cast on a typological chronology by the coexistence of two supposedly sequential features in one part of one building, just as Taylor himself acknowledges the presence of single and double openings together on the same level on the tower at Bardsey.

Similarly, the documentary evidence for the Old Minster at Winchester, Ramsey, Durham and Sherborne provides a reasonable framework of dates for other buildings like Dover, Breamore, Wooton Wawen and Norton, with no indication that any one example could be a century or two distant from the rest. Finally, in all instances where a church with a tower is demonstrably early, as at Monkwearmouth or Jarrow, the tower is an addition.

Nor is it possible to compromise by having towers like those at Barnack,

Barton-on-Humber and Earls Barton, all in the Danelaw, built for purposes of defence in the second half of the ninth century. As Taylor has pointed out, such towers, with their wooden floors and accessibility from the nave or the chancel, would have been a death-trap rather than a haven in the event of a raid.[32] On these grounds then, Taylor's ninth-century date for Barnack in particular and for the earliest Anglo-Saxon towers in general must remain unproved, though not disproved.

Chapter Nine

ANGLO-SAXON ROMANESQUE: THE DECORATION

Apart from some free-standing columns and baluster shafts, chamfered and carved stringcourses and perhaps some friezes of sculpture at places like Reculver, Monkwearmouth, Hexham and Breedon, buildings which can be securely dated to the pre-Danish period are devoid of architectural decoration. The buttresses of the Kentish group appear to be functional rather than decorative, and doorways have nothing more than a rebate, if that. Conversely, after the Danish invasions decoration is the rule rather than the exception, with stripwork forming panels and blind arcading, building up in some cases to a pattern covering a whole wall, and hood-mouldings, half-shafts and soffit rolls forming a rich decorative mass on a doorway or chancel arch.

One cannot always be certain that these elements only came into use in the later period, but the weight of the evidence suggests that this should be one's first assumption, any proposed dating of a particular building to the early period requiring powerful supporting argument. The study of early medieval architecture is bedevilled by the fact that the Romans invented almost every single feature used in building before the mid twelfth century, including attached shafts, detached shafts, compound piers, horseshoe arches, triangular-headed arches, hood-mouldings, chamfered imposts, long-and-short quoins, carved tympana and historiated capitals. They could therefore have been used at any time in the first millennium in what might be called the Roman vernacular tradition.

Nevertheless this state of affairs should not be allowed to detract from the fact that fashions exist at certain periods and not at others and that all things are not likely, even if possible, at any one time. A case in point is the double-splayed window, every English instance of which has with good reason been dated to the ninth, tenth, eleventh or twelfth century.[1] It would be counter-productive to propose, on the basis of the third-century examples in the Villa dei Sette Bassi in Rome, the acceptability of seventh-century dates for Anglo-Saxon buildings with this type of opening.[2] By the same token, while the half-shaft and the carved tympanum occur in Roman buildings and even enjoy an unbroken survival through the whole of the Middle Ages in the Caucasus, there is every reason to believe that their popularity in western Europe only dates from the eleventh century. This is not to say that the English examples of any particular feature must all derive from precedents on the Continent, only that they should not without overwhelming evidence be attributed to a very different period.

Only four buildings of the post-Danish period bearing architectural decoration can be securely dated by documentary evidence, namely

Sherborne, between 1045 and 1058, Westminster Abbey, before 1065, Odda's Chapel at Deerhurst of 1056 and Kirkdale between 1055 and 1065, and only one or two others such as Great Paxton, St Benet's at Cambridge and St Martin's at Wareham can be dated by means of copious stylistic and technical links with other buildings. On this meagre basis, but with important contributory evidence from the Continent, especially for the late tenth and early eleventh century, it is possible to attribute the use of the curved profile, whether as half-shaft (Sherborne, Westminster), hood-moulding (Cambridge), hollow roll (Odda's Chapel), soffit roll (Wareham), or detached shaft (Kirkdale), largely if not entirely to the eleventh century and later. From this it may not be unreasonable to assume that decoration which restricts itself to the rectangular profile is liable to be characteristic of an earlier approach, acknowledging that individual examples of this earlier type could have been built well after the introduction of the curved form.

The weakness of typological chronologies outlined at the end of the last chapter with respect to the dating of towers also of course applies in the case of the curved profile, but there is one major difference. What is proposed here is not a set of evenly spaced steps of half a century each between four forms of an element differentiated by sometimes minor variations, but a single, overriding change in taste which affected almost every decorative form employed, and which probably took place over no more than three or four decades.

In order to test this hypothesis against the material, the elements and the buildings have been divided up as follows. Britford and Brigstock may be early examples of stripwork with a square section, as it is there restricted to jambs and arches, while its spread over whole wall surfaces is exemplified by the towers at Barnack, Barton-on-Humber and Earls Barton. The sources of this type are partly Roman, partly indigenous and partly continental and involve a particular examination of long-and-short work and the hood-moulding. This part of the discussion centres on the Danelaw, but Bradford-on-Avon may offer a distant parallel to Earls Barton. The curved profile plays the major part at Stow, Sherborne, Cambridge, Great Paxton, Worth and St Mary's at Deerhurst.

At **Britford** in Wiltshire little remains visible of the Anglo-Saxon fabric except the entrances to two porticus north and south off the eastern end of the nave, rather like those in the seventh-century church at Winchester or the late Saxon one at Worth. Each face towards the porticus has stripwork running up the wall beside the jambs and round the arch as a hood-moulding, while the soffit face has a double order of slabs, some of which are enriched with vine scrolls in low relief. This carved ornament has been dated around 800 by Clapham, to the reign of Alfred by Rice, and to the tenth century by Baldwin Brown, all dates open to many qualifications and uncertainties.[3].

St Andrew's at **Brigstock** in Northamptonshire has a large and imposing arch between the nave and the western tower. The jambs, the arch and the imposts are of a simple rectangular section outlined or contained in a strip of masonry, as at Britford but without any carving. An early date has been proposed on the basis, in part, of a comparison between the single-splayed windows at Brigstock and those at Monkwearmouth, Jarrow and Escomb. Against this, however, it can be argued that windows of this character occur throughout the Anglo-Saxon period.[4] It is only the presence of through-stones which provides a specific link, but the openings at Brigstock contain anything from a dozen to a score of such stones while those at Monkwearmouth have six at most. The western annex at Brigstock is also much larger in relation to the nave than those at Monkwearmouth and Jarrow, and while it is comparable with that added at Escomb or that at Seaham, there is no evidence that these two communicated with the nave, in sharp contrast to the large arch provided here. Brigstock remains, then, an undated building.

A much more extensive use of stripwork is made at St John the Baptist at **Barnack** (Northants/Cambs). For the most part this is a building of the thirteen, fourteenth and fifteenth centuries, but it is dominated by its single Anglo-Saxon feature, the tower at the western end of the nave (fig. 79). This massive object, which at 65 ft (19.8 m) rivals the crossing tower at Dover in height, is about 24 ft by 26 ft (7.3 m by 8 m) in size externally. The nave, of which the north-west and south-west quoins remain, was slightly wider than the tower. As the western wall of the nave and the eastern wall of the tower are one and the same, it follows that the north and south faces of the tower are wider above the roof of the nave than they are below. This has an extraordinary effect on the disposition of the decoration and is very revealing of the attitude of the

79 Barnack (Northamptonshire/Cambridgeshire), St John. Tower from south-west, tenth–eleventh century

designer. Each of the north, south and west faces is divided into four panels by three strips, with the middle strip in the centre of each face, as that is established at ground level. This means that on the north and south faces the panels become asymmetrical as they rise into the second storey where more of the tower is free-standing.

The same effect is created by the distribution of the openings, only one of which, the lowermost on the west front, lies in the centre of the wall. The others appear to be placed where it is convenient and to avoid the stripwork, and come in a bewildering variety of forms which bear no relationship to differences in function. The triangular-headed doorway in the west wall of the upper storey probably performed the same function as that suggested at Deerhurst, namely giving access to a wooden balcony used for the display of relics. The two storeys are separated by a curious multiple band consisting of two stringcourses of square section with a recessed strip between them, which causes the upper storey to be set back from the lower. Despite the continuity of the vertical stripwork this feature acts as a complete break in the elevation. The stripwork in the upper storey rises from corbels which are like wheels set on their sides, protruding beyond the stringcourse so that, in a most unarchitectural way, the bottom face of each is visible.

The central strip on the western faces rises not from the stringcourse but from the top of a slab carved with scrolls and leaves, illustrating once again that the builder had no compunction about disrupting the vertical elements of his design. This *ad hoc* approach also marks the slabs on the side walls, each of which is set in the middle of the panel to the east of the central strip. This almost has the effect of aligning them with the centre of the wall at this upper level, but of course they lie a little too far to the east, as is shown by their relationship to the bell openings in the thirteenth-century octagonal spire. Equally oddly, on the eastern face the three strips descend not to the varying points at which they would meet the roof, but to the level of the central one at the apex of the gable, leaving the other two visually unsupported.

From this description it appears that a wish to articulate and to clarify is accompanied and thwarted by a willingness to treat architectural features as if they were part of a piece of sculpture, or conversely as if they had nothing but a purely utilitarian function. The result is at one and the same time structured and whimsical, articulate and wayward.

The interior is dominated by the tower arch, which is not only quite large in absolute terms, being 13 ft (3.9 m) wide and 20 ft (6 m) high, but massive in character as well (fig. 80). The nave face has a thick strip on each jamb which is carried up round the arch turned in non-radial voussoirs. The most striking features are the capitals or imposts, which extend right back to the side walls of the nave. They can be understood as a variation on the theme of the band which separates the storeys on the exterior, since the size is about the same and both are composed of upper and lower protruding slabs with a recessed element between.

As we have seen in the last chapter there are no convincing arguments for dating Barnack in the ninth century from the fact that it has a tower, and the same is true of the stripwork and of the long-and-short technique in which it is constructed. Attempts have been made to date the building by the carved slabs in the upper storey, but one is on no more secure ground than with the architecture. Most Anglo-Saxon sculpture is found on movable objects like cross-shafts and screens and hence is even more difficult to attach to documentary dates than the buidings are. It is therefore not surprising that

80 Barnack (Northamptonshire/ Cambridgeshire), St John. Tower arch, tenth– eleventh century

dates which have been proposed range from the early ninth century to the late tenth, and there is little to prevent them being later still.[5] Given this degree of uncertainty it seems safer to maintain a post-Danish date for Barnack.

This is supported by the related church of St Peter's at **Barton-on-Humber** in Lincolnshire which has the distinction of being one of only three surviving Anglo-Saxon churches with a tower for a nave (fig. 81).[6] There are two narrower square-ended annexes, namely the chancel now beneath the later churches which turned the old nave into a western tower, and the western one, the surviving floor of which preserves the base of a font and marks it as a baptistery. The arches to these two rooms are decorated with stripwork like that at Brigstock, though the imposts are chamfered and acknowledge the passage of the strip (fig. 82). Only the faces towards the nave are enriched

81 Barton-on-Humber (Lincolnshire/ Humberside), St Peter, late tenth–eleventh century. Plan, and north elevation of tower-nave, 1:400 (Rodwell, *Medieval Archaeology*, 1981; Taylor, 1978)

82 Barton-on-Humber (Lincolshire/ Humberside), St Peter, late tenth–eleventh century. Arch in west wall of tower-nave

83 Sabratha (Libya), Roman Theatre. Arches

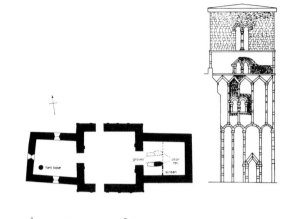

in this way, indicating the greater importance of the chancel and of the baptistery.

The western annex is built of rubble and is devoid of decoration except for the effect of the long-and-short quoining on the exterior, while the tower, excluding the upper of the two bell-stages, rises about 50 ft (15 m) and is built in the same way, except that its north and south faces are articulated by stripwork. The original topmost storey stands on a plain stringcourse and has a double bell-opening in each of the decorated walls, with triangular heads, hood-mouldings and squat baluster shafts. The lower and major storey has a row of triangular-headed panels standing on top of a row of blind arches, staggered so that the upper pilasters rise from the crowns. The discomfort of this relationship is not disguised but underlined by the provision of large block-like protruding bases, even more obvious than the half-round slabs at Barnack. The disposition of the openings also reveals the same partial control as in the other church.

As to the date, Rickman was the first to argue that the Norman character of the upper bell-storey made the separate phase beneath it Anglo-Saxon, while the absence of cylindrical elements in the stripwork suggests a date at least a number of decades before the Conquest. This is supported by the results of radio-carbon tests recently carried out on fragments of scaffolding, joists and shutters from the baptistery, which provide brackets of the mid and late tenth century.[7] This, however, is a surprisingly narrow range for the technique, so that dates as far apart as the first half of the tenth century and the first half of the eleventh might be safer, with a preference for the later end, especially given the later date implied by the chamfers on the arch imposts and the suggestion of a curved moulding on the imposts of the north door.[8]

The decoration of the tower-nave of All Saints at **Earls Barton** in Northamptonshire is by far the most extreme and wilful of the buildings examined so far (fig. 84). The chancel, the chancel arch and the roof are lost but everything else remains intact, including the eastern quoins, which show that the tower was wider than the eastern arm, if there was one. The elevation is divided into four storeys separated by stringcourses and each set back from the one below. The openings are oddly placed and the panels formed by the strips are even more erratic than elsewhere, with five on the first and second storeys of the north face and six on the south, then seven on the third storey. It does not seem to matter whether the strips meet at their intended places, as in the storey immediately above the clock on the south face, or on the west face where two strips rise from corbels above the doorway, even though extended down they would have fitted neatly against the stripwork of the opening. The arches and triangular heads are separated from the panels by stringcourses and, in the case of the triangles, turned into part of an overall lozenge pattern.

The tops of the windows in the ground floor are carved out of huge single blocks of stone in the form of depressed arches which look more organic than structural. The leading edge of the arch has three mouldings which are closer together at the springing than at the crown, creating an effect like a sail. The shafts supporting them are bulbous in form, as if they had been inflated and then constricted with pieces of string. The result is very much a sculptor's view of the turned shaft as found at Monkwearmouth and Jarrow. They are however almost disciplined compared with the shafts in the bell-openings. The six on the south face are of varying kinds, set without any order, from double and treble bands to single cigar-like shapes with bulging sides which one hesitates to call an entasis.

The language is the same as that of Barnack, but it is more exuberant,

84 Earls Barton
(Northamptonshire), All
Saints, eleventh century.
Tower from north-west

84 Earls Barton (Northamptonshire), All Saints, eleventh century. Tower from north-west

suggesting a later date. In this regard the west doorway is of special interest. It has Escomb-fashion jambs, massive imposts and a containing strip, as at Brigstock, Barnack and Barton-on-Humber. The only differences are the arcading carved in low relief on the imposts and the one large and two small semi-cylindrical rolls decorating the face of the arch (fig. 87). The roll appears on none of the other churches in this group and instead suggests contact with buildings which definitely belong to the eleventh century.

The sources of stripwork and in particular long-and-short stripwork, as represented by the preceding five buildings, have been hotly disputed. Some have seen in it an attempt to emulate wooden structures on the part of builders more used to working in that medium, supporting their case with the fact that, apart from Britford, the examples are all in the Danelaw, where in the tenth century new stone buildings would have been even less common than elsewhere.[9] This however is highly unlikely. The decoration of Earls Barton is the most suggestive of timber, yet it appears to be later than Brigstock and Barnack. Equally, though the church at Greensted does not represent the only type of wooden construction, it is significant that it offers no points of comparison whatever.

The Romans are a much more likely source as they used long-and-short work to increase the strength of rubble walls, and, in the few cases where it can be ascertained, Anglo-Saxon strips also extend about a foot into the wall, further than would be necessary for applied decoration.[10] What began as a practical aid was swiftly prized by the Anglo-Saxons for its ornamental possibilities. England was not alone in adopting the technique, as there are continental examples, for instance at Limburg in the 1020s and at St Pantaleon in Cologne in the late tenth century, including short sections with no 'ears' bonding them into the wall, a type that is not common in England, but one which is found on the north face of Barton-on-Humber.

The relevance of the German instances has in the past been seen in extreme terms: on the one hand the English examples are simply derivative and on the other they are part of an independent tradition.[11] However, a statement that two similar traditions are independent requires as much justification as the claim that they are related, since once a technique was in use in one part of northern Europe it is unlikely to have remained unknown for long elsewhere. Therefore, regardless of who re-invented long-and-short work, if the earliest German examples appear to belong to the late tenth century, then it is no more than prudent to accept a broadly similar date for the English equivalents, none of which have any documentary anchors.[12]

Like long-and-short work the hood-moulding plays a particular part in the history of stripwork, characterising as it does Anglo-Saxon architecture from Britford and Barnack to Odda's Chapel and beyond. It has an almost standard pedigree, with numerous Roman examples on, for instance, the Porta Nigra in Trier, the Severan Theatre at Sabratha in North Africa, where the strip is also carried down each jamb very much in the Anglo-Saxon manner (fig. 83), the Temple of Hadrian in Ephesus, the small temple at Baalbek, and so on. The form continues in use throughout the first millennium, on the seventh-century baptistery at Poitiers, the eighth-century 'Tempietto' at Cividale, the ninth-century stucco arches in the apse of Germigny-des-Prés, and on a group of early Romanesque churches of the late tenth or early eleventh century in the Poitou and the Touraine. Despite the distance in date, of all these examples the Anglo-Saxon hood-mouldings most resemble those on the Roman monuments, especially those at Trier.

Returning to our main theme, south of the Thames the most interesting building comparable to Barnack and Earls Barton is more of an analogy than a parallel. The chapel of St Laurence at **Bradford-on-Avon** in Wiltshire survives in an even more complete state than Great Paxton, with standards of design and workmanship which are remarkably high, indicating that despite its diminutive size it was a building of some consequence (figs 85, 86). Perhaps for these very reasons it is also one of the most controversial of Anglo-Saxon churches and worth an extended investigation.[13]

William of Malmesbury, writing around 1120, says that there was at Bradford 'a little church which he [Aldhelm] is generally stated to have built in the name of the most blessed Laurence', and Aldhelm, who was bishop of Sherborne, died in 709.[14] On the written evidence alone, then, the chapel should be a building of the early eighth century. It is, however, decorated with

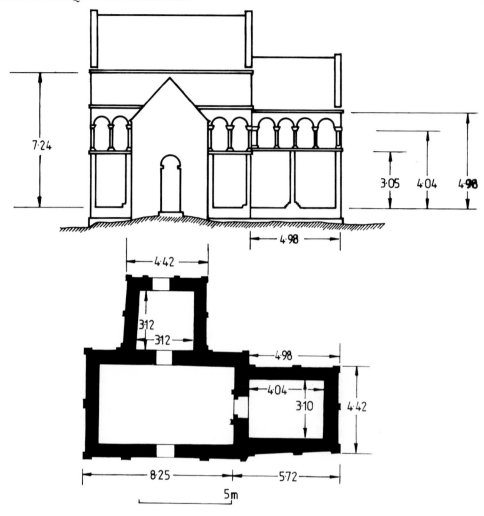

85 Bradford-on-Avon (Wiltshire), St Laurence, eleventh century. Plan and elevation, 1:200

numerous features which would be hard to parallel before the tenth century, so that a date around the year 1000 has often been argued on the basis of style. The later date, and in the eleventh century rather than the tenth, appears to be the correct one.

What follows is a description with an assessment of the finer points of the design, then an attempt to establish a date with particular reference to the decoration. The plan consists of a short rectangular nave with a rectangular chancel to the east and two square porticus to north and south, the southern of which has been destroyed. Both sides of all walls are faced with well-cut ashlar.

The design is an exercise in planes defining volumes. On the exterior the three subsidiary blocks bear an unambiguous relationship to the nave, creating an effect not unlike that of Escomb, except that here the blocks are much more insistent and easier to read because of the pilasters, sunken panels, stringcourses and blind arcading which both enliven and articulate their surfaces. The whole building rests on a massive projecting plinth of square section. On top of this stands a second much thinner plinth which again encompasses all the walls and from which the pilasters rise. These have the same

depth as the plinth and mark each corner and the centre of each face, except where that is prevented, as in the case of the side walls of the nave, where instead each porticus is flanked by a pilaster marking the return. Most of the pilasters rise from stepped bases, that is they broaden out laterally in steps while retaining the same depth, stressing the plane of the wall already underlined by the plinth and by the pilasters themselves.

The top of this first storey is marked by a stringcourse of square section echoing the projecting plinth. On this stands the flat blind arcading forming the second storey, the top of which is defined by the eaves of the chancel roof. Every length of wall contains four arches, with the central support standing above the central pilaster. This is even true of the side walls of the nave, where each porticus is flanked to east and west by two arches. The nave walls rise another storey above those of the chancel, and the porticus roofs fit between the line of the capitals of the blind arcading and the eaves of the nave roof. The supports of the blind arcading on the eastern wall of the chancel are composed of flat sets of three tightly packed shafts, setting off this end of the chapel from the blind arcading on the nave and porticus. There is a fragment of the same decoration on the pilaster of the lower storey clasping the north-east corner, as if it had been intended to make the chancel even more ornate.

Although there are some irregularities in the setting out, it is nonetheless clear that specific dimensions have been selected and used in various places, which means that the building has been designed not simply with an eye to form, but geometrically. The north porticus is about 10 ft 3 in, (3.12 m) square on the interior and 14 ft 6 in. (4.42 m) on the exterior. The chancel has the same inner and outer widths, but as befits its status it is longer, 13 ft 3 in. (4.04 m) internally and 18 ft 9 in. (5.72 m) externally, that is to the nave face of the chancel arch, and thirdly the internal length of the chancel is the same as the internal width of the nave, so that the three constituent rectangles are related in three ascending steps. These same figures occur again on the exterior elevation, with the top of the second plinth, that from which the pilasters rise, acting as a base line. The lower storey between the plinth and the first stringcourse measures a little over 10 ft (3.1 m) like the internal widths of the chancel and porticus, while from the same plinth to the base of the arcading in the next storey is the 13 ft 3 in. (4.04 m) of the chancel length and nave width. The height to the top of the second storey, that is to the eaves of the chancel roof, is 16 ft 4 in. (4.98 m), a new dimension but one which turns out to be the length of the chancel visible on the exterior, so that in elevation its side walls are square. Finally the height to the eaves of the nave roof, again from the plinth, is 23 ft 9 in. (7.24 m) which may be intended as a combination of 10 ft 3 in. (3.12 m) and 13 ft 3 in. (4.04 m). With the exception of the last figure it seems difficult to deny that the coincidences were intended, and even in the case of the 23 ft 9 in. length the formula is similar to that proposed for the height of the nave at Great Paxton.

It only remains to note that the interior and exterior widths of the porticus and chancel, of the length of the chancel, and of the width of the nave all relate in the same way as the width of the chancel to the width of the nave at Escomb, that is as the side of a square to its diagonal or one to the square root of two, or 10 ft 3 in to 14 ft 6 in. (3.12 m to 4.42 m), and 13 ft 3 in. to 18 ft 9 in. (4.04 m to 5.72 m).

On the interior the three archways between the four chambers are narrow and low, compartmenting the spaces, an effect which is underlined by the great relative height of the building, the nave for instance being almost twice as high as it is wide. The decoration is considerably simpler than on the exterior, with only a single plinth like the upper of the two outside, and no pilasters. The nave face of the chancel arch is decorated with a strip on each jamb which, above the imposts, changes into an arched moulding with the profile of the triple shafts used outside (fig. 88). The interior face of this arch is plain, since the stripwork as usual announces the more important space while decorating the less. The same rule, already noted at Barton-on-Humber and relevant at Dover, applies to the two doorways in the north porticus, which have the same decoration as the chancel arch and again on one face only. The opening in the outer wall has the stripwork on its outer face, making the porticus more important than the world outside, and that on the inner wall has its decoration on the face to the porticus, making the nave in turn more important. The doorway to the south porticus has no sign of stripwork on either face. Assuming that this is not the result of damage and repair, it could mean that, unlike in the north porticus, there was no opening from the exterior and hence no need to make the doorway into the nave into a marked entrance.

Having established the character of the building and the elements of which it is composed, it is now possible to re-examine the question of its date. The plan of the chapel finds its closest parallel at Bishopstone in Sussex. This is usually dated in the early period, but the presence of long-and-short quoins must cast doubt on the attribution. In any case Bradford-on-Avon is only a variant of the simple two-cell rectangular church which is so long-lived, from Escomb to Odda's Chapel and for that matter Barton-on-Humber, that a late date at least cannot be ruled out.

Monkwearmouth, Jarrow and Escomb are built of good-quality masonry, but it bears no comparison with the squared ashlar of Bradford-on-Avon, the best parallels for which are at Diddlebury, Dymock and Titchborne, all of the eleventh century. Taylor has also called the masonry of St Laurence's the only Anglo-Saxon fabric of an excellence comparable to that of St Rule's tower at St Andrews, which may be as late as the twelfth century.[15] The stepped bases to the pilasters tell the same story as they occur on the Bayeux tapestry in the 1070s and at Dunham Magna and Coln Rogers, 'overlap' buildings of similar date. Blind arcading of various kinds is used at Ravenna in the fifth century, Poitiers in the seventh, and Gernrode in the tenth, but the particular type of St Laurence's only occurs in similar though more sophisticated form on the later eleventh-century choir of Milborne Port, which is also built in good ashlar.

Apart from the plan, which is neutral in the matter, all these parallels point to the eleventh century, and, while it is more circumstantial than the reference to Aldhelm, the documentary evidence does provide a suitable occasion at a convenient date. In 1001 King Ethelred gave the manor and monastery at Bradford-on-Avon to Shaftesbury Abbey as a refuge from the Danes and to house the bones of King Edward the Martyr. It is not difficult to see St Laurence's as specifically rebuilt for this purpose, especially given the possibility that in its pristine state it had no windows. The reference also establishes another link with Milborne Port since, according to Domesday, the nuns of Shaftesbury held property there.[16]

It might be objected that a local tradition could not have gone so awry as to mislead William of Malmesbury only a century later, but pre-literate peoples in the nineteenth and twentieth centuries have been known to incorporate events of the previous fifty or a hundred years into myths or tales which purport to originate in the distant past. Equally, the desire to attribute a standing building to the founder of the institution manifests itself far beyond the bounds of oral traditions, and is not unknown even among architectural historians. Lastly, William of Malmesbury is careful to say only that the opinion about the date was generally voiced, which implies that he considered it open to doubt.

If anything, indeed, 1001 is uncomfortably early given the rolls on the arches and pilasters, which find their closest parallels some decades later, and the institutional and stylistic links with Milborne Port. This church is no more securely dated than Bradford-on-Avon, but it has to be seen in a Saxo-Norman context probably around 1090 and certainly no earlier than 1060.[17] The question of the date of St Laurence's must remain open, but within the confines of the eleventh century.

Before leaving this church mention should be made of the large carved crucifixion which originally dominated the eastern wall of the nave. Only two angels now remain, symmetrically flanking the centre near the top of the wall. At first sight there might appear to be far too much room between the chancel arch and the angels, but if the latter are assumed to have been positioned above the arms of the cross, as in the late tenth-century Sherborne Pontifical, then the 10 or 11 ft (3 m) available would comfortably accommodate the cross which stands on the western doorway at Headbourne Worthy in Hampshire, a building with pilasters and stepped bases, and probably datable, like Bradford-on-Avon, to the first half of the eleventh century.

The rood now in the cloister at Romsey, also in Hampshire, is equally of a suitable size. It is undated, but like all Anglo-Saxon roods it probably derives directly or indirectly from the popularisation of the theme on a large and public scale in the time of Charlemagne. St-Riquier, for instance, is known to have had a rood before the arch at the east end of the nave. It is not unlikely therefore that the rood at Romsey, which is a large-scale piece of mason's work and not an item of church furniture, formed part of a building erected at the time of the reform of the nunnery in 967. As the angels in St Laurence's have been justifiably compared with those supporting Christ in majesty on the title page of King Edgar's foundation charter for the New Minster in Winchester, of 966 or a little later, these examples have the makings of a small group of carvings in south-west England made in the last third of the tenth century and the first of

87 Earls Barton (Northamptonshire), All Saints, eleventh century. West doorway
88 Bradford-on-Avon (Wiltshire), St Laurence, eleventh century. Chancel arch

the eleventh, in the wake of the monastic reform movement.[18]

The western doorway at Earls Barton and the chancel arch at Bradford-on-Avon bear a number of striking similarities and differences (figs 87, 88). In both the arch springs from massive, simple imposts and the opening is outlined by stripwork of both square and cylindrical section. They differ in that the strips at Earls Barton project at least their own width from the wall and rise from solid, inarticulate bases, while those at Bradford-on-Avon are broad pilasters an inch or so deep set on a shallow and restrained plinth course. Equally the rolls of differing sizes on one arch contrast with the controlled, almost regimented triple form on the other. It is possible that the two are contemporary, but whereas Earls Barton lies at the end of a series Bradford-on-Avon is more like a beginning, its clarity pointing the way to the main developments of the middle of the century, exemplified by the half-roll used on a much more architectonic scale, to which we must now turn.

The half-roll or half-shaft on the jamb is usually accompanied by a pilaster, one form setting off the other and articulating the wall surface in a way not open to pilasters by themselves, let alone to stripwork. The formula is employed at Stow, probably between 1034 and 1049, and at Sherborne after 1045, where the two elements are elided, producing a richer profile (figs 69, 71, 89:1, 2). The tower arch of St Benet's in Cambridge is decorated on both faces with the strip and the half-shaft, the two set very close together, especially on the western face,

89 Profiles, 1:100. 1. Stow, respond of crossing arch. 2. Sherborne, respond of north-west doorway. 3. Cambridge, St Benet, respond of tower arch. 4. Wittering, chancel arch. 5. Bernay, crossing arch. 6. Caen, St-Étienne, crossing arch. 7. Durham Cathedral, arcade arch. 8. Stow, western arch of crossing. 9. Lincoln Cathedral, arch of façade niche. 10. Wharram-le-Street, arch of west doorway. 11. Broughton, arch of south doorway. a: pilaster strip; b: half-shaft; c: angle roll; d: hollow roll; e: soffit.

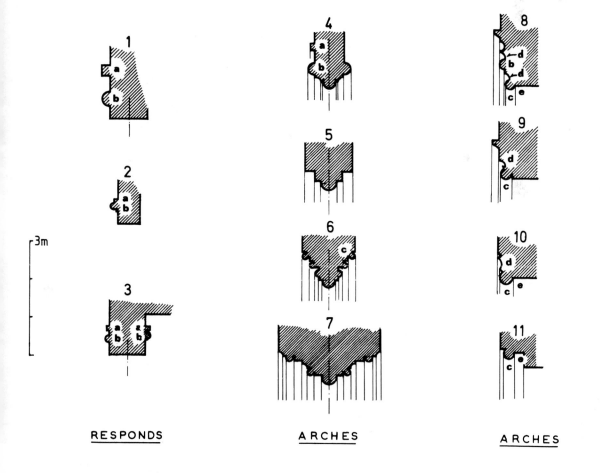

RESPONDS   ARCHES   ARCHES

making them appear as two parts of a single moulding, as at Sherborne (fig. 89, 2, 3,). A number of elements connect this arch with the decoration at Great Paxton not far to the west (figs 1, 78). The impost in the Cambridge church consists of a large central roll between slabs enriched with quirks, like a cousin to Barnack, and where the half-shaft meets this impost it produces a bulbous capital like those on the piers of the nave in Great Paxton. Similarly the animals carved in low relief on the springers of the arch recall the heads and sprigs of leaves which nestle between the bases and the capitals. The two buildings also share a certain refinement and precision which is less evident at Stow.

Except for the imposts at Cambridge the curved forms in these examples are all restricted to the face of the opening, leaving the soffit of the arch and the equivalent surfaces of the jambs undecorated. In two churches, St Nicholas's at Worth and St Mary's at Deerhurst, each jamb of the opening into the chancel is decorated with a large half-column, though the arch itself remains plain. Worth is very difficult to date. Its plan is a mixture of the seventh-century Old Minster in Winchester and the late tenth- or eleventh-century church at Dover, with an apse which can be paralleled at Ethelwold's tenth-century extension to the Old

90 Worth (Sussex), St Nicholas, mid eleventh century. Interior to east

Minster. The other openings can be characterised as nothing more specific than late Saxon, so it may be that the chancel arch represents the best means of establishing at least the earliest possible date within that period, and on the same basis as at Stow it would be surprising if the half-columns were any earlier than the second quarter of the eleventh century (fig. 90). The same of course should apply to Deerhurst, and as we have attributed the second major phase of building there to the time of Oswald around 970 the arch must be an insertion, for which there is fortunately some evidence in a disturbance in the fabric of the wall above it.[19]

Chapter Ten

THE REIGN OF
EDWARD THE CONFESSOR

Edward the Confessor's most important act of architectural patronage was the rebuilding of **Westminster Abbey**. It is not known when work began on the new project, except that it must have been after the start of the reign in 1042. One must therefore work backwards from the consecration which took place on 28 December 1065, though the evidence is conflicting as to how much of the church was complete by this date. The king died on 5 January and it is therefore possible, as William of Malmesbury thought, that the timing of the ceremony had more to do with reasons of state than the progress of the building programme. On the other hand Edward intended the church as his place of burial and he did not die a young man. This, taken in conjunction with the fact that there was no subsequent consecration, makes it virtually certain that a large part of the building was up by 1065, including the eastern arm, the transept and the easternmost bays of the nave. This could imply a start not later than the early 1050s, while contemporary observations on the demolition of the old church suggest the fabric was complete to the west end by 1085.[1]

The material remains lying under Henry III's thirteenth-century church are sparse, but can be fleshed out from various documentary sources. The two areas excavated, at the east and west ends, indicate that the building was only a little shorter than the present one, 314 ft (95.75 m) from the chord of the apse to the façade (fig. 91). The eastern arm consisted of two bays defined by pilasters and attached half-shafts on bases with chamfered and lightly moulded plinths. There was an apse to the east which could have been accompanied either by smaller apses at the ends of the aisles or by an ambulatory. The crossing and transept arms must have occupied the same position as the present ones since the dormitory range to the south belongs to the eleventh-century layout, as does the large cloister which it helps to define. At the west end the fragments permit the reconstruction of a tower at the end of each aisle and a nave of 12 bays with supports alternating between compound piers and supports standing on square plinths. From the descriptions it is clear there was a crossing and a lantern tower above the liturgical choir, with galleries in the transept arms and numerous spiral staircases and chapels.

Because of its stupendous length and the presence of twin towers and alternation at the west end of the nave, it has on occasion been suggested that the design was radically altered after 1065, but there are grounds for assuming that, in its length at least, the building is as it was intended to be from the start. The proportional relationship between the length of the nave and the length of the eastern arm is, as far as can be determined from the uncertain evidence, the same as that used in the majority of the larger Anglo-Norman churches such as Canterbury, Winchester, Ely and Norwich.[2] In other words if this parallel is correct then the distance from the chord of the apse to the western side of the crossing, which everyone agrees was established before 1065, presupposes the length of the nave as excavated and makes a change of plan unlikely.

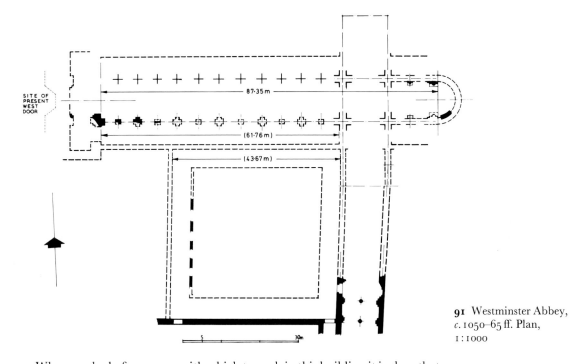

91 Westminster Abbey, *c.* 1050–65 ff. Plan, 1 : 1000

When one looks for sources with which to explain this building it is clear that they are not going to be found in England. Transepts, crossings, upper chambers flanking the choir and claustral squares can all be adduced, but they are either of a very different type or a very different scale, or both, which is also true of decorative details on doorways and bases. Instead, everything points to Normandy and in particular to the abbey church at Jumièges on the Seine near Rouen, begun around 1040 and consecrated in 1067 (fig. 56d). This building survives complete in plan and as a standing structure west of the western walls of the transept. The eastern arm is of two bays with an apse, and the arms of the transept were filled with low vaults like those in the aisles of the nave, supporting galleries at first-floor level, probably with chapels off them to the east, above those at ground level. From these platforms rise spiral stair-cases leading to wall-passages and the lantern tower. The supports in the nave alternate between compound piers and columns, the latter standing on square plinths almost undistinguishable from those at Westminster, and the former having attached half-shafts like those in the presbytery there. While the west end of the nave unlike Westminster takes the form of a small westwork, it is nonetheless dominated by two towers standing over the ends of the aisles. Finally, like Westminster and most Norman churches, but unlike practice in England, the church was built as a whole after the complete demolition of its predecessor.[3]

Jumièges was begun under Abbot Robert, who in 1044 became bishop of London, providing an unusually straightforward avenue for the transfer of influence. He went on to become archbishop of Canterbury before departing in haste during the anti-Norman upheavals of 1051, returning to Jumièges where he died in 1052. It was no accident that as important a see as London and then the highest ecclesiastical office in the land should have been held by a Norman at this time. In 1016, during the second Danish wars, Edward had been both a claimant to the throne and the son of a Norman mother so that, with the accession of Cnut, he spent his exile in Normandy, continuing his education at the ducal court in Rouen.[4] Given this background, Westminster Abbey becomes simply one of a number of things which indicate the importance of the duchy in English affairs in the early years of his reign. Indeed this is one of the most cogent reasons for assuming that the new building was begun before the reaction of 1051.

Because its character is so much at variance with what preceded it in England and conversely so closely related to work in Normandy, Westminster is usually treated as the first monument of the Anglo-Norman period and omitted from discussions of Anglo-Saxon architecture. Yet the logic of this decision applies equally well to Augustine's buildings in Kent, which were also importations made Anglo-Saxon only by reason of their location and their patrons, and Westminster has if anything a stronger claim to the apellation than SS Peter and Paul and its sister churches, as the following may indicate.

Of course Edward was affected by his upbringing, but it would be quite wrong to see him as anything other than an English king and accepted as such by his contemporaries. In fact as the son of Aethelred he was more English than his three predecessors, Cnut, Harold Harefoot and Harthacnut, and while his introduction of Normans and their manners may have annoyed certain sections of the nobility, no less would have followed had he favoured, as he might, the Flemings, Lotharingians or Scandinavians in his employ. In addition, as a member of one of the oldest royal houses in Europe he was of much greater stature than the parvenu dukes of Normandy, a point which receives eloquent physical expression in the scale of Westminster. Despite its dependence on Norman buildings in detail, its great length (314 ft or 95.75 m between the chord and the façade) cannot be paralleled at Jumièges (241 ft or 73.50 m), at the cathedral of Rouen (not more than 260 ft or 80 m), or at any contemporary building in the region, and is only surpassed, among contemporary buildings, by the cathedral at Speyer (about 390 ft or 119 m), another royal mausoleum recently begun and only finished a few years before 1065.

One can only assume that, although neither the resources nor the ambition were lacking to him, Duke William chose not to build on this scale in order to avoid a charge of hubris from neighbouring crowned heads. Certainly once he was king of England the architectural projects with which his name might be linked, like the new cathedral at Winchester (420 ft, 128 m), make even Edward's church look if not small at least restrained. It is therefore true to say that the fact that Westminster Abbey was built in England gave it a scope which it would not have had in Normandy, a somewhat ironic conclusion given the reputation of the Anglo-Saxons for producing nothing but under-sized buildings.

It is not just at this rather rarefied level that Westminster can be spoken of as English, since the stone of which it was built came from Reigate. It may appear to be the soundest of economic good sense to use a nearby quarry, but after the

Conquest vast quantities of stone were imported from Caen, and it is even possible that Westminster was more easily accessible from Caen than from Reigate. However, the important point is that the architectural revolution which Westminster represents was as much technical as stylistic, involving the use of large numbers of blocks of similar size and shape instead of the masonry varying from the large slab to the small piece of unsquared stone typical of Anglo-Saxon building methods. The change implies an equal revolution in the methods of quarrying and preparing the stone for transportation, methods which must have been used at Reigate.

In addition, the three men most likely to have been responsible for the design and construction of the abbey were Teinfrith 'the churchwright', Leofsi Duddlesunu and Godwine Greatsyd, at least two of whom are indubitably English and none Norman. Obviously they were not trained at Barnack or Bath, and one must assume that they learnt their trade across the Channel, either when they were there with Edward before 1042 or when despatched on his orders thereafter. Despite this training they were nonetheless English and were therefore well placed to influence English architectural manners. In view of this and of the great prestige which Westminster must have enjoyed it is surprising to find how small an effect the new work had before the Conquest.

In 1049 Wulfric, abbot of **St Augustine's** in Canterbury from 1047 until his death in 1059, attended a council in Reims at which he obtained the permission of Pope Leo IX to enlarge the principal church of the monastery. On his return he demolished the east end of SS Peter and Paul and the west end of St Mary's and linked the two by means of a large centralized building which was still unfinished at his death (figs 18, 92).[5] The walls of this survive to a height of 5 ft (1.5 m) below the nave and crossing of the later Norman church. The building is octagonal on the exterior and circular on the interior, with an internal diameter of 54 ft (16.5 m). On the western side a flight of steps leads up from this aisle towards the level of the floor in the nave of SS Peter and Paul, so that the surviving part must have been a crypt.

On the exterior each of the six free-standing faces appears to have been decorated with a broad flat buttress set in the centre of the wall rather than at the corner. These buttresses provide evidence of a change of plan, since where they survive they have been covered with a layer of masonry which thickens the wall by about two feet, and on the south face forms a semicircle which probably acted as the base of a spiral staircase. To the west this second phase broadens out as if to become the east end of a new set of nave and aisles.

Among the possible sources for this building Wilfrid's centralized church at Hexham, Alfred's at Athelney and the wooden church at Potterne can be excluded because each had four porticus projecting from the core, while the form of St Dunstan's tower-church of St John the Baptist at Glastonbury is unknown. Ethelwold's church at Abingdon had an ambulatory and hence is more relevant, but a similar building of more recent date was the rotunda at Bury St Edmunds, rebuilt in the 1020s by Cnut as a martyrium for Edmund, the East Anglian king and saint murdered by his Scandinavian ancestors. It had a circular core and an ambulatory and may even, like Wulfric's rotunda, have been added to an earlier building.[6]

All these structures are lost and known only from descriptions, but extant parallels at Essen, Dijon and Charroux indicate that the integration of centralized and longitudinal forms was a subject of some interest in the first half of the eleventh century. Between 1039 and 1058 Abbess Theophanu built a western apse onto the ninth-and tenth-century church at Essen, basing it on

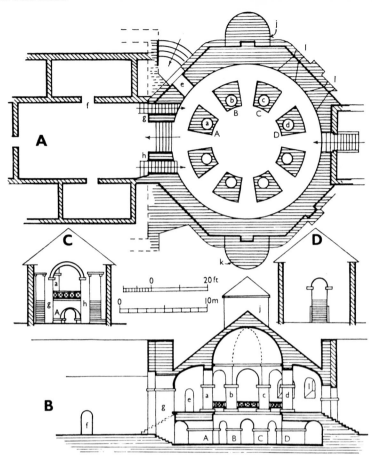

92 Canterbury (Kent), St Augustine, Wulfric's rotunda, between 1049 and 1059. Plan and reconstructed section, 1:400 (Taylor, 1969)

three-eighths of the palace chapel at Aachen. The result is stunning but only tangentially relevant to St Augustine's.

On the other hand the church of St-Bénigne at Dijon built by William of Volpiano between 1001 and 1018 has often and with good reason been proposed as the immediate source of Wulfric's ideas. The rotunda at the east end of this building had an internal diameter of 55 ft (16.75 m), it was flanked by a pair of spiral staircases to north and south, and it was set between a larger church to the west and a smaller to the east, the latter dedicated to the Virgin, all of which characteristics it shares with Wulfric's building. Despite this the parallel is misleading.

The chief source of information concerning the eastern parts of the church at Dijon is the set of engravings published by Dom Plancher in the first half of the eighteenth century. These show, just to the west of the rotunda, a series of columns forming the main apse opening towards the west, making the rotunda into an adjunct to the church, lying east of the apse and tangential to it. As such it is immediately recognisable as a member of a group of buildings which have been mentioned a number of times already, and of which two representative examples are St-Pierre at Geneva of the sixth century and the cathedral at Hildesheim of the ninth (fig. 85). This is the family of which St-Bénigne has always been considered a member, but as such it has little to do with Wulfric's work.

In all these cases the rotunda is a subsidiary building lying to the east of the church. This is not the case at Canterbury. Wulfric demolished the apse of SS Peter and Paul, and the evidence is unequivocal that he did not intend to reinstate it in either phase of planning. Because of this the high altar must have been intended to stand either in the rotunda or in St Mary's, an arrangement which is entirely at variance with the disposition of St-Bénigne as usually reconstructed.

On the other hand it can be compared with the large church of St-Sauveur at Charroux in western France, consecrated in 1047. While dependent on St-Bénigne for the outlines of its design, it differs in having the rotunda set firmly in the centre with all four arms radiating from it (fig. 93), providing a model for Wulfric's alterations.[8] Further, Charroux prompts the suggestion that Wulfric may have seen his rotunda as a kind of crossing, without north and south arms to be sure, but acting as a central focus from which the nave and chancel extended. As such he would have been attempting to do in a limited way what Scotland, the first Norman abbot, achieved, that is the imposing of an essentially Romanesque order onto an older Anglo-Saxon site. If so, then this would be the one respect in which the work of St Augustine's resembles Westminster.

93 Charroux (Vienne), St-Sauveur, consecrated 1047. Plan, 1:1000

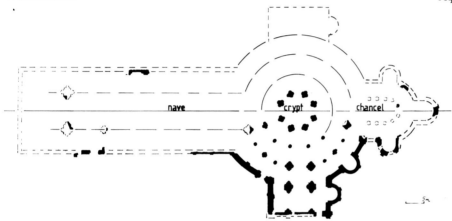

Apart from Sherborne Cathedral and perhaps Great Paxton there are only two more churches which can be securely dated in Edward's reign, and these are on a tiny scale compared with all the others. The small building known as **Odda's Chapel** lying to the south-west of St Mary's at **Deerhurst** can be dated from an inscription to the fourteenth year of the reign, that is to 1056.[9] It has a rectangular nave and a rectangular chancel linked by an archway with a most unusual horseshoe-shaped head which, with its hood-mould, springs from richly moulded imposts. These have four elements in vertical section, a block above and a chamfer below, with between them a larger and a smaller concave roll (fig. 94). The earliest example of this last feature so far discussed is on St-Étienne at Caen of the 1060s and hence slightly later than the chapel, raising an interesting problem which will be examined in more detail in the next chapter.

St Gregory's at **Kirkdale** in Yorkshire can be dated to the time of Earl Tostig, between 1055 and 1065, from an inscription on a sundial over the south door. The nave contains two interesting openings in the form of the west doorway and the chancel arch, both of which have jambs decorated with shafts set into recessed orders, a feature which has not occurred in any building

94 Impost mouldings, 1:10. Left: Sherborne Cathedral, north-west doorway; right: Deerhurst, Odda's Chapel, chancel arch. a: quirk; b: hollow roll; c: chamfer

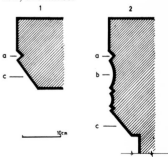

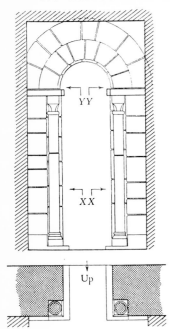

95 Kirkdale (Yorkshire), St Gregory, between 1055 and 1065. West doorway. Plan and elevation, 1:50 (Taylor and Taylor, 1965)

examined so far (fig. 95). Such nook-shafts, as they are called, decorate the windows of the lantern over the crossing at Jumièges, and so may well have come to Yorkshire by way of Westminster.

One other possible candidate for inclusion as a dated monument of the reign is the central chamber of the crypt of St Peter's, now the cathedral, at **Gloucester**. This is normally attributed along with the rest of the crypt to the new abbey church begun by Serlo in 1089, but doubts have been expressed as to whether the structure is of one period.[10] The level of the floor in the central part, as defined by the bases of the columns, is considerably lower than that of the aisles and radiating chapels, suggesting that it belongs to a separate build. This possibility is supported by the appearance of two layers in the arcade walls, with the outer built on to the inner, that is the wall of the central chamber. If one assumes that the outer layer along with the ambulatory chapels is Serlo's, then the earlier phase could either be a false start in 1089 or a remnant of the church built by Ealdred, bishop of Worcester, and consecrated, according to the Anglo-Saxon Chronicle, in 1058. The normal attribution of this work to the late eleventh century gives some indication of the thoroughly Norman character of its volute capitals, tooling, vaulting and general layout. Since Westminster did not have a crypt it could not have been the model, so that, if Ealdred's authorship could be proved, the building would constitute a second independent instance of Norman influence before the Conquest.

One can only speculate about the lost buildings of the period, but some are worth mentioning in any case. One of the two churches at Evesham was enlarged and reconsecrated in 1054, but nothing is known of its form. Edward's queen, Edith, built a stone church for the nunnery at Wilton which was consecrated by Herman bishop of Sarum in 1065, and given the royal connection there may have been something of Westminster in the design.[11] The church of the secular house founded around 1060 by Harold at Waltham is in this sense somewhat ambiguous, in that while there is no doubt of its importance and its connections with the court, its founder might have been less anxious than either Edward or Edith to emulate Norman ways.[12]

In this chapter and the preceding three the material of the late Anglo-Saxon period has been treated in two different ways. Chapters eight and nine examined particular features of planning and decoration regardless of their date, while chapters seven and ten have dealt with buildings datable respectively to the monastic revival of the second half of the tenth century and to the reign of Edward. The singling out of these particular years raises the question of the significance of the period between, namely the first forty years of the eleventh century.

There are good grounds for believing that the building boom which attended the monastic reform movement did not survive the turn of the millennium, both because of lay resistance and counter-pressure to monastic encroachment and because of the revived dangers of Danish attack.[13] Even after the establishing of the new order under Cnut in 1016 and despite the fact that the king is eulogized for having built and restored numerous churches, there is little evidence of such activity. In 1019 he founded St Benet of Hulme in Norfolk, from where in 1020 monks were sent to replace the canons at Bury St Edmunds and where in turn Edmund's rotunda was re-built. Beyond this there are only one or two references. Things only appear to change under Edward, when the number of dated monuments increases and Westminster Abbey adds a new and potentially distorting element to the picture.

Some support for this thesis of a lull in the early eleventh century can be gleaned from the history of the crossing since the 'Breamore' type clearly belongs to the period of the reform, while conversely all the evidence for the salient type points to its use specifically in the middle of the eleventh century, at Stow and Sherborne for example.

The picture provided by decoration, however, is less clear cut. It would be convenient to argue that the earlier group comprising Britford, Brigstock, Barnack, Barton-on-Humber and Earls Barton, with square section stripwork, has its centre of gravity in the reform period while the later use of the roll at Stow, Sherborne and so on again belongs to the reign of Edward. Earls Barton, however, does not fit happily into this scheme because of the half-roll on its western arch. Taken at face value this suggests a date at least in the 1030s, and this in turn forces an acknowledgement that its forerunner at Barton-on-Humber can easily be dated into the first third of the eleventh century. Bradford-on-Avon supports similar misgivings since, despite a documentary reference of 1001, it too has half-rolls, and in addition blind arcading best paralleled much later in the century. At present the idea of a recession must remain unproved.

An overview such as that just presented forcefully underlines the extent to which Anglo-Saxon church architecture changed between *c*. 970 and *c*. 1060. What can be called the clutter and lack of organisation of the internal arrangements at Deerhurst, or the rather *ad hoc* accumulation of spaces at Ethelwold's Winchester contrast sharply with the order and clarity of Sherborne or Stow. The same move from a functional approach to one in which the overall form of the building takes precedence is evident in the change from the varying positions and sizes of arches and porticus at Wooten Wawen, Norton and Dover to the more regular arrangements of Stow and Great Paxton. In other words, there is such a thing as a Romanesque style in Anglo-Saxon building. This, and the presence of Westminster, throws up a problem of terminology. 'Norman' is used in this country as a synonym for what in France or Germany would be called 'Romanesque'. This usage is proper and unambiguous in its context, but in the standard distinction (not to say confrontation) between 'Anglo-Saxon' and 'Norman', it has the effect of making the former by definition pre- or non-Romanesque. It would be less restricting if 'Norman Romanesque' were to be used for the architecture of that style in Normandy, 'Anglo-Norman Romanesque' for its equivalent in England, and 'Anglo-Saxon Romanesque' for pre-Conquest English buildings in the same broad category.

Westminster Abbey occupies a special place here since all three phrases are applicable to it, the first on the grounds that it is in most essentials a Norman building constructed in England, the second because it is the start of the Anglo-Norman school, and the third by reason of its patron and location. But to the question 'To what extent was the Abbey responsible for the growth of an indigenous Anglo-Saxon Romanesque?', the answer seems to be, not at all. Clapham expressed the view that had the Conquest not intervened the Anglo-Saxons would have developed their own version of the Romanesque style after the manner of their kinsmen in the Rhineland.[14] On the contrary, they did not wait until after the 1060s but brought the change about considerably earlier and, what is more, independently of Westminster.

Chapter Eleven

THE 'OVERLAP'

Only two kinds of building have been examined in the last four chapters, those with definite documentary evidence dating them before 1066, like Sherborne, Westminster and Kirkdale, and those with no Norman features, like Great Paxton, which may therefore be presumed to date before the Conquest. The shortcomings of this out-of-date dynastic technique for dividing up architectural history are well known, exemplified as they are in the works of Bannister Fletcher where English medieval architecture ceases and Tudor begins in 1485, and of Commendatore Rivoira whose history of Roman architecture marches inexorably with the Caesars. The cream of the Anglo-Saxon architectural profession did not perish on the battlefield at Hastings, nor did the survivors flee westwards in the face of new continental fashions.[1] On the contrary the break in 1066 has been adopted here because its very artificiality forces a confrontation with the issue of what constitutes an Anglo-Saxon style, and how it came to an end.

'Anglo-Saxon' and 'Norman' are usually seen as two separate and indeed almost opposing entities which enjoy, or suffer from, an overlap during which one replaces the other.[2] Since influence from Normandy begins before the Conquest and the Anglo-Saxon style can be presumed to have continued after 1066, this overlap is usually taken to extend from about 1050 to about 1100, that is, Baldwin Brown's and the Taylors' period C3. This view inevitably presents Anglo-Saxon features after 1066, or even after 1050, in a passive role, surviving for a few years through force of inertia and lasting longest in rural backwaters. There is of course some truth in this view, but on examination it applies, perhaps surprisingly, to only two or three features such as long-and-short quoining and the salient crossing, while the last phase of Anglo-Saxon architecture as a whole is much more varied and interesting than this terminology would imply. After a brief look at these two survivals we shall examine a few aspects of this exceedingly complex period.

Long-and-short quoining is one of the hall-marks of the late Anglo-Saxon period, but it falls out of use soon after the introduction of Norman masonry techniques. It continues longest in regions lacking good free-stone, but even in those it is soon replaced by quoining of blocks of more nearly equal size. Post-Conquest examples can be cited at the chapel in Winchester Castle built for, or ready by, the council held there in 1072, and in the parish church of St John Timberhill in Norwich, founded between the Conquest and the compiling of Domesday by 1086.[3] While it is therefore incorrect to speak of this technique as a sure sign of Anglo-Saxon date, it may not be misleading to refer to it as a mark of Anglo-Saxon workmanship.

The crossing with salient corners occurs at a handful of places which are either post-Conquest or not definitely pre-Conquest, such as Hadstock, Milborne Port, Wimborne Minster, Sherborne (in the twelfth-century eastern crossing which is presumed to reflect that of Aelfwold), Stanton Lacy and, at the west end of the church, at Netheravon. There may well be later examples of both these features, but they leave no mark on future developments.[4]

Apart from these two survivals, features which are relevant to the period of the Conquest can be divided into two main categories, those which are used in both major and minor churches and those which are restricted to the latter. In the first category the cushion capital and the complex arch profile are of particular interest, while the importance of considering minor churches as a group in their own right, and not simply as an appendage to the larger buildings, can be illustrated by a discussion of round towers, double-splayed windows and crossing towers with low chambers. All of these elements will now be examined in turn.

Just as long-and-short work and the salient crossings are entirely Anglo-Saxon, so other features of the period such as the volute capital and various masonry techniques are, as one would expect, purely Norman in origin, and others again, like the quirked and chamfered impost, are apparently both Saxon and Norman. In addition, however, there is a small category of elements which are surprisingly and paradoxically neither Saxon nor Norman, and of these the cushion capital is the most acute example.

As described in chapter six, it appears to be an invention of the early eleventh century in Saxony, remaining the rule in the German Empire for the next 200 years. In Anglo-Saxon England there are a number of what can only be called pseudo-cushions, which are even more ambiguous than some of those on the Continent of the ninth and tenth centuries, and should not be confused with the real thing. The early ninth-century panel of a female saint at Breedon-on-the-Hill is framed by an arch supported on such capitals, and the shaft of the Gosforth cross makes the transition from a square section to a cylindrical by means of four lunettes. Some of the frames in the Anglo-Saxon Copenhagen Gospels, of the late tenth-century, have capitals depicted as a semi-circle, but if they do represent real forms they would resemble not so much cushion capitals as the 'tectonic' type found in, for example, the late ninth-century crypt of St George's at Reichenau-Oberzell or the late eleventh-century crossing of South Lopham in Norfolk. Lastly the capitals in the triple arcade in the west wall of the nave at Brixworth, part of the alterations of the late tenth or early eleventh century, while appearing to have a cushion-like form in reality have sloping sides which are either straight or concave.

For capitals which will hold their own with German cushions one has to wait until the Conquest, after which they appear almost immediately, in the crypt of Lanfranc's cathedral at Canterbury begun in 1070 and on the north gate of the contemporary castle at Exeter.[5] The latter underlines the problem as well as the character of the period in having fully formed cushion capitals (an imperial feature) alongside long-and-short quoins (an Anglo-Saxon feature) in the context of a castle (a Norman building type). After this the progress of the form is, if anything, even more triumphant than in the Empire, with scallops appearing around 1080 in St John's chapel in the Tower of London and versions decorated with figures and animals in Anselm's crypt at Canterbury in the 1090s. The earliest examples on the southern side of the Channel belong to this late date and are clearly imports from England, so that the Norman

Conquest appears to introduce into England a feature unknown in Normandy.

Taylor has argued that the fully formed cushion capital existed in England before the Conquest and that it was invented independently here and in the Empire.[6] This assessment, however, underestimates the evidence against a pre-Conquest date for such buildings as the Lincolnshire group of western towers, and the nature of those capitals of cushion-like form described above which can definitely be ascribed an Anglo-Saxon date.[7] In addition, suggesting independent origins for such a well-defined feature introduces an unwarranted complication into the picture presented by the material: the Empire provides such an obvious source that, if anything, a case has to be made out against it. There is even a convenient means of transfer in the persons of William's Flemish allies and mercenaries, the most important group in his forces after the Normans.[8]

A completely different kind of uncertainty attaches to the profiles of arches and responds. These owe nothing to the Empire and are as complicated in Anglo-Saxon England as they are in Normandy, if not more so, indicating a close interdependence across the Channel as much before the Conquest as after it. The point can be illustrated by a juxtaposition of arches in St-Étienne at Caen, reliably dated to the 1060s and 1070s, and All Saints at Wittering, two buildings usually considered eminently representative of the Norman and the Anglo-Saxon styles respectively (figs 96, 97).

The chancel arch at Wittering is perhaps the most splendid and certainly the

96 Wittering (Northamptonshire), All Saints, 1050–80. Chancel arch. Plan, elevation and section, 1:100 (Taylor and Taylor, 1965)
97 Caen (Calvados), St-Étienne, c. 1070. Crossing arches

0   5   10   15 ft

most powerful of all the late Anglo-Saxon archways. The nave face is framed with the standard half-roll frame flanked by one of square section, as in St Benet's at Cambridge and at Stow. The roll is however proportionately thicker than in any other example and is matched not only by an opposite number inside the chancel, but by a roll on the soffit carried on half-shafts, the whole forming a trilobe in section. As if this were not enough, the angles between the lobes are filled with a large hollow roll set at an angle like a chamfer. The rich sculptural effect of this massing is impossible to parallel outside England, and the elegance and restraint of the crossing arches at Caen stand in marked contrast to the crude, bulging vigour of Wittering. Yet examined in detail the forms turn out to be very similar indeed. The innermost order in both cases is a trilobe, the hollow roll between the lobes at Wittering occurs on the western doorways at Caen, and the chamfer on the abaci on the crossing. It is clear that despite the differences in their appearance these two monuments should not be discussed separately.

In order to establish the context of their relationships it will be useful to examine the constituent parts one at a time, namely the rolls on (1) the face, (2) the soffit and (3) the angle, then (4) the chamfer and finally, (5) the hollow roll.

1. The half-roll on the face of the arch is unknown in Normandy apart from Caen, but appears in England as early as the second quarter of the eleventh century. It is developed, in conjunction with the pilaster strip, from Stow to Sherborne and Cambridge by the closer juxtaposition of the two elements until they read as a single moulding (fig. 89; 1–3). At Wittering the half-shaft amalgamates with the hollow roll and the roll on the soffit rather than with the strip, but the principle is the same and 'amalgamation' is exactly what happens on the jambs at Great Paxton.

Cambridge, Great Paxton and Wittering are also linked by the likelihood that the stone of which they are constructed comes from the quarry at Barnack, which might explain the common elements in their designs. On the other hand Wittering is distinguished by one characteristic which should be connected with how the stone is quarried. While all three openings use through-stones those at Cambridge are large and those at Great Paxton huge, while Wittering is built of small, manageable blocks laid without a trace of the Escomb-fashion technique which characterises the other two. In this Wittering is more like Caen.

2. As we have already seen in chapter 6 the soffit roll at Caen has a respectable pedigree from Auxerre in the 1020s via Bernay in the middle of the century (figs 45, 46, 97). There are no dated examples in Anglo-Saxon England, but Great Paxton suggests that the earliest instance is likely to be later than the 1040s. This is because, despite the extremely rich sets of shafts on the jambs of the crossing, there is no decoration at all on the soffit of the single surviving arch. Such an assumption is of course questionable on the basis of only one building, especially as in Normandy Jumièges, which is probably later than Bernay, does not have the roll, but support for it can be found in a second English church.

The chancel arch of St Martin's at Wareham in Dorset is outlined by the standard half-roll, though not on the jambs and without the strip, while on the soffit is another larger roll supported on half-shafts and on quirked and chamfered imposts (fig. 98). Three features link this building closely to nearby Sherborne (fig. 69). Both stand on a double plinth the upper element of which is chamfered, the imposts of the chancel arch at one and the entrance to the north aisle at the other have the same profile, and the masonry bears the same

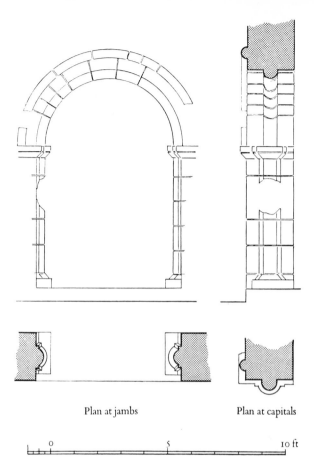

Plan at jambs   Plan at capitals

0   5   10 ft

98 Wareham (Dorset), St Martin, *c.* 1050–80. Chancel arch. Plan, section and elevation, 1:50 (Taylor and Taylor, 1965)

erratically diagonal tooling. The presence of the soffit roll at Wareham might be taken to indicate a later date, but this is a circular argument, in addition to which the extant arch at Sherborne is of minor importance compared with a chancel arch and hence might be expected to be plainer. More significant is the fact that all the voissoirs at Wareham are radial while those in the cathedral are, though neat, not regular. This sort of technical characteristic should not be affected by the position of the feature in the church, and as the more advanced form is in the lesser building and the two churches are in the same diocese the implication is that Wareham should be later, that is at least in the 1050s if not in the 1060s. Following the trend of this argument Wittering could be dated to the very same decade as St-Etienne.

3. There appear to be no immediate precedents for the angle rolls which occur on almost every arch at St-Etienne.[9] The type becomes popular on both sides of the Channel in the last third of the eleventh century in numerous Norman and Anglo-Norman churches (fig. 89c) and produces a particularly interesting variant used in some smaller buildings in England. In this the curve continues round to a soffit set much further back than in the Norman examples or, to put it the other way round, instead of being a semi-cylindrical roll on the angle with an equal relationship to both the vertical face and the soffit, it is a three-quarter roll set right on the edge of the soffit (fig. 89: 10, 11).

A possible explanation or forerunner for this variant may be the profile of the stripwork at Sherborne, in which the half-shaft is elided with the strip in such a way as to produce a longer curve on one side than on the other (figs 69, 89:2). The connection is not close, but the profile is on a doorway and could have acted as an influence when the Norman angle roll was first introduced. Wharram-le-Street and Broughton, among a number of others, have this feature. The second is undated, but thanks to John Bilson's ingenious analysis the arches of Wharram-le-Street can be dated to within a few years of 1120, indicating that despite or because of its non-Norman quality the form was used over a long period of time.[10] Another version of the type occurs on the crossing arches at Stow and on the west front of Remigius's cathedral at Lincoln, both probably of the 1090s (fig. 89: 8, 9).

4. Apart from the Roman examples at Chesters, or those at Monkwearmouth and Escomb which are Roman at one remove, there are no instances of chamfers in England before those at Barton-on-Humber, probably datable late in the tenth century or early in the eleventh. Next, those at Jumièges, Stow, Sherborne and Great Paxton belong in the second quarter if not the middle of the century. The variant with a quirk occurs at Odda's Chapel at Deerhurst and in the north-west doorway at Sherborne, both of the 1050s (fig. 94). Significantly, the latter example is hardly distinguishable from the profile of the early twelfth-century hood-mould of the enlarged south-western doorway in the same building. Finally Bernay and Caen have some examples with a hollow chamfer in addition to the quirk, very similar to those on the doorways in the north transept at Wimborne Minster, which may be part of the early twelfth-century building programme or retained from an earlier phase.

5. With the hollow roll we return to a feature used at both Caen and Wittering. Unlike the angle-roll it has Roman or at least late antique predecessors with a wide distribution, occurring in North Africa, Syria and Armenia between the fourth century and the seventh.[11] The earliest dated example in the present context is that on the imposts of the chancel arch in Odda's Chapel at Deerhurst, of 1056 (fig. 94). While this is unlikely to be the place at which it was revived or re-invented, it is clear from what has been said above that the source does not have to lie in Normandy.

To summarise, of the features to be found on the arches at Caen and Wittering, the half-roll on the face of the arch is an Anglo-Saxon feature, that on the soffit is, in the present context, Norman, the angle roll appears to be Norman rather than English, and the hollow roll English rather than Norman, while the chamfer is both Norman and English, a promiscuous result which, if nothing else, should call into question any idea of a simple replacement of an old style by a new. The richness and variety of the mouldings at Caen are unparalleled in other Norman and north French churches not only of an earlier date but also later, at least until the eighties, when similar examples occur at Cerisy-la-Forêt and St-Nicolas in Caen. In England on the other hand the predilection for decorative forms was much more wide-spread. While acknowledging the likely importance of the soffit rolls at Bernay, it is still possible to argue that the stripwork and half-shafts at Stow and Sherborne could easily have led to experimentation with the soffit and the leading edge in the fifties and sixties, to the extent that Rigold felt able to describe the architectural manners of Caen as 'Saxon-like'.[12]

At this point we are confronted by a conundrum, or even a mystery. Given the possibility of an English influence on Caen in the 1060s, one would expect similar decoration on the earliest buildings erected by the Normans in England after the Conquest, but at Winchester and Ely in the seventies and eighties the arches are completely plain apart from the doubling of the order. It is only in the last decade of the eleventh and the first of the twelfth, at Gloucester and Durham (fig. 89:7) and in the second phase of work at Ely, that decoration comparable to that at Wittering and Caen begins to re-appear.

How is one to explain this odd disjunction? It seems unlikely that William, after indulging himself as patron of St-Etienne should have ordered an end to a 'superfluite of too gret curious werkes of entaille and besy moldying' as Henry VI did at his chapel in Cambridge in the fifteenth century,[13] and another possibility suggests itself, among buildings of the second or even third rank. The kinds of profile used in Caen in the sixties and Durham in the nineties are also found at numerous smaller places like Sompting, Clayton and Milborne Port. Although these cannot be accurately dated, among other reasons, characteristics like a stronger admixture of Norman elements than at Wittering suggest dates after rather than before the sixties. They can therefore be seen as a sort of pool or reserve which continued both Anglo-Saxon and Saxo-Norman traditions until these became of interest once again to the designers of the larger buildings a generation later, at Durham for instance, just as Anglo-Saxon sculpture lies behind much of the carving at Ely and Canterbury in the 1080s and 1090s.[14]

This view, if it is correct, points to the conclusion that there are good reasons for studying minor churches as a group, independent of the major buildings. This is indicated very clearly by a number of features which, unlike cushion capitals and profiles, are at all dates almost entirely restricted to the minor churches. Three are particularly worthy of comment, namely the round tower, the double-splayed window, and the crossing tower with a low upper chamber.

Of the nearly 200 examples of single, round western towers in England, barely half-a-dozen can be dated with any conviction before the Conquest, while the majority can be shown to belong to the late eleventh, twelfth and even thirteenth centuries.[15] The feature can thus hardly be called a survival, nor can its restriction to minor churches be taken as a sign that it represents the backwaters of architectural development, since many examples, like Little Saxham (Suffolk) are of the very highest quality and anything but rustic.

The great majority of western round towers are to be found in East Anglia, to the extent that they are the mark of a regional school of minor churches extending from, at a guess, the first half of the eleventh century to the first part of the thirteenth. The type does not occur in Normandy at any date, and while it is possible to suppose that it is an indigenous development in an area lacking good building stone, this argument does not explain why other such areas did not adopt it. Nor does it take account of the remarkable similarities which exist between the East Anglian examples and the round towers of north-west Germany (the earliest of which may be that at Heeslingen, now demolished but probably erected in the time of Abbess Hathui between 973 and 1013) which continued in fashion until the late twelfth century.[16] The parallel extends beyond the shape and the western position of the tower, so that a building like Ratekau near Lübeck has a round, double-splayed window in its southern quadrant, exactly comparable to that at Roughton in Norfolk.

It would not be surprising if there was a connection between these two areas, as the route by water from the Yare to Hamburg could hardly be more direct, forming as it did an avenue of trade over many subsequent centuries. In addition, the bishop of London who re-christianized East Anglia in the second half of the tenth century had the German-sounding name of Theodred and was accompanied by a number of other churchmen with German apellations.

Between them they could have established ecclesiastical connections which were maintained into the eleventh century.[17]

The Conquest then had no significance for the round tower, introduced, as it seems to have been, well before the 1060s yet reaching the zenith of its popularity in the twelfth century, making it at the same time both Anglo-Saxon and Anglo-Norman.

Apart from Roman examples the earliest double-splayed windows are Carolingian, occurring at St Lucius in Chur before 820, and in the crypts of St Michael's in Fulda and St Michael's at Rohr later in the century, after which they remain common in Germany until the twelfth century. No English instances can be definitely dated to the pre-Danish period, but they appear in the late tenth or early eleventh century in the baptistery at Barton-on-Humber and thereafter become almost the standard window type. After the Conquest some scattered examples occur in castles, such as those at Lydford, Porchester, Castle Rising, Richmond and Sherborne, and because of this apparently restricted distribution they have looked like a technique retained to perform a special function in very thick walls. This, however, is misleading, since many buildings which may be post-Conquest have been excluded from the count simply because their double-splayed windows were taken as a sign of Anglo-Saxon date, as for instance at Hales, where the twelfth-century date of the building can only be denied by the expedient of proposing the wholesale addition of the numerous Norman features which characterise almost every part of the church.

In most churches with a crossing, whether they are Anglo-Saxon or Anglo-Norman, the interior space rises higher than that of the surrounding arms, often ending in a lantern tower providing a well of light and adding to the central importance of the feature. It therefore seems perverse when the upper floor, which is present in most crossing towers, is placed so low down that it reads as a part of the internal elevation of the nave and other arms. In the twelfth-century church at Melbourne, for instance, the arches of the crossing are no higher than those of the nave arcade and they support a passage in the thickness of the wall the arcading of which is a continuation of that of the triforium. Similar arrangements exist at Attleborough and Melton Constable in Norfolk and Oulton in Suffolk, without the wall-passage but with equal indications of advanced date, at Lympne in Kent which is even simpler and less decorated, and at Thaon in Normandy.[18] In attempting to explain these oddities it is more useful to consider them in the same context as earlier buildings which have related features but are more predominantly 'Saxon' in character, such as Newton-by-Castle-Acre and the west tower at Sherborne, than to attempt to construct a divide between pre- and post-Conquest or Anglo-Saxon and Norman.

Case-histories of individual buildings illustrate the same point. St Botolph's at **Hadstock** in Essex has a salient crossing with plinths of four decreasing stages (fig. 99).[19] This arrangement is very like that at Stow, datable to the second quarter of the eleventh century, but a similarly early date is difficult to argue for Hadstock because the edges of the imposts are decorated, not with a chamfer, but with a roll, suggesting a date no earlier than the third quarter. Some of the features of these responds also occur on the doorway in the north wall of the nave, which is a veritable compendium of forms. A stripwork hood-moulding of Anglo-Saxon vintage encloses an arch with an angle roll of Norman derivation (fig. 100). The jambs are decorated with nook-shafts, a feature used around 1060 at Kirkdale and also of Norman derivation, while the

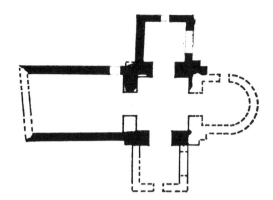

99 Hadstock (Essex), St
Botolph, *c.* 1050–80.
Plan, 1:400 (Rodwell,
1976)

100 Hadstock (Essex), St
Botolph, *c.* 1050–80.
Doorway in north wall of
nave

capitals, though cushion-like, have a facetted quality which sets them apart from those of Canterbury and Exeter. The roll is also applied in rather gross fashion to the imposts, in a way reminiscent of the imposts on the chancel arch at Worth, and finally the palmette decoration on the imposts and capitals can be compared with that on the twelfth-century west doorway of Leominster Priory.

The lower 60 ft (18.3 m) of the impressive western tower at **Clapham** in Bedfordshire is unbroken except for a western door and a number of unadorned double-splayed windows. Above this is a bell-storey, set back a few inches and provided with recessed and dressed double bell-openings. Ever since Rickman in the early nineteenth century, this tower and that at Barton-on-Humber have been seen as undocumented but nonetheless primary evidence for work of an Anglo-Saxon date, because in both a Norman bell-storey appeared to be a later addition to an earlier and, therefore, Anglo-Saxon, base. At Barton-on-Humber there is no doubt that the upper bell-storey belongs to a separate phase of building, but at Clapham examination made possible by scaffolding erected during a recent restoration has revealed that there is no break at all between the masonry of the topmost storey and the rest.[20] With the wisdom of hindsight one can point to a major flaw in the original view, namely that if the top storey had been a later addition then, unlike at Barton-on-Humber, there would have been no bell openings in the earlier tower. To judge from the capitals in the topmost storey, some of which have small heads in place of volutes, the work belongs in the late eleventh century if not the twelfth, a date which then applies to the double-splayed windows as well as to everything else in the structure.

It would be a mistake if this re-assessment were to lead to the straight removal of Clapham tower from a position of any relevance to the history of Anglo-Saxon architecture. It is no longer Anglo-Saxon, that is true, but in its new light it becomes a significant member of that school of minor churches, inhabiting the hundred years from the second quarter of the eleventh century to the second quarter of the twelfth, which is neither simply 'Saxon' nor simply 'Norman'. Other buildings which belong in this category are legion, including (apart from those like Wittering, Hales and Attleborough already mentioned in connection with profiles, double-splayed windows and crossing chambers), places like Bosham, Langford, Ickleton, North and South Elmham, Kirk Hammerton (with a south doorway flanked by stripwork and a west doorway by nook-shafts), Weaverthorpe, and almost all the Lincolnshire and Northumbrian towers.[21] Indeed it is probably true to say that half, if not the majority, of the surviving buildings commonly grouped under the label 'Anglo-Saxon' belong in this category.

The Taylors' catalogue contains just over 400 entries, of which they attribute about 320 to period C (950–1100), and in turn no fewer than 178 to C3 (1050–1100) and the small Saxo-Norman category. Many of the 320 are not attributed to phase 1, 2 or 3 within period C and hence could on investigation be dated to C3, as has been done here with Hadstock for instance, while in other cases attributions to periods A and B can be challenged and altered to C3 or beyond, as has happened with South Elmham, increasing still further the proportion of buildings in the latest category.[22] It is here, rather than in the years before 1066 (or 1050) that the material collected in volumes I and II of the Taylors' study can be usefully subjected to statistical treatment, and the tools developed in volume III utilized to greatest effect.

In its treatment of ecclesiastical architecture the present volume is in effect an attempt to clear the ground and to define groups of related monuments, or at least problems. Thus only those buildings with very sound dating arguments for the early period have been considered in chapters three, four and five (see map, fig. 12), and the same process of winnowing has been applied to the tenth and eleventh centuries so that chapters seven to ten only deal with buildings either known to be earlier than 1066 or almost certainly earlier. What is left over after this exercise defines the area of a different problem, namely the school of minor church building between the third quarter of the eleventh century and the third quarter of the twelfth (see p. 178). A dynastic definition of the contents of the book was in part decided upon to avoid having to face this huge project here, which it is hoped will be dealt with elsewhere.[23]

The positive effects of the Anglo-Saxon tradition are not restricted to minor buildings since, as we have already seen with regard to profiles, many of the features which differentiate Anglo-Norman Romanesque architecture from contemporary work in Normandy are directly attributable to the development of earlier indigenous forms. Clapham long ago called attention to the possibility that the western towers in the Anglo-Norman churches at Winchester, Ely and Bury could have been derived from their Saxon predecessors. Similarly, Bony has gone so far as to suggest that the architect of Durham Cathedral was an Anglo-Saxon because the sculptural quality of the design is inexplicable in a strictly Norman context, while Zarnecki has demonstrated the Anglo-Saxon origins of the revival of sculpture in the late eleventh century.[24]

To these examples may be added the particularly subtle treatment of the crossing in many Anglo-Norman buildings. At St Albans and Durham, for instance, with a transept wider than the nave, the piers of the crossing are asymmetrically designed with the east-west responds longer than those to north and south, with the result that all four openings end up the same size. At Durham, in addition, each extra section of wall on the east-west responds is decorated with a half-shaft which picks up the rhythm of the shafts on the soffit faces of the jambs of the openings leading off east and west, and causes the eye to move more easily along this axis than along the other. Nothing like this happens at Bernay, Jumièges or St-Etienne at Caen, but it is of course an important feature at Great Paxton, while the placing of the half-shaft on the face of the respond is itself entirely Anglo-Saxon in origin. The unusual design of the nave piers at Great Paxton also crops up during the twelfth century in the naves of churches like Rochester and Kirkstall. It is of course possible that the links between these forms are not direct, but due to the fact that Great Paxton, Durham and Rochester lie, like Reims, on the periphery of Lotharingia (fig. 39). In the same way, in chapter seven Deerhurst and Winchester were related to Celles and St Pantaleon in Cologne, among other churches with dwarf transepts and western forebuildings (figs 54, 55), while the spiral columns and piers at Repton, Durham and Canterbury can be related to those Lotharingian experiments at Utrecht and Deventer (figs 63, 66).

The vigorous development of Anglo-Saxon forms is also evident in the relationship between complex stripwork such as that of Strethall in the late eleventh century and the forms of twelfth-century responds at Castle Acre and again at Kirkstall or between the nave piers of Great Paxton and those of the thirteenth century at St Benet's in Cambridge (figs 78, 1). A hood-moulding on the exterior of a building may perform the function of a dripstone in protecting the masonry of the openings below it, but on the interior it can only be decorative. It is therefore significant that interior hood-mouldings are the rule in Anglo-Saxon and Anglo-Norman buildings but the exception on the Continent.[25] Lanfranc's cathedral at Canterbury, despite its use of cushion capitals, owed a great deal to his previous church, St-Etienne in Caen, yet its north-western tower, which survived until the nineteenth century, rose with a set-back at each new storey, unlike the western towers at Caen but comparable to that at Earls Barton.

The development of Saxon motifs beyond the Anglo-Norman period, sometimes as an accepted part of the architectural language available and sometimes as a conscious revival, is more tendentious but still arguable. Thus a number of the capital, base and moulding forms of early English Gothic have been compared to Saxon forerunners like, again, the bulbous capitals or the bases resembling Pontefract cakes on the piers at Great Paxton, or the base mouldings of the porticus arches at Britford. Beyond even this, the rectangular east end and prominent western tower are as much characteristic of the late medieval parish church as they are of the late Saxon period. This however, is moving too far into the realms of speculation, and so to conclude we can return to the late eleventh century and note that at Canterbury, whereas Lanfranc, like most of the first generation of builders after the Conquest, swept away the standing Anglo-Saxon church and replaced it with a unitary structure, already by 1096 Anselm, Lanfranc's successor, reverted to the piecemeal Anglo-Saxon approach and enlarged the east end, even though the enlargement was as big as the church to which it was an addition. Again, after the fire of 1174 the east end was remodelled and extended rather than rebuilt, and even then the monks bewailed the fact that so much of the old building had to be destroyed. In the light of all this it becomes possible to ask, not 'How long did the influence of Anglo-Saxon England survive the Norman Conquest?' but rather, how long did that of Normandy do so?

CONCLUSION

At this point it is appropriate to ask what, if anything, unifies the six centuries of Anglo-Saxon architecture. Is there any common feature other than the Anglo-Saxon identity of the people who built Yeavering and Bradford-on-Avon, or West Stow and Stow? The question is complicated by the fact that dealing with secular and ecclesiastical architecture together in one volume has underlined the great divide between them, or at least between the timber and masonry traditions, making any affirmative answer appear extremely unlikely.

Yet if there is a positive reply, even if it goes only a little way towards bridging this gap, it is to be found in the attitudes of the English towards Rome. It is easy to picture the Anglo-Saxons as in some sense representing an opposing principle to the Romans: barbarians who did not even enter their final home while it was still under Roman rule, and hence had to learn all their civilization the hard way, at one remove, whose approach to the solving of problems, to social organisation and to building was the antithesis of that of the Romans, and who valued the individual above institutional and administrative order. But this remnant of classicist-romanticist dualism is, if not entirely erroneous, at least seriously misleading.

Regardless of how they were prepared for it, the Anglo-Saxons took to Christianity and the Roman order which accompanied it as quickly as the Franks, Goths and Langobards, while their understanding of governmental efficiency was in no way inferior to that of most of the Continent, until by the tenth century the royal house of Alfred was a model for western Europe.

In order to illustrate the links with Rome, both in terms of continuity within Britain and of contemporary influences from outside, what follows is an examination of place-names, tribal and personal names and terms of rank, allusions in poems to secular buildings and in particular towns, and finally of the Church as an agent first of Romanisation and then of continuity.

Before the Anglo-Saxons left the Continent they had had more than a little contact with the Romans. The boundary of the Empire, of *Germania Inferior*, extended beyond the Rhine to the southern edge of Friesland, Roman power penetrated beyond the Weser and organised trade as far away as Denmark, and Tacitus, in the first century AD, wrote an account of the Germans including comments on the coastal lands between the Rhine and the Elbe, the area populated by the Frisians and the Saxons. An indication of the extent of this contact is provided by the place-name element -wick or -wich, the Anglo-Saxon *wic* which is supposed to be a loan word from the Latin *vicus*, acquired before the Saxons arrived in Britain.

Equally, on this side of the Channel the survival of Celtic and Roman names indicates a strong degree of continuity between the fourth century and the seventh. It is only in Sussex that Celtic place-names are completely lacking, which suggests that the slaughter of the conquered peoples recorded in the Anglo-Saxon Chronicle only gives an accurate picture for a small part of the country. Outside Sussex for instance almost all the river names are Celtic (or at least not Anglo-Saxon), like Caesar's *Tamesis* and *Sabrina* and Ptolemy's *Tava* for the Thames, the Severn and the Tay, while even the Isle of Wight, in close proximity to Sussex, derives its name from a Celtic form known as *Vectis* in Latin. Similarly, although most of the smaller settlements have Anglo-Saxon or Viking names, more than three-quarters of the recorded town names of pre-Saxon Britain survive today, as with for example London, Lincoln, York and Gloucester, the last being *Glevum* plus *ceaster*, an Anglo-Saxon term itself derived from *castra*.[1]

Tribal names are more equivocal in that only three of the 21 existing in Celtic Britain have passed over into English, namely those of the Dumnonii (or is it the Dobunii?), the Cornovii and the Cantiaci, as Devon, Cornwall and Kent. The first two, lying in the extreme west, are not surprising, but by the same token the survival of the name of the Cantiaci is particularly impressive. Mixed sources for aristocratic names are equally unexpected but not at all uncommon. Caedwalla, a seventh-century king of Wessex, traced his descent from the Anglo-Saxon Cerdic, yet his name is an anglicized version of the British 'Cadwallan', and even 'Cerdic' is thought to be Welsh in origin. Rulers styled themselves kings of Britannia and used the title *Bretwalda*, consisting of *Bret* for Britain or Briton and *walda* from the Anglo-Saxon *wealdan*, to rule, and hence meaning 'Ruler of Britain'. Lastly the missionary brothers Cedd and Chadd with their Celtic appellations were nonetheless Englishmen, and Caedmon, the first English poet, had an equally British name.[2]

In other words, not only the peoples over whom they ruled but the Anglo-Saxon ruling houses themselves were distinctly diverse. We have the whole spectrum of concentrations from a completely Germanic settlement in Sussex, through mixed peoples and rulers in most of the southern part of the country, to an Anglo-Saxon upper class ruling a Celtic populace in Northumbria.

So much for the evidence to be had from names. The romantic notion of the Germanic invaders of Britain as awe-struck barbarians confronted by the artifacts of an alien and overpowering culture rests to a large extent on the seventh- or eighth-century poem called *The Ruin* which describes decaying stone cities as the work of giants, including such phrases as

The city buildings crumble, ... hoar frost clings to the mortar ... The architect conceived a remarkable plan: ingenious and resolute, he bound the foundations with metal rods into linking rings. The city halls were beautiful, the bath-houses plentiful ... Over the redstone arch the roof framework is a skeleton, untiled ... Stone houses stood here, and a hot spring gushed from the earth ... That city was a noble place.[3]

The references to arches, stone houses and baths make it certain that Roman remains form the subject, yet there is no need to see in these lines anything more than the elegaic emotion evoked by ruins in most ages, the image of fallen greatness made sharper by the portrayal of the builders as giants. The author, far from speaking for the whole of his people, appears, like a citizen of the nineteenth century, to be savouring the melancholy power of the monuments by dramatizing them in his imagination.[4] Indeed the mundane nature of some of the details suggests an intimate knowledge rather than distant wonder, with references to metal clamps and frost in the mortar which reveal a technologist in the poet. In addition, the poem *Andreas*, which makes no reference to giants, speaks in matter-of-fact terms of the 'stone-adorned streets within the city' and of mighty pillars and standing columns, while the remains of certain types of wooden structures found in towns of the fourth century indicate the presence of Germanic mercenaries in a Roman context.

Thus even though there is little or no support for the continuous life of cities between the fifth century and the eighth, there is incontrovertible evidence for their continued existence as places, inhabited by Anglo-Saxons, among others. Bede describes how Cuthbert on a visit to Carlisle in 685 was conducted round the walls of the city, which were 'built in a wonderful manner by the Romans', thereby acknowledging the citizens' easy yet appreciative familiarity with the Roman past.[5] He numbers the emperors from Augustus to his own time, explains the varying lengths of the day during the year in terms of a spherical world with poles, gives an account of the Romans in Britain which is entirely matter-of-fact and records the dimensions of Hadrian's Wall, just as if he were a citizen of late Antiquity like Isidore of Seville, except that he is somewhat better informed (*HE*, 1, 23, 1, 12, 3–11).

There is also reason to believe that *The Ruin* has a Christian content, the work of giants paralleling the Tower of Babel and illustrating the destructive consequences of pride, and it is of course the case that Christianity (at least of the non-Celtic kind)[6] meant Latin culture. Gregory's intention that two metropolitans should be re-established at the Roman centres of London and York is a direct indication of this. In the event it proved over-optimistic since Augustine, confronted with the bellicose intractability of the East Saxons and not being cast in the heroic mould, preferred the status quo of success at Canterbury to the imponderables of a spiritual assault on the old capital. On the next echelon down, however, the consistency is impressive, with the majority of sees established in the seventh century being associated with Roman sites, as at Rochester, Winchester, Dorchester, Leicester, Worcester, York and probably Felixstowe, while missionaries acquired Roman forts at Reculver, Bradwell-on-Sea and Burgh Castle, among others. Few of these proselytizers would have been so foolish as to set themselves up in places shunned by those they wished to convert, and their success proves that they did not do so. Roman Christianity may have been southern and urban, but it did not for that reason find itself at odds with the Anglo-Saxons.

This thesis is supported not only by the well-attested Roman sources of early Anglo-Saxon ecclesiastical architecture, whether these were acquired locally, or direct from Italy or via Gaul, but also by the surprising degree of continuity evident in this type of building from the seventh century to the eleventh. This is so despite the far-reaching changes introduced after the Danish invasions, and may be explained by a basic conservatism which shows itself in the Anglo-Saxon preference for piecemeal addition, rather than demolition and rebuilding. Thus many a builder working in the eleventh century did so in direct contact with a piece of seventh- or eighth-century fabric, a fact which might help to explain the survival of the Roman element right up to the coming of the Normans. This continuity can be illustrated by a comparison of arches, plans and slabs.

The seventh-century chancel arch at Escomb and the small arch in the eleventh-century north transept at Stow both have tall proportions, through-stone jambs laid Escomb-fashion, a stepped extrados and arches springing from chamfered imposts (figs 29, 72); Despite the absence of a plinth at Escomb and the use of non-radial voussoirs at Stow, the similarity across three and a half centuries is remarkable. Over an even longer period, the arches at Worth with their thin through-stone voussoirs are almost indistinguishable from those of the Roman Newport Gate at Lincoln, just as miniature arches on the Romano-British chimney pots resemble the hood-mouldings and imposts of Anglo-Saxon arches such as those at Barnack or Barton-on-Humber.[7] The same similarity between the earliest and the latest Anglo-Saxon buildings is evident in plans, Escomb and Kirk Hammerton for instance having a great deal in common, in which regard it is ironic that one of the handful of dated Anglo-Saxon buildings, Odda's Chapel at Deerhurst, should have such an ageless form.

The Anglo-Saxons were impressed enough by Roman methods of construction to adopt the technique of using large, unwieldy blocks of stone, such as those forming the lower courses of the eastern quoins at Escomb, the imposts of the tower arch at Barnack, or the 4 ft (1.2 m) square slabs of the responds at Great Paxton. The burden of manhandling these objects is one which any Norman mason would have avoided at all costs, and as there is no great advantage to be had from it, and the Anglo-Saxons seem to have imposed it on themselves through choice rather than incompetence, it can be seen as the result of an admiration for the work of people whom they saw as giants among builders.

This traditionalist character in the architecture is no doubt in part responsible for the distinction commonly drawn between the Anglo-Saxon period on the one hand and what is sometimes called the medieval period on the other. Yet such a formulation overstates the significance of the Conquest, both because Anglo-Saxon architecture was up-to-date and inventive as well as traditionalist, and because the starting of the Middle Ages only after 1066 is so at variance with the pattern applied to the rest of Europe. There the date at which Antiquity ends and the Middle Ages begin is placed between the fourth century and the eighth. The earlier bracket is marked by the public advent of Christianity (the strongest unifying force of the whole period however it is defined), and the later one by, according to one view the destruction of the infrastructure of the Roman Empire through the expansion of Islam, forcing northern Europe to look to its own resources.

Anglo-Saxon England belonged at first to the Germanic world, became part of the Roman one in the sixth and seventh centuries and, in the course of the eighth and ninth, along with the rest of Europe entered the Middle Ages. The buildings and the society of tenth- and eleventh-century England are as much medieval as those of Capetian France, and a dramatic separation of past from future at the Conquest only serves to perpetuate an image of Anglo-Saxon architecture as insular and entirely backward-looking, a view which, as I hope this book has shown, is by no means the whole story.

APPENDIX

Anglo-Saxon and Saxo-Norman churches with material remains, listed by period*

1 Pre-Danish

Seventh or early Eighth Century

Bradwell-on-Sea
Bywell, St Peter
Canterbury, St
    Martin
Canterbury, St Mary
Canterbury,
    St Pancras
Canterbury, SS Peter
    and Paul
Corbridge (?)
Escomb
Glastonbury I
Hexham
Jarrow

Ledsham
Lyminge
Minster-in-Sheppey
Monkwearmouth
Reculver
Ripon
Rochester
Seaham
Winchester, Old
    Minster I

Late Eighth or Ninth Century

Brixworth
Cirencester

Deerhurst, St Mary I
Wing

2 Pre- or Post-Danish

Bishopstone
Heysham, St Patrick
London, All Hallows

Muchelney
Titchfield
Wareham, St Mary

3 Post-Danish

Tenth Century

Britford (?)
Deerhurst, St Mary II
Glastonbury II
Gloucester, St Oswald
Greensted (?)
North Elmham,
    wooden cathedral

Peterborough
Potterne
Repton
Tredington (?)
Winchester, New
    Minster
Winchester, Old
    Minster II

First Half of the Eleventh Century

Barnack
Barton-on-Humber
Bradford-on-Avon
Breamore
Brigstock
Deerhurst, St Mary
    III

Dover
Earls Barton
Norton
Wooton Wawen
Worth

4 Second Quarter of the Eleventh Century to the Early Twelfth Century

Attleborough
Bosham
Broughton
Cambridge, St Benet
Canterbury, St
    Augustine
Clapham
Clayton
Coln Rogers
Deerhurst, Odda's
    Chapel
Diddlebury
Dunham Magna
Dymock
Gloucester, St Peter (?)
Great Paxton
Hadstock
Hales
Ickleton
Kirkdale
Kirk Hammerton
Langford
Little Saxham
Lympne
Melbourne
Melton Constable

Milborne Port
Netheravon
Newton-by-Castle-
    Acre
North Elmham, ruined
    stone church
Norwich, St John
    Timberhill
Oulton
Roughton
St Andrews, St Rule's
    Tower
Sherborne
Sompting
South Elmham
South Lopham
Stanton Lacy
Stow
Strethall
Titchborne
Wareham, St Martin
Weaverthorpe
Westminster
Wharram-le-Street
Wimborne Minster
Winchester, Castle
    chapel
Wittering

* These four lists only contain the names of buildings
mentioned in this book. See pp. 171–2.

GLOSSARY

AMBULATORY: curved aisle forming a full circle or a semi-circle (figs 92, 93).

ANGLE ROLL: three-quarter cylinder set on the leading edge of an arch (figs 89c, 97).

BASILICA: in *modern usage*, a building, normally on a large scale, formed of a central hall flanked on each side by a subsidiary structure of similar length, with the central space taller than the flanking parts, and lit by windows set on the wall above them (figs 40, 78). Latin *basilica*, in *ancient and early medieval usage*, means a meeting hall of any size or shape.

BROACHED: describes the surface of a masonry block worked with deep, parallel gashes (fig. 29).

COLUMN: in *modern usage*, a supporting member of cylindrical form (fig. 41), as opposed to a pier of rectangular section. Latin *colum (p)na*, in *pre-modern usage*, means a support, whether a column, a pier, or a buttress.

CROSSING: area created by the intersection of the walls of the nave and transept arms (fig. 43).

CRYPT: chamber, usually vaulted, lying under or beyond a sanctuary; need not be below ground level. RING CRYPT: vaulted passage under a sanctuary following the curve of the inside face of the apse (fig. 40). OUTER CRYPT: vaulted structure subsidiary to the sanctuary but lying outside the apse wall (fig. 33).

DRAFTED: chiselled finish in the form of a strip on a block of masonry.

HOOD-MOULDING: moulding following the curve of an arch (figs 80, 82).

LANTERN TOWER: tower, usually over a crossing, with a ceiling high enough to permit daylight into the interior of a church (fig. 43).

LONG-AND-SHORT WORK: stones of alternately tall and flat, slab-like proportions, laid to form a corner or pilaster (fig. 79).

NOOK-SHAFT: shaft in a nook or rebate normally flanking an opening (figs 95, 100).

OPUS SIGNINUM: hard-wearing surface of crushed brick.

ORDER: a smaller form applied to a larger, creating a stepped profile, as in an arch with two orders (fig. 78). Not to be confused with a type of elevation, as in 'the Greek orders'.

PILASTER: member of rectangular section attached to a wall (fig. 86).

PIER: free-standing support with rectangular section (fig. 55) (see also COLUMN). COMPOUND PIER: one with features added to the core, forming cruciform, lobed and other sections (figs 56d, 78).

PORTICUS: room of variable size and function attached to a church; Latin *porticus*, fourth declension, singular and plural (figs 13, 15, 20).

QUIRK: sharp inset between two other parts of a profile (fig. 94a).

QUOIN: external angle of a corner, or one of the cut stones forming such a corner (fig. 79).

SOFFIT: the under-side of an arch, hence 'soffit roll' (figs 45, 46, 89).

STRINGCOURSE: horizontal course of masonry standing proud of the wall surface (figs 63, 79).

STRIPWORK: strips of masonry decorating any part of a building (figs 79, 84). Taylor, iii, 1978, pp. 915–38, restricts the term to strips around openings such as doorways, using 'pilaster strips' for other forms.

THROUGH-STONE: stone extending the full thickness of a wall, especially on the jambs or soffit of an arch (figs 80, 90).

VOUSSOIR: one of the blocks forming an arch, often wedge-shaped (figs 80, 96).

WESTWORK: a large, centralised structure of the Carolingian period, with a crypt, first-floor platform, galleries and towers, set at the west end of a church. Sometimes used in a less specific sense for any more or less ambitious construction in this position (figs 52, 50).

ABBREVIATIONS

Ant. J.	*Antiquaries Journal*
Arch. J.	*Archaeological Journal*
ASC	*Anglo-Saxon Chronicle*
BAA	*British Archaeological Association*
BAR	*British Archaeological Reports*
CBA	*Council for British Archaeology*
HE	*Bede's Ecclesiastical History of the English People*
JBAA	*Journal of the British Archaeological Association*
Med. Arch.	*Medieval Archaeology*
RS	Rolls Series

NOTES

Reference to the appropriate entry in Taylor and Taylor, 1965, is assumed in all notes on individual Anglo-Saxon churches.

Introduction
1. The description is that of A.L. Rowse, 1944. Even Baldwin Brown, p. vi, reminds himself that behind the beauties of the English village lie 'Anglo-Saxon crudities'.
2. M. Hunter, *Proceedings of the Cambridge Antiquarian Society*, 66, 1975–6, p. 138, n. 43.

1 Halls, Houses and Palaces
1. A.E. van Giffen, *Germania*, 20, 1936, pp. 40–6; B. Hope-Taylor, *Yeavering, An Anglo-British Centre of Early Northumbria*, London, 1977, figs 97–100. For the pre-historic material in general see B. Trier, *Das Haus in Nordwesten der Germania Libera*, Münster, 1969; W. Horn and E. Born, *The Plan of St Gall*, Los Angeles, 1979, ii, pp. 23–75; A. Zippelius, *Bonner Jahrbücher*, 153, 1953, pp. 13–45; W. Sage, in *Karl der Grosse*, ed. W. Braunfels, iii, *Karolingische Kunst*, Düsseldorf, 1965, iii, pp. 573–90.
1a. M. Welch, in P. Brandon, ed., *The South Saxons*, London, 1978, p. 21.
2. *Monumenta Germaniae Historica*, AA, iv, part I, p. 219. J. Strzygowski, *Early Church Art in Northern Europe*, London, 1928, p. 84.
3. E.T. Leeds, *Archaeologia*, 73, 1923, pp. 147–92, and 92, 1947, pp. 79–93.
4. S.E. West, *Med. Arch.*, 13, 1969, pp. 1–21.
5. P.V. Addyman and D. Leigh, *Med. Arch.*, 16, 1972, pp. 13 ff; 17, 1973, pp. 1–25.
6. B. Hope-Taylor, op. cit.
7. R. Cramp, *Med. Arch.*, 1, 1957, pp. 73–6.
8. G. Bersu, *Germania*, 20, 1936, p. 229; Sage, op. cit., pp. 576 and 589; Cramp, op. cit., p. 68. The ninth-, tenth- or eleventh-century church at Greensted (Essex) may be the earliest standing example.
9. F.H. Thompson, *Archaeologia*, 105, 1975, pp. 134–40.

10. Whitelock, 1979, no. 129, pp. 594–6. For the continental material see J. Gardalles, *Cahiers de Civilisation Médiévale*, 19, 1976, pp. 115–34.
11. P. Rahtz, *The Saxon and Medieval Palaces at Cheddar*, (*BAR* 65), 1979.
12. H. Schmidt, *Med. Arch.*, 17, 1973, pp. 55–60; T. Capelle, *Frühmittelalterliche Studien*, 3, 1969, pp. 244–56; P. Holdsworth, *Med. Arch.*, 20, 1976, pp. 36–9; Addyman, 1972, pp. 282, 289 and 300.
13. Whitelock, 1979, no. 7, pp. 293 and 298.

2 Towns and Fortifications
1. M. Barley, ed., *European Towns*, CBA, London, 1977; Biddle, in Wilson, 1976.
2. J.S. Wacher, *The Towns of Roman Britain*, Batsford, 1979. M. Biddle, in M. W. Barley, ed., *The Evolution of Towns*, CBA, Research Report 14, 1975, pp. 19–32.
3. D. Hill, *Med. Arch.*, 13, 1969, pp. 84–92.
3a. M. Biddle and D. Hill, *Arch. J.* 51, 1971, pp. 73–8; Biddle, op. cit., 1975, pp. 21–7, and Biddle, in Wilson, 1976, pp. 129–134.
4. *Med. Arch.*, 3, 1959, pp. 120–38; C.A.R. Radford, *Med. Arch.*, 14, 1970, pp. 85 and 87.
4a. J. B. Ward-Perkins, *Cities of Ancient Greece and Italy*, New York, 1974, passim and figs 22–72. J. S. Wacher, *The Civitas Capitals of Roman Britain*, Leicester, 1966. Biddle, op. cit., 1971, p. 71 and 1975, pp. 27 and 31. O. A. Dilke, *The Roman Land Surveyors*, Newton Abbot, 1971.
5. P. Wade-Martins, *Excavations in North Elmham Park, 1967–1972*, Norfolk Archaeological Unit, Gressenhall 1980, pp. 125 ff. M. Welch, op. cit., p. 22; Horn and Born, op. cit., 1979, i, pp. 223–4 and ii, passim.
6. Whitelock, 1979, no. 7, p. 298, and no. 99, pp. 540–1.
7. Re the *burh* see W. Levison, *England and the Continent in the Eighth Century*, Oxford, 1946, and R. Allen Brown, *Arch. J.*, 126, 1969, pp. 140–4.
8. Whitelock, 1979, no. 7, p. 299.
9. J.M. Hassall and D. Hill, *Arch. J.*, 127, 1970, pp. 188–92.

10. N. Brooks, in P. Clemoes and K. Hughes, ed., *England Before the Conquest*, Cambridge, 1971, pp. 69–84.

11. C. Fox, *Offa's Dyke*, London, 1955.

3 Church Building in the Kingdoms of Kent, Essex and Wessex

1. S.E. Rigold, *JBAA* (3), 24, 1961, pp. 55–9, and 37, 1974, pp. 97–102.

2. C.R. Peers, *Archaeologia*, 77, 1927, pp. 241–55; H.M. Taylor, *Arch. J.*, 125, 1968, pp. 291–6, and 126, 1969, pp. 225–7; S.E. Rigold, in D. Johnston, ed., *The Saxon Shore*, CBA, Research Report 18, 1977, p. 73a.

2a. See pp. 41–2.

3. A.D. Saunders, *Med. Arch.*, 22, 1978, pp. 25–63.

4. See Clapham, 1930, p. 42, and Taylor and Taylor, 1965, i, pp. 92–3, for the early date and Baldwin Brown, 1925, p. 102, and Rigold, op. cit., 1977, pp. 72–3, for the later.

5. F. Jenkins, *Med. Arch.*, 9, 1965, pp. 11–15.

6. E. Fletcher and G. Meates, *Ant. J.*, 49, 1969, pp. 282–4; H.M. Taylor and D.D. Yonge, *Arch. J.*, 138, 1981, pp. 118–45.

7. H.M. Taylor, *Arch. J.*, 126, 1969, pp. 257–60.

8. M. Biddle, *Ant. J.*, 48, 1968, pp. 270–80, and 50, 1970, pp. 314–21. B. Kjølbe-Biddle, *World Archaeology*, 7, 1975–6, p. 93, reconstructs an apse over the rectangular substructure of the eastern porticus. B.A. Yorke, *Procs. Hants. Field Club*, 38, 1982, pp. 75–8, proposes that the church was founded in the 660s. For the palace see M. Biddle in Parsons, ed., 1975, p. 125.

9. C.A.R. Radford, in *Medieval Art and Architecture at Wells and Glastonbury*, BAA, 1981, pp. 116–18.

10. F. Oswald, *Frühmittelalterliche Studien*, 1, 1967, p. 157; Oswald, 1966, Trier, St Maria in ripa.

11. M. Deansley, *Trans. Royal Historical Society*, 23, 1941, pp. 25–69; Radford, 1973, p. 120.

11a. See p. 63.

12. H.M. Taylor, in *Anglo-Saxon England*, 3, 1974, pp. 163–74; ibid *Ant. J.*, 53, 1973, pp. 52–8; F. Oswald, *Frühmittelalterliche Studien*, 3, 1969, pp. 313–26.

13. Krautheimer, 1975, figs 152–3.

14. Ep. 32, 13. See C. Davis-Weyer, *Early Medieval Art 300–1150* (Sources and Documents), Englewood-Cliffs, 1971, p. 21.

15. A. Grabar, *Martyrium*, 2 vols., Paris, 1946, passim; F. Deichmann, *Mitteilungen des deutschen archäologischen Instituts. Römische Abteilung*, 77, 1970, pp. 144–69; and R. Krautheimer, *Corpus Basilicarum Romae*, 5 vols, Vatican City, 1937–77, for cemetery basilicas such as San Lorenzo (with which St Peter's should probably be numbered).

16. Grabar, op. cit., i, p. 550.

17. See also, however, ii, 3. C. Thomas, *Early Christian Archaeology of North Britain*, Glasgow, 1971, chapters 3–6.

18. S.S. Frere, *Archaeologia*, 105, 1975, pp. 277–302.

19. S.E. Rigold, *JBAA* (3), 31, 1968, pp. 27 and 31.

20. W. Levison, *England and the Continent in the Eighth Century*, Oxford, 1946, p. 34, chapter 4, and Appendix i; Knowles, 1966, pp. 547–9; Knowles, 1971, p. 9; Rigold, op. cit., 1968, p. 31. On Frankish buildings see E. James, *The Merovingian Archaeology of South-West Gaul*, BAR, S–25, i, Oxford, 1977, chapter 8 and in H.B. Clarke and M. Brennan, *Columbanus and Merovingian Monasticism*, BAR, S–113, 1981, pp. 33–55.

21. See L. Blondel, in *Frühmittelalterliche Kunst in den Alpenlöndern*, Lausanne, 1954, pp. 271–307.

4 Church Building in the Kingdom of Northumbria

1. Cramp and Rahtz, in Wilson, 1976, pp. 223–9, and appendices B and C.

2. R. Cramp, *Arch. J.*, 133, 1976, pp. 230–7, and in Wilson, 1976, pp. 229–34.

3. R. Cramp, *Arch. J.*, 133, 1976, pp. 220–5.

4. J. Higgitt, *Ant. J.*, 59, 1979, pp. 343–4.

5. Cramp, in Wilson, 1976, pp. 234–41, and *Arch. J.*, 133, 1976, pp. 224–5.

6. Horn, 1973, pp. 34–5.

7. Clapham, 1930, p. 42; Taylor, iii, 1978, p. 1062.

8. Baldwin Brown, 1925, pp. 53 and 139–40, and figs 25, 26, 30 and 64B. See also Asser's description of Alfred's building activities, p. 22.

9. 13.24 and 13.19 m = average 13.22; 13.22 ÷ 3 = 4.40; 4.40 ÷ root 2 = 3.11 m. For other uses of this proportion see p. 148 and p. 155 n. 2.

10. M. Pocock and H. Wheeler, *JBAA* (3), 34, 1971, pp. 11–21.

11. *Historia Abbatum*, cap. 5, in C. Plummer, ed., *Venerabilis Bedae Opera Historica*, Oxford, 1896, I, p. 368.

12. R. Cramp, in *Famulus Christi*, ed. G. Bonner, London, 1976, pp. 11–12, and *Early Northumbrian Sculpture*, 1965, p. 4 and fig. 3.

13. Krautheimer, 1975, fig. 138.

14. Oswald, 1966: Kapellenfleck.

15. W. Levison, op. cit., 1946, pp. 77 and 92.

16. Oswald, 1966: Büraberg, Regensburg and Pier.

17. See M. J. O'Kelly and D.B. Hague in *Scottish Archaeological Forum*, 5, 1974, pp. 1–35, for numerous, though undated, chapels in Ireland and Wales of the same two-cell type as Escomb.

18. This description and the plan in fig. 31 are based, with some minor variations, on R.N. Bailey and D. O'Sullivan, *Archaeologia Aeliana*, fifth series, 7, 1979, pp. 144–57, and E. Cambridge, ibid., pp. 158–68. These articles propose a dramatic reduction in the amount of masonry previously accepted as Saxon.

19. B. Colgrave, ed., *The Life of Bishop Wilfrid by Eddius*, Cambridge, 1927, cap. 22. The translation is

Colgrave's, except for the phrase 'carried by various supports'. See glossary: COLUMN.

20. J. Raine, *The Priory of Hexham*, I, 1864, p. 12: *Parietes autem quadratis, et variis, et bene politis columpnis suffultos, et tribus tabulatis distinctos, immense longitudinis et altitudinis, erexit. . . . In ipsis vero cocleis, et super ipsas ascensoria ex lapide, et deambulatoria, et varios viarum anfractus, modo deorsum, artificiosissime ita machinari fecit, ut innumera hominum multitudo ibi existere, et ipsum corpus ecclesiae circumdare possit, cum a nemine tamen infra in eum existentium videri queat.* Baldwin Brown, p. 152, translates *Parietes . . . suffultos* as 'walls of squared stone . . . and finely polished columns,' specifically denying that it can mean 'square piers'. Against this reading, there is no word for 'stone', and *quadratis* agrees with *columpnis*.

21. R.N. Bailey, *Archaeologia Aeliana*, fifth series, 4, 1976, p. 66.

22. Raine, op. cit., pp. 14–15.

23. Krautheimer, 1975, pp. 282–4, and *Corpus Basilicarum Romae*, Vatican City, i, 1937, pp. 15 ff, and ii, 1959, pp. 1 ff.

24. F. Deshoulières, in *Mélanges en l'honneur de M. Fr. Martroye*, Paris, 1940, pp. 5–6.

25. J. Puig y Cadafalch, *L'Art Wisigothique*, Paris, 1961, pp. 34–6.

26. J. Raine, ed., *The Historians of the Church of York and its Archbishops*, RS 71, 1879, i, 394.

5 Mercia and the Anglo-Saxon Basilica

1. Whitelock, 1979, no. 81, pp. 512–13; L. Butler, P. Rahtz and H.M. Taylor, *Ant. J.*, 55, 1975, pp. 346–65; H.M. Taylor, *Deerhurst Studies*, 1977, passim.

2. E. Jackson and E. Fletcher, *JBAA* (3), 28, 1965, pp. 29–33.

3. E. Fernie, *Archaeologia*, 104, 1973, pp. 235–60.

4. Wilfrid's church at Ripon, the *Alma Sophia* at York, Canterbury Cathedral, Lady St Mary in Wareham and All Hallows in London may all have been basilicas, but too little is known of them to make them useful here.

5. D. Parsons, in *Mercian Studies*, ed. A. Dornier, 1977, pp. 173–90; ibid, *JBAA*, 133, 1980, pp. 30–6; J. Stones, *JBAA*, 133, 1980, pp. 37–63, with full bibliography to date.

6. Taylor, iii, 1978, p. 793.

7. Excavations in progress at Brixworth can be expected to produce a great deal more information on the material history of the building.

8. H.M. Taylor, *North Staffs. Journal of Field Studies*, 9, 1969, p. 38.

9. See Oswald, 1966 for Reichenau, and for Cologne Cathedral, Neustadt, St Aurelius at Hirsau, Steinbach, and Petersberg-bei-Fulda.

9a. Hubert, et al., *Carolingian Art*, London, 1970, pp. 304–5 and 365; *Congrès Archéologique*, 93, 1930

(Orléans) pp. 5–34; A. Katchatrian, *Cahiers Archéologiques*, 7, 1954, pp. 161–170 and fig. 6.

9b. R. Crozet, *Symposium Sobra la Cultura Asturiana de la Edad Media*, Oviedo, 1964, pp. 21–5. F. Lesueur, *Bulletin Monumental*, 124, 1966, pp. 178–80.

10. Parsons, *JBAA*, 133, 1980, pp. 34–5. E.C. Gilbert, *Art Bulletin*, 47, 1965, pp. 14–15, dates Brixworth between 750 and 820, but the grounds on which this view is based are unclear.

11. D. Brown and A. McWhirr, *Ant. J.*, 46, 1966, pp. 240–54, and in *Archaeology and History of Cirencester*, BAR, 30, 1976, pp. 33–59, including B. Evans, pp. 46–59.

12. Horn, 1973, p. 51, n. 57.

13. E. Jackson and E. Fletcher, *JBAA* (3), 25, 1962, pp. 1–5; H.M. Taylor, *Arch. J.*, 136, 1979, pp. 43–52.

14. *Vita Sancti Dunstani*, RS 63, 1874, c. 16, p. 271.

15. See Glossary: COLUMN.

16. Taylor, iii, 1978, p. 1042.

17. Krautheimer, 1975, chapters 2–5, and 7, and pp. 160–76 and chapter 14; Ward Perkins, 1970, fig. 86 and pl. 118.

18. E. Jackson and E. Fletcher, *JBAA* (3), 31, 1968, pp. 19–26. There is some uncertainty about the dates at which the land around Lydd was above sea level (D. Hill, *An Atlas of Anglo-Saxon England*, Blackwell, Oxford, 1981, figs 15, 21 and 253), but there is no reason to believe that it was more available to the Saxons than to the Romans. For the German buildings see Ward Perkins, 1970, figs 137 and 197.

6 Early Romanesque Architecture in Northern Europe

1a. O.M. Vieillard-Troïekouroff, *Karl der Grosse*, ed. W. Braunfels, iii, *Karolingische Kunst*, Düsseldorf, 1965, pp. 336–55. See also Fulda Abbey, in Oswald, 1966, and M. Fischer and F. Oswald, *Rheinische Ausgrabungen*, 2 (*Bonner Jahrbücher*, 26, 1968), pp. 268–80.

1b. Surveys of the whole period include K.J. Conant, *Carolingian and Romanesque Architecture 800–1200*, Harmondsworth, 1974; H.E. Kubach, *Romanesque Architecture*, New York, 1975; H. Saalman, *Medieval Architecture 600–1200*, London, 1962.

2. J. Hubert, et al., *Carolingian Art*, London, 1970, pp. 1–4 and 362–3, and figs 2 and 339–41; C. Heitz, *Architecture et Liturgie*, Paris, 1963; Heitz, 1980, pp. 54–7 and fig. 38; D, Parson, *JBAA*, 130, 1977, pp. 21–51, casts some doubt on an eighth-century date for St-Riquier as usually reconstructed.

3. On Cologne see Oswald, 1966; Heitz, 1980, pp. 87–92; J. Achter, in *Das Erste Jahrtausend*, Düsseldorf, ii, 1964, pp. 948–91; Clapham, 1930, fig. 21.

4. On outer crypts see Hubert, op. cit., pp. 50–5, 363 and figs 345–9, 354, 359; H. Claussen, in *Karolingische und Ottonische Kunst*, Wiesbaden, 1957, pp. 118–40.

5. Oswald, 1966; Grodecki, 1958.

5a. H. Beseler and H. Roggenkamp, *Die Michaelskirche in Hildesheim*, Berlin, 1954; Oswald, 1966; Grodecki, 1958, pp. 81–4 and 193–6.

5b. This account of what constitutes the Romanesque style specifically omits the vault. The great Anglo-Norman churches of the late eleventh and early twelfth centuries are without doubt fully Romanesque, yet the majority are unvaulted. Preoccupation with vaults, for instance, by Clapham, 1934, passim, has led to the exclusion of buildings which otherwise satisfy the criteria, such as St Michael's at Hildesheim, and many of the Anglo-Saxon churches discussed in Chapters 8, 9, 10 and 11.

5c. For Paderborn see Oswald, 1966; for Portofino, C. Ceschi, *Architettura Romanica Genovese*, Milan, 1954, and for Lomello, H. Thummler, *Römisches Jahrbuch*, 3, 1939, p. 141 f.

6. On Lotharingian buildings see Oswald, 1966, Genicot, 1972, Kubach, 1972, and Grodecki, 1958.

7. On Capetian France see R. de Lasteyrie, *L'Architecture Religieuse en France à l'Époque Romane*, Paris, 1929; the relevant volumes of the *Congrès Archéologique de France*; Heitz, 1980, and for documentation, J. Ottaway in *Cahiers de Civilisation Médiévale*, 23, 1980, pp. 141–72 and 221–39.

8. P-M. Brun and P. Rousseau, in R. Louis, ed., *Études Ligériennes*, Auxerre, 1975, pp. 443–9 and 454–76; *Congrès Archéologique*, 93, 1930 (Orléans), pp. 52–70; F. Lesueur, *Bulletin Monumental*, 115, 1957, pp. 169–206; *Bulletin Monumental*, 134, 1976, p. 62.

9. F. Lesueur, *Bulletin Monumental*, 89, 1930, pp. 435 ff.

10. On Normandy see Liess, 1967.

10a. Liess, 1967, pp. 167–83, pls. 14–30; L. Grodecki, *Bulletin Monumental*, 108, 1950, pp. 32 ff.

11. Liess, 1967, pp. 215–46; J. Vallery-Radot, et al., 'Colloque', *Bulletin Monumental*, 127, 1969, pp. 126–41; G. Lanfry, *L'Abbaye de Jumièges*, Rouen, 1954; R.D.H. Gem, in *Procs. of the Battle Abbey Conference*, 3, 1980, pp. 54 ff.

12. D.C. Douglas, *William the Conqueror*, London, 1969, pp. 76 and 80; Liess, 1967, pp. 183–201; E. Carlson, *Gesta*, 10, 1971, pp. 23–30.

7 From Alfred to the Monastic Revival

1. Knowles, 1971, pp. 10–11; 1966, pp. 32–6, 551–2, 695.

2. P. Grierson, *Trans. Royal Historical Society*, 23, 1941, p. 88; D. Bullough, in Parsons, 1975, p. 32, fig. 1.

3. *Gest. Pont.*, RS 52, 1870, p. 199.

4. *Medieval Latin Word List*, 1965, and Lewis and Short. See also the eighth-century *magistri comacini* as 'masters of the scaffolding' rather than 'masters from Como'. On the other hand Wulfstan, in his late tenth-century description of parts of the Old Minster at Winchester, uses *machina* for a masonry structure; see R.N. Quirk, *Arch. J.*, I, 14, 1957, p. 44., n. 2, and p. 59.

5. Concerning the possible relevance of the reliquary in Venice, there is a suggestive mention in the New Minster *Liber Vitae*, of the head of St Valentine being presented to the monastery by Emma, Cnut's wife, enclosed in a 'Greek shrine'; see R.N. Quirk, *JBAA*, (3), 24, 1961, p. 19.

6. R. Quirk, op. cit. *JBAA*, (3), 24, 1961, pp. 17–21; M. Biddle, *Ant. J.*, 49, 1969, pp. 313 ff; ibid. in Parsons, 1975, pp. 128–36. It is possible that this plan is the result of a re-building of the 950s, or even of the 980s, when a dramatic new tower was built.

7. C. Heighway, et al., *Ant. J.*, 58, 1978, pp. 107–19; 60, 1980, pp. 207–26.

8. D.H. Farmer, in Parsons, 1975, pp. 10–19; T. Symons, in Parsons, 1975, pp. 37–59; Knowles, 1966, pp. 42–4; and, for Ethelwold, R. Quirk, op. cit. *Arch. J.*, 14, 1957, p. 29, and P. Grierson, op. cit., 1941, p. 90.

9. A. Klukas, *Altaria Superioria*, Ph.D., Pittsburg, 1978, pp. 210–66.

10. C.A.R. Radford, in *Medieval Art and Architecture at Wells and Glastonbury*, BAA, 1981, pp. 116–18; *Vita Sancti Dunstani*, RS 63, 1874, p. 271, cap. 16; *Est ibi ecclesiae ligneae, ut ante dixi, lapidea contermina, cujus auctorem Inam regem non falsa confirmat antiquitas. Hanc ille adjecta turri ad multum spatium prorogavit; et ut latitudo longitudini conquadraret, alas vel porticus quas vocant adjecit.*

11. Horn, 1973, p. 42 and C. Malone and W. Horn in Born and Born, op. cit., 1979, ii, pp. 315–56.

12. H.M. Taylor, *Arch. J.*, 126, 1969, pp. 101–30; R.D.H. Gem, *Arch. J.*, 127, 1970, pp. 196–201. For the seal see T.A. Heslop, in *Medieval Art and Architecture at Canterbury before 1220*, BAA, 1982, pp. 96–7 and pl. XXVIIB.

13. Taylor, *Arch. J.*, 1969, pp. 129 and 106, paragraphs 15 (g) and (h).

14. Taylor, loc. cit., paragraph 15 (j).

15. R.N. Quirk, *Arch. J.*, 114, 1957, pp. 28–68; M. Biddle, *Ant. J.*, 48 1968, pp. 270–80; 49, 1969, p. 316; 50, 1970, pp. 314–21.

16. C. Heitz, *Architecture et Liturgie*, Paris, 1963, pp. 151 ff.

17. Krautheimer, 1975, p. 256 and figs 296, 312 and 309.

18. R. Girard, *Congrès Archéologique*, 130, 1974 (Dauphiné), pp. 243–63.

19. W. Sanderson, *Trans. American Philosophical Society*, 61, 1971, p. 7; Klukas, op. cit., pp. 217 and 265–6.

20. L. Butler, P. Rahtz and H.M. Taylor, *Ant. J.*, 55, 1975, pp. 346–65; H.M. Taylor, in Parsons, 1975, pp. 162–8; H.M. Taylor, *Deerhurst Studies*, 1977; Knowles, 1966, pp. 52–3, and 1971, p. 64; Radford, 1973, p. 138; Whitelock, 1979, no. 235, p. 908.

21. Similar openings exist at Wing and Repton, the latter with a surviving gable.

21a. There is insufficient space in the text for setting out and supporting the more radical view that all the dressed openings in the building belong in the reign of Edward the Confessor, an argument based in particular on the close similarities between the arches of the porticus galleries and the chancel arch of Odda's Chapel of 1056.

22. Taylor, in Parsons, 1975, p. 163, including similar arrangements at Earls Barton, Barnack and Aachen.

23. Taylor in Parsons, 1975, pp. 162–3. For Tredington see Taylor, *Arch. J.*, 128, 1971, pp. 222–3.

24. Whitelock, 1979, no. 235, p. 908; for 966 see Symons, in Parsons, 1975, p. 40.

25. G. Lambrick, *Med. Arch.*, 12, 1968, pp. 42–60; M. Biddle, *Med. Arch.*, 12, 1968, pp. 60–7; *Chronicon Monasterii de Abingdon*, two vols., RS2, 1858.

26. R. Krautheimer, 'Introduction to an "iconography of medieval architecture" ', *Journal of the Warburg and Courtauld Institutes*, 5, 1942, p. 8 and passim.

27. Oswald, 1966: Muizen; Genicot, 1972, pp. 90–1; W. Kleinbauer, *Gesta*, 4, 1965, pp. 5, 10 and 11.

28. Baldwin Brown, 1925, pp. 232–3; Clapham, 1930, p. 36; Taylor, *Arch. J.*, 126, 1969, p. 118.

29. *Chron.*, ii, 272: *Monasterium Abbendoniae, quod construxit Heane primus abbas ejusdem loci tale erat:- habebat in longitudine c. et xx pedes, et erat rotundum, tam in parte occidentale quam in parte orientali. Fundatum erat hoc monasterium in loco ubi nunc est cellarium monachorum, ita quod altare stetit ubi nunc est lavatorium. In circuitu hujus monasterii erant habitacula xii et totidem capellae, et in habitaculis xii monachi ibidem manducantes et bibentes et dormientes; nec habebant clausum sicut nunc habent, sed erant circumdati muro alto qui erat eis pro claustro . . . Diebus Dominicis et praecipuis festivitatibus simul conveniebant, et in ecclesia Missam celebrabant, et simul manducabant.*

30. Horn, 1973, figs 13, 23, 26, 27, 29, and p. 25; Baldwin Brown, 1925, p. 118.

31. See *Chron.* i. p. 129, and ii, p. 259. Radford, op. cit. (at Glastonbury, above), 1981, p. 122, records that excavations in progress at Fleury have revealed a complicated east end of the mid tenth century.

8 Anglo-Saxon Romanesque: the Crossing

1a. On the Romanesque style, see chapter 6, and especially note 5b.

1b. Taylor and Taylor, 1965, i, p. 96.

2. A case in point is Milborne Port, a late eleventh-century church with arms off-set to the east.

3. *Chron. Abbatiae Ramesiensis*, RS83, 1886, pp. 38 ff.; *Historians of the Church of York*, RS71, 1879, i, p. 434. For *columnas* as 'piers', see glossary, COLUMN.

4. Clapham, 1930, pp. 90, 94 and 98.

5. C. Plummer and J. Earle, *Two Saxon Chronicles Parallel*, 1892, i, p. 160.

6. *Liber Eliensis*, ed. E. Blake, Camden Miscellany, 92, 1962, pp. 131–2: *. . . muros ecclesie dilatare et ad australem plagam ampliare incepit et suis expensis reliquo operi unitos consummavit.*

7. R.D.H. Gem, *Arch. J.*, 128, 1971, pp. 225–8; C.A.R. Radford, *Arch. J.*, 136, 1979, pp. 77–89.

8. H.M. Taylor, in *England before the Conquest*, ed. P. Clemoes and K. Hughes, Cambridge, 1971, pp. 351–89; ibid, *Repton Studies*, i, 1977, ii, 1979; ibid., *St Wystan's Church at Repton*, 1979.

9. Florence of Worcester, *Chronicon*, ed. B. Thorpe, London, 1848, i, p. 72.

10. Knowles, 1971, p. 480.

11. The mausoleum at the east end of the seventh-century church at Glastonbury also had the chancel extended over it, perhaps casting doubt on its identification as the burial place of King Ine.

12. E. Fernie, in *Medieval Art and Architecture at Durham Cathedral*, BAA, 1980, pp. 49–58; *Medieval Art and Architecture at Canterbury before 1220*, BAA, 1982, pp. 27–38.

13. *ASC*, 874.

14. *Evesham Chronicle*, RS29, 1863, pp. 325–6 and 83. See also D.W. Rollason, 'Lists of saints' resting places in Anglo-Saxon England', *Anglo-Saxon England*, 7, 1978, pp. 61–8.

15. Oswald, 1966, s.v.

16. E. Jackson and E. Fletcher, *JBAA* (3), 25, 1962, pp. 6–8, answered by H.M. Taylor, *Arch. J.*, 136, 1979, pp. 45–9.

17. J. Gibb and R.D.H. Gem, *Arch. J.*, 132, 1975, pp. 71–110.

18. Radford, 1973, p. 131; R.D.H. Gem, S. Heywood, and P. Everson, *JBAA*, forthcoming. For 1091 see Knowles, 1971, p. 483.

19. On the excavations and restorations in the nave and chancel see G. Atkinson, *Associated Architectural Societies, Reports and Papers*, 1, 1850–1, pp. 319–25. See also H.M. Taylor, *Arch. J.*, 131, 1974, pp. 362–6.

20. Taylor and Taylor, 1965, i, p. 469.

21. Bakewell, Taylor and Taylor, i, 1965, p. 36; Tamworth, Taylor, iii, 1978, p. 1076; R.D.H. Gem, in *Ethelred the Unready*, BAR 59, 1978, pp. 107–9, calls attention to Cholsey, Cadbury and Edith's chapel at Wilton.

22. Krautheimer, 1975, p. 79 and fig. 34.

23. L. Cobbett and C. Fox, *Procs. Cambridge Antiquarian Society*, 25, 1924, pp. 75–7; C.A.R. Radford, *Arch. J.*, 124, 1967, pp. 256–7.

24. For more examples of piers of this type, see B. Cherry, *JBAA*, 131, 1978, p. 28, n. 70.

25. Parallels have also been drawn between the shafts of the piers at Great Paxton and arrangements of logs in wooden buildings. For Greensted see H. Christie et al., *Ant. J.*, 59, 1979, pp. 92–112, and for North Elmham, S. Rigold, *Med. Arch.*, 6–7, 1962–3, p. 106.

26. G. Forsyth, *St Martin's Church at Angers*, Princeton, 1953, fig. 59.

27. Oswald, 1966, s.v.

28. Clapham, 1930, pp. 116–18.

29. For Fortunatus see chapter 1, n. 2.

30. Taylor, iii, 1978, pp. 889 and 898.

31. Taylor, iii, 1978, pp. 882–3 and 1069; H.M. and J. Taylor, *North Staffs. Journal of Field Studies*, 8, 1968, pp. 16–17.

32. Taylor, iii, 1978, p. 889. B. Davidson, *Arch. J.*, 124, 1967, pp. 208–10, supports a defensive function. The cross-shaped openings in the lowest windows might support this view, but the unrebated doorway at ground level contradicts it.

9 Anglo-Saxon Romanesque: The Decoration

1. Taylor, iii, 1978, pp. 1068–9, 853–8; Clapham, 1930, p. 113.

2. G.T. Rivoira, *Roman Architecture*, Oxford, 1925, pp. 148 and 152.

3. Clapham, 1930, p. 50 and pl. 10; D.T. Rice, *English Art 871–1100*, Oxford, 1952, pp. 90–1; Baldwin Brown, 1925, pp. 207–8, 225.

4. Taylor, iii, 1978, p. 1079; see p. 847 and table 7 for megalithic single-splayed windows.

5. H. and J. Taylor, *North Staffs. Journal of Field Studies*, 8, 1968, p. 16, early ninth century; R. Cramp, in Parsons, 1975, pp. 192–3, early tenth century; Taylor, iii, 1978, p. 1069, mid ninth century to early tenth century; Baldwin Brown, 1925, p. 276, late tenth century; Clapham, 1930, pl. 38, tenth century.

6. The other two are Earls Barton and Broughton.

7. T. Rickman, *An Attempt to Discriminate the Styles of Architecture in England*, Oxford, 1881, (1819), p. 45; H.M. Taylor, *Arch. J.*, 131, 1974, pp. 369–73; W. and K. Rodwell, *Current Archaeology*, 78, 1981, p. 212.

8. Re chamfers see p. 167.

9. E.G. Rice, op. cit., 1952, p. 53; J. Strygowski, op. cit. (in chapter 1), 1928, pp. 98–9.

10. J.G. Wilkinson, *Associated Architectural Societies, Reports*, 7, 1863, pp. 49–51; G. Dehio and G. von Bezold, *Die Kirchlike Baukunst des Abendlandes*, i, pl. 38 (1); E. Jackson and E. Fletcher, *JBAA* (3), 9, 1944, pp. 18–26; H.M. Taylor, *North Staffs. Journal of Field Studies*, 10, 1970, pp. 21–47.

11. For the view that they are derivative, see Baldwin Brown, 1925, chapter 9, and independent, Taylor, iii, 1978, pp. 955 and 927, and Taylor, op. cit., 1970, pp. 32–6.

12. Pre-Danish dates have been claimed for stripwork at Ledsham (Taylor and Taylor, i, 1965, pp. 378–84) and Monkwearmouth (Taylor, iii, 1978, p. 919; R. Cramp, *Med. Arch.*, 13, 1969, pp. 37 and 56).

13. H.M. Taylor, *Arch. J.*, 129, 1972, pp. 89–118; 130, 1973, pp. 141–71.

14. *Gest. Pont.*, RS 52, 187:, p. 346.

15. E. Mercer, *JBAA* (3), 29, 1966, pp. 61–70; Taylor, *Arch. J.*, 130, 1973, p. 154; Taylor, ii, 1965, p. 712, and iii, 1978, p. 926.

16. Taylor, *Arch. J.*, 1930, p. 152. J.M. Kemble, *Codex Diplomaticus Aevi Saxonici*, iii, London, 1845, no. 706, pp. 318–19. P. Sawyer, *Anglo-Saxon Charters*, London, 1968, no. 899, considers the charter genuine. See also Taylor, i, 1965, p. 428, and iii, 1978, p. 912.

17. Zarnecki, 1966, pp. 98–9.

18. For the Sherborne Pontifical and the charter, see M. Rickert, *Painting in Britain, the Middle Ages*, Penguin, 1965, pls. 24–5. For Headbourne Worthy see Quirk, *JBAA*, 1961, pl. VI(I). For other examples of roods, see J. and H. Taylor, *JBAA* (3), 29, 1966, pp. 4–12.

19. H.M. Taylor, *Deerhurst Studies*, i, 1977, fig. 1.

10 The Reign of Edward the Confessor

1. J.G. Robinson, *Archaeologia*, 62 (1), 1910, pp. 81–100; L. Tanner and A.W. Clapham, *Archaeologia*, 83, 1933, pp. 227–36; R.D.H. Gem, *Procs. Battle Abbey Conference*, 3, 1980, pp. 33–64.

2. E. Fernie, *Medieval Art and Architecture at Ely Cathedral*, BAA, 1979, pp. 2 and 4; *Medieval Art and Architecture at Canterbury before 1220*, BAA, 1982, p. 36; *Medieval Art and Architecture at Winchester Cathedral*, forthcoming; and 'The proportions of the St Gall plan', *Art Bulletin*, 60, 1978, p. 587 and fig. 5.

3. Liess, 1967, pp. 215 ff; Gem, op. cit., 1980, p. 54. On the other hand, it may be significant that the proportional system employed at Westminster plays no part at Jumièges.

Gem argues that when the nave of Jumièges was begun after 1052, it was built to a new design, making it possible that the nave at Westminster was earlier. Yet there is no evidence in the fabric of any break in building at the western piers of the crossing, and the difference between the supports in the presbytery and the nave does not necessitate a break. Such differences are more the rule than the exception in Norman and Anglo-Saxon churches, and would therefore appear to represent what was intended from the start.

4. F. Barlow, *Edward the Confessor*, London, 1979, pp. 7, 31, 36, 39.

5. C.R. Peers and A.W. Clapham, *Archaeologia*, 77, 1927, pp. 201–18; H.M. Taylor, op. cit. *Arch. J.*, 126, 1969, pp. 229–33.

6. Gem, 1975, pp. 35–7; R.D.H. Gem and L. Keen, *Suffolk Inst. of Archaeology and History*, 35, 1981, pp. 13–19.

7. E.g. by Clapham, 1930, p. 151; J. Hubert, in *Frühmittelalterliche Kunst in den Alpenländern*, 1954, pp. 310 and 313; R.D.H. Gem, in *Medieval Art and Architecture at Canterbury*, BAA, 1982, p. 16, suggests Ottmarsheim as the model. For the recent excavations at St Bénigne see C.M. Malone, *Bulletin Monumental*, 138, 1980, pp. 253–91. These vindicate the reconstruction of A. Martindale, *JBAA* (3), 25, 1962, pp. 21–55, against that of K.J. Conant, *Carolingian and Romanesque Architecture 800–1200*, Harmondsworth, 1974, pp. 150–3.

8. *Congrès Archéologique*, 109, 1951 (Poitiers) pp. 353 ff.

9 Taylor, iii, 1978, pp. 738–9 and fig. 643.

10. A.W. Clapham, *English Romanesque Architecture after the Conquest*, Oxford, 1934, pp. 32–4 and 64–5. This possibility was, to my knowledge, first raised by A.P.

Baggs at the BAA conference at Gloucester in 1981.

11. F. Barlow, ed., *The Life of Edward the Confessor*, Nelson, 1962, pp. 46–50. Gem, 1975, p. 30; Knowles, 1966, pp. 75–6.

12. For the foundation see J.M. Kemble, *Codex Diplomaticus Aevi Saxonici*, iv, London, 1846, no. 813, pp. 154–5: Edward, 1062. P. Sawyer, *Anglo-Saxon Charters*, London, 1968, no. 1036, records that most authorities since Stubbs consider the charter spurious.

13. Knowles, 1966, pp. 66–70, and Gem, 1975, passim.

14. Clapham, 1930, p. 77.

11 The 'Overlap'

1. As suggested by D.T. Rice, *English Art 871–1100*, Oxford, 1952, p. 153, and K.J. Conant, op. cit., (ch. 10, n.7), p. 454. For a similar criticism to that voiced here see Zarnecki, 1966, pp. 97 and 102.

2. Taylor and Taylor, i, 1965, pp. xxv, xxvii, and 2; Conant, loc. cit. Clapham, 1930, p. 11, is more circumspect, while Baldwin Brown, 1925, pp. 231 and 379–80, offers a characteristically acute assessment.

3. M. Biddle, *Ant. J.*, 55, 1975, pp. 106–9 and pls xxi–iii; A. Carter, in *Anglo-Saxon England*, 7, 1977, p. 194, n. 4.

4. Triangular-headed arches and bulbous bases may also count as survivals after the Conquest.

5. H.J.A. Strik, in *Medieval Art and Architecture at Canterbury*, BAA, 1982, p. 25 and fig. 5; D. Renn, *Norman Castles in Britain*, London, 1968, p. 185.

6. Taylor, iii, 1978, p. 1050.

7. See below, note 21.

8. P. Grierson, *Trans. Royal Historical Society*, 23, 1941, passim, esp. pp. 95–103.

9. The angle roll is probably Roman, as there is an early-Islamic example at Khirbet-al-Mafjar, near Jericho. Another on the southern arcade of the courtyard forming part of the mid eleventh-century rebuilding of the church of the Holy Sepulchre in Jerusalem provides a possible link with western Europe.

10. J. Bilson, *Archaeologia*, 73, 1923, pp. 55–72.

11. See e.g. Tebessa, Qalat Siman and Zvartnots.

12. *JBAA*, 132, 1979, p. 114.

13. L.F. Salzman, *Building in England down to 1540*, Oxford, 1952, p. 522. 'Entaille' means 'carving'.

14. G. Zarnecki, *The Early Sculpture of Ely Cathedral*, London, 1958, pp. 10 ff.

15. S. Heywood, *Minor Church Building in East Anglia during the 11th and early 12th centuries*, MA Report, University of East Anglia, 1977, pp. 22–39.

16. Heywood, op. cit., p. 25; Oswald, 1966, s.v. Destroyed 1897.

17. For Theodred and his colleagues see Whitelock, 1979, pp. 553–4.

18. My thanks are due to David Butcher for drawing Oulton to my attention. See also the strange example at St-Aubin in Burgundy (Heitz, 1980, fig. 144).

19. W. Rodwell, *Ant. J.*, 56, 1976, pp. 55–71, and E.C. Fernie, *JBAA*, 1983, forthcoming.

20. S.E. Rigold, op. cit. *JBAA*, 132, 1979, p. 113, notes that the possibility was first pointed out to him by T.P. Smith.

21. Baldwin Brown, 1925, pp. xiv–xv, is particularly enlightening on a post-Conquest date for the Lincolnshire towers.

22. It is of some historical interest that, before the publication of their first two volumes, the Taylors had intended to entitle their work *Anglo-Saxon and Saxo-Norman Churches of England* (see Quirk, *JBAA*, 1961, p. 37). Parallel to the changed final title there is an ambivalence in the use of category C3. While the Taylors adopted this period from Baldwin Brown with the brackets 1050 and 1100 (i, p. xxv), in the text buildings classified in this way are in many cases (e.g. Weybourne and Wharram-le-Street) referred to as 'pre-Conquest'. Uncertainty is increased by the use of the category 'Saxo-Norman', which is not clearly differentiated from period C3, and in practice produces the suggestion that C3 means 1050 to 1066 and Saxo-Norman 1066 to 1100.

23. In the form of Stephen Heywood's doctoral dissertation, *The Saxo-Norman Overlap and Minor Church Buildings in England c. 1050–1150*, University of East Anglia, in progress.

24. Clapham, 1930, p. 94 and op. cit., 1934, p. 38; J. Bony, 'Durham et la tradition Saxonne', in *Études Offertes à Louis Grodecki*, Paris, 1981, pp. 79–85; Zarnecki, 1966, and op. cit., 1958.

25. Taylor, iii, 1978, p. 936, reaches the same conclusion.

Conclusion

1. P.H. Blair, *An Introduction to Anglo-Saxon England*, Cambridge, 1977, pp. 22 and 280–1, and *Roman Britain and Early England 55 BC–871 AD*, Edinburgh, 1963, pp. 7 and 177.

2. Blair, op. cit., 1963. pp. 31, 59, 211 and 202; Colgrave, in *HE*, preface, p. 380 n. 3, iii, 21 and 23, iv, 24, and p. 414 n. 1; M. Deansley, *English Historical Review*, 58, 1943, pp. 132–3.

3. K. Crossley-Holland and B. Mitchell, *The Battle of Maldon and Other Old English Poems*, Macmillan, 1965, pp. 69–70.

4. Contrast Blair, op. cit., 1977, p. 280, with P.J. Frankis, 'The thematic significance of *enta geweorc* and the related imagery in *The Wanderer*', *Anglo-Saxon England*, 2, 1973, p. 258.

5. B. Colgrave, ed., *Two Lives of St Cuthbert*, Cambridge, 1940, pp. 242–4.

6. Frankis, op. cit., pp. 253 ff., and J. Higgitt, 'The Roman background to medieval England', *JBAA* (3), 36, 1973, pp. 6–7.

7. A.W. Lowther, 'Romano-British chimney pots and finials', *Ant. J.*, 56, 1976, pp. 35–48, and pl. V.

BIBLIOGRAPHY

P.V. ADDYMAN, 'The Anglo-Saxon house: a new review', *Anglo-Saxon England*, 1, 1972, pp. 273–307.

G. BALDWIN BROWN, *The Arts in Early England*, volume II, *Anglo-Saxon Architecture*, London, 1925

Bede's Ecclesiastical History of the English People, ed. B. Colgrave and R.A.B. Mynors, Oxford, Clarendon Press, 1979

J. BONY, review of Taylor and Taylor, 1965, *Journal of the [American] Society of Architectural Historians*, 26, 1967, pp. 74–7

A. W. CLAPHAM, *English Romanesque Architecture Before the Conquest*, Oxford, Clarendon Press, 1930

R.D.H. GEM, *The Origins of the Early Romanesque Architecture of England*, doctoral dissertation, Cambridge, 1973

R.D.H. GEM, 'A recession in English architecture during the early eleventh century', *JBAA*, third series, 38, 1975, pp. 28–49

J.-L. GENICOT, *Les Eglises Mosanes du XIe Siècle*, Louvain, 1972

L. GRODECKI, *L'Architecture Ottonienne*, Colin, Paris, 1958

C. HEITZ, *L'Architecture Religieuse Carolingienne*, Picard, Paris, 1980

W. HORN, 'On the origins of the medieval cloister', *Gesta*, 12, 1973, pp. 13–52

D. KNOWLES, *The Monastic Order in England*, Cambridge University Press, 1966

D. KNOWLES and R.N. HADCOCK, *Medieval Religious Houses*, Longman, 1971

R. KRAUTHEIMER, *Early Christian and Byzantine Architecture*, Penguin, 1975

H.E. KUBACH and A. VERBEEK, *Romanische Kirchen an Rhein und Maas*, Neuss, 1972

R. LIESS, *Die Frühromanische Kirchenbau des elften Jahrhunderts in der Normandie*, Fink, Munich, 1967

F. OSWALD, et al., *Vorromani sche Kirchenbauten*, Prestel-Verlag, Munich, 1966

D. PARSONS, ed., *Tenth Century Studies*, Phillimore, London, 1975

C.A.R. RADFORD, 'Pre-Conquest minster churches', *Arch. J.*, 130, 1973, pp. 120–40

H.M. and J. TAYLOR, *Anglo-Saxon Architecture*, volumes I and II, Cambridge University Press, 1965

H.M. TAYLOR, *Anglo-Saxon Architecture*, volume III, Cambridge University Press, 1978

J.B. WARD-PERKINS and A. BOETHIUS, *Etruscan and Roman Architecture*, Penguin, 1970

D. WHITELOCK, ed., *English Historical Documents, I, c.500–1042*, Eyre and Methuen, 1979

D.M. WILSON, ed., *The Archaeology of Anglo-Saxon England*, Cambridge University Press, 1976
P. Rahtz, 'Buildings and rural settlement', pp. 49–98
M. Biddle, 'Towns', pp. 99–150
B. Cherry, 'Ecclesiastical architecture', pp. 151–200
R. Cramp, 'Monastic Sites', pp. 201–252
G. ZARNECKI, '1066 and architectural sculpture', *Proceedings of the British Academy*, 52, 1966, pp. 87–104

INDEX

Figures in *italics* refer to the illustration
numbers

DATE DUE

11/22/18			